D1054328

THE SALES COACH

Selling Tips from the Pros

by

Linda Blackman
Joe Killian
Steve Richards
Mary Maloney Cronin
Deb Haggerty
David Goldman
Jeffrey Tobe
Dave Jakielo
Anne Louise Conlon Feeny
Sandie Akerman

COPYRIGHT © 1997 BY JEFFREY TOBE

All rights reserved including the right to reproduce in whole or part in any form or by any means.

Requests for permission to make copies of any part of the work should be mailed to:

Jeffrey Tobe
1144 Colgate Drive
Monroeville, PA 15146

ISBN: 1-889944-02-5
Manufactured in the United States of America

Foreword

In an age where sales books are as plentiful as sales trainers, it was our intent to bring you the best of the best. Each one of the contributors to *The Sales Coach...Selling Tips from the Pros*, is a seasoned sales professional, speaker and trainer. The idea for the book was born from our frustration in not being able to find a "handbook" that could be used by a sales professional at any time in their sales career. This book is to be read and then referred to whenever you hit that proverbial "wall." When you need information on a specific skill in which you have weakened, or when you just need to affirm that you are on the right track, *The Sales Coach* can help. We have attempted to bring you a book that flows for you, the reader, but we have also tried to maintain the integrity of each contribution without altering the author's "style"of delivery. It is our hope that there is something for everyone in this book.

We hope you enjoy this handbook, and we look forward to bringing you many more in the "Coach" series with contributions from industry pros around the world.

"By opening this book, you have opened up new opportunities in your quest to be the best. Use the information in this handbook to expand your mind <u>and</u> your bottom line.

The Sales Coach is one of the best books on selling on the market today. It is loaded with practical ideas and techniques that you can use to be a more effective salesperson in any situation."

-Brian Tracy
Brian Tracy International
author: PSYCHOLOGY OF SELLING

Table of Contents

Presentational Selling™
by Linda S. Blackman 1

Time Management: A Strategy for Personal Sales Success
by Joe Killian 41

Goal Setting or, How Did I Get to Where I am Today?
by Steve Richards 79

How to Market Yourself
by Mary Maloney Cronin 97

Networking: Necessity or Nuisance?
by Deb Haggerty 127

Are You Listening?
by David Goldman 153

Put a Little C.O.L.O.R. in your Selling
by Jeffrey Tobe 171

Selling Through Negotiating
by Dave Jakielo 201

Dick and Jane Communication
by Anne Louise Conlon Feeny 225

How Customer Service Relates to Sales:
A Case Study
by Sandie Akerman 257

Chapter 1

The Hottest New Results-Producing Way To Sell: Presentational Selling™

by
Linda S. Blackman

You are always selling product,
concept, service, or self.

—Linda Blackman
The Image Guru®

Yes! It's true! There really is a natural salesperson in you. And, it's my job to bring that naturalness out even more. By reading the words on this page, you have made a powerful commitment to catapult yourself into the nineties and beyond as a top salesperson who knows how to reach out and help your customer by using the wonderful techniques that follow.

But first—What is Presentational Selling™? Simply put, Presentational Selling means everything you do and say is for the benefit of your audience. In this case, your audience is your client or customer. Through your ability to help your client or customer, you automatically and continually skyrocket your career regardless of what you are selling. Presentational Selling consists of 12 key components:

1. *Knowing What YOU Want*
2. *Determining Your Unique Selling Proposition*
3. *Selling Through Questioning*
4. *Targeting the Need*
5. *Using Your Signature Stories*
6. *Dressing to Sell*
7. *Being Specific*
8. *Learning the Signs of Body Language*
9. *Establishing the Qualities of a Loving Relationship*
10. *Identifying the Adjectives that Describe You*
11. *Building and Keeping the Relationship*
12. *Bonus Items*

I tell you about each of the components in detail with examples in the following pages. Plus, as an added bonus for you, I provide you with "Accomplishment Pages" to complete and customize in order to enhance your natural selling ability.

1. Knowing what YOU want

You're probably thinking, "Excuse me? You're asking me to know what I want? What are you talking about? I thought I only needed to know what my customer wants!"

That's exactly my point! That's traditional thinking. Here we're talking about Presentational Selling! Unless you know what you want out of every selling opportunity, whatever it is you have to offer cannot be presented with "your all" and you cannot reach your full potential. I'm not just talking about selling to earn a living. Simply wanting to sell to make a buck may get you something in the short term but not in the long term. In an ideal world, wouldn't you want a career that fulfills you in every possible way, plus be able to help the people who seek your advice and wisdom? Unless you sell with this attitude and know what you want, you cannot reach your full potential. Within the next several pages, I will give you a guaranteed success formula that I've been using for over 20 years.

The formula came to me during my years as a student at Northwestern University. You see, knowing who you are is very closely linked to knowing what it is you want to do. If you want to be the best possible salesperson, you must first get in touch with yourself before you can reach out to fully help others. Here's the valuable lesson Cathy Martin taught me.

Cathy was my guidance counselor at Northwestern University. I was assigned to her when I transferred to Northwestern in the middle of my sophomore year. Cathy invited me into her office and asked me: "What do you want to do?" I thought I was ready to boldly answer the question. So I did. I proudly told Cathy:"I want to be in broadcasting."

Cathy seemed unimpressed. She asked: "Exactly what do you want to do in broadcasting?" I responded humbly: "I'll do anything." Cathy retorted back quickly: "So will a lot of other people. Broadcasting is a very competitive field. You need to know what you want to do in order to succeed. You need to decide right here, and now, what it is you want to do."

I looked Cathy squarely in the eye and stated with conviction: "I want to be a television news anchor and reporter."

She smiled and said: "Good. Now you know what you want to do. When you walk out of my office, you tell everyone you know what you want to do with your life—that you want to be a TV anchor and reporter. And, on those days you're feeling uncertain, you share that uncertainty with your family, your friends, and with me. But, to the rest of the world, you address them with certainty in all that you do."

I walked out of Cathy Martin's office. I had direction. A mission to become a broadcast journalist EXTRAORDINAIRE.

Here's a brief synopsis of the impact Cathy's words had on my career. Eventually, in December, 1973, I graduated half a year early to get a jump on the June graduates. Within four months, after countless rejections, I got my first job as a TV reporter. In fact, I was one of the very first, as well as youngest, female co-anchors in the United States. Eventually, I went on to become a coast-to-coast TV news reporter, anchor and talk show host. Today, as a professional speaker and trainer, I run my own company which helps people become great at selling, make better presentations and talk to the media.

Often I think back to the valuable lesson Cathy Martin taught me: She motivated me to set a goal... to become all that I could be... to achieve my dream. It all happened to me. It can happen to you! Follow this simple formula: Visualize what you want. Verbalize what you want. Maximize your knowledge. Realize that no one can help your customer or client quite the way that you can. Now, let's put this formula to work for you.

Visualize—Visualize what you want. I mean, right now, close your eyes and think about the type of salesperson you want to be. Don't read on until you have visualized. See your new self clearly. In a moment, you'll be able to commit your visualization to writing...

Now, time to commit your visualization to writing. Grab a sheet of paper and write down whatever you saw in your mind's eye. If you see yourself being understanding, cocky, helpful or whatever came to your mind—good for you for honestly identifying how you see yourself.

Verbalize—Get ready, say who you are. For example, "I am an understanding, fast-talking salesperson who has a tendency not to let my customers explain what's important to them. Because I am understanding, people feel I am empathetic and provide the solution they need." Further, be willing to verbalize who you are by saying the truth as you see it... "I can be more effective to my customer by continuing my same level of being understanding. However, I will be even more effective by slowing down how rapidly I speak and by pausing to ask for some feedback." Your verbalization is an affirmation of you saying and doing what you know is right, not only for yourself, but for the person you are helping. How?... by providing them exactly what they need.

Maximize—Time to maximize your knowledge of your product line. Know all that you can. Study the competition. Work with those at your company who are the pros. As you learn from the pros, think of yourself initially as the understudy. Know that it's just a matter of time before you will take the lead—in this case, by becoming the leading salesperson. Be humble. Learn your customer's needs, hopes, pains and joys. The more you know, the more you can deliver their needs ...not just one time, but all the time.

Realize—Realize that no one can help your customer quite the way you can. No one has had the same life and experiences that you have had. It is individual qualities and life experiences that make you unique. Now, you are ready to determine your unique selling proposition.

ACCOMPLISHMENT SHEET
Knowing What YOU Want

Visualize— How do you currently see yourself when you sell to those you are helping?

Verbalize— Say out loud what you have visualized. Then, say out loud what you like and don't like about what you've said. Then commit your words to writing, right here.

Maximize— What else should you know about your product line or service?

Which competitors should you study to learn what they offer and what your customers may find attractive about them?

Who are the pros at your company who you should ask to help you?

Identify and talk to mentors in your field who can help you.

What should you additionally be learning from your customers?

Realize—**You are unique and each customer should be unique to you too!**

---

2. Determining your unique selling proposition

What is a USP? It is a <u>U</u>nique <u>S</u>elling <u>P</u>roposition. It's what sets you apart from all the others in your field to make you special; make you different...unique.

Think back to the spectacular advertising campaign launched by Domino's Pizza. They promised pizza to your home within 30 minutes or the pizza was free. That became their USP. For Avis Car Rental it became, "We try harder." What is it about you that makes you unique? Brainstorm. Go to the USP Accomplishment Sheet and write down what makes you different from others in your field. Here are the areas for you to focus on: Credentials, Speed, Accuracy, Successes, Results, Testimonials and How you can do it differently from your competition.

USP's are often found by taking the obvious and putting on some slight twist to make you different. My daughter Felise taught me this lesson one Halloween when she was seven years old. Halloween, by far, had become a favorite holiday for Felise. This particular year, she wanted to dress as a bride. So she did. But, when she came downstairs in her pristine white gown and veil, she donned a paste-on tattooed rose on her cheek. When I asked her why, she explained to me that each year she had watched her older brother, Ian, dress in very creative costumes. He always got more candy than she did or anyone else for that matter. This year she proclaimed that there may be other brides but nobody would be a tattooed-cheek bride. Felise was right! She collected more candy than her brother that year in her orange plastic Jack o'lantern. (I sometimes think that my thighs are still working off all the candy she collected that Halloween.) Felise was a seven-year old with a unique selling proposition who was able to identify who her customers were and what would make them respond to her USP.

Now, it's your turn.

ACCOMPLISHMENT SHEET
Determining your Unique Selling Proposition

What are your personal credentials?

What is your company known for?

Is speed important in your business? If yes, how so and how can you make speed unique in what you do?

Is accuracy important in your business? If yes, how so and how can you make accuracy unique in what you do? (Then try such words as *quality, selection, toughness, price, style, taste, freshness* or whatever is important to your potential customer.)

What are your successes and your company's successes?

What wonderful comments have people said about you that can be used as testimonials?

What do you do that your competition does not? What do you do better?

Use your answers to the above to help determine what is unique about you. Then, answer....What is my and/or my company's Unique Selling Proposition?

3. Selling through questioning

When a customer comes to you or you approach them, you must find out: What brings them to you? What's bothering them? Where is their pain? Or, is this possibly just a general checkup to make sure they don't need to purchase any more than they currently have? We call these "probing questions"...generally, questions that cannot be answered "Yes" or "No." Ask! Ask! Ask these probing questions!

Always find out as much as you can about your customers. For example, their likes and dislikes, types of events they like to attend, significant others, and children. Knowing such does not make you nosey—it makes you a caring person. Because, you see, you now can send them articles about what's important to them. Perhaps tickets to a favorite symphony or ball game. Share with them news about a new study on children who are the same ages as their toddlers or college-bound kids. You become a partner in the sense of being concerned overall for what's best for them.

For example, think of someone who is in the market to buy a personal computer. We'll call him Joe Sampson. You are the salesperson at ComputerAll.

As Joe walks into ComputerAll, you of course want to help him, but in addition, you must also be able to identify the competition. Who is the competition? Traditional thinking is: The competition might be another computer company. The competition could be a discount office supply warehouse that carries the same computer—but for 10 percent less than your price—Joe is looking at in your shop. The possibilities are virtually endless on who or what the competition may be.

But, with Presentational Selling, you have the opportunity to get more facts because your use of caring yet probing questions that let you see beyond the types of assumptions most people make. With Presentational Selling, you learn about your customer, your competition, and more.

Often, salespeople don't consider that the competition may not be obvious. In the case of Joe Sampson, we have a new small business owner who was going to buy eight new computers accompanied by all the supporting hardware and software. Was is the operative word here because, as Joe was driving over to ComputerAll, he passed AutoDeal where he stopped in. Joe saw his dream mobile being featured—a preowned van, which could be bought for a great price, but only for cash. He had to have it! But, Joe has to have the computer equipment first. Then, he tells himself he must have the van. The deal is too good to pass up.

Joe enters your domain! He is in ComputerAll. His eyes busily scan and absorb all that can be observed. You approach him with those dreaded four words: "May I help you?" He responds with those dreaded two words: "Just looking." You vow to check back. You do. Joe is gone.

Let's do an instant replay. Joe enters your domain! He is in ComputerAll. His eyes busily scan and absorb all that can be observed. You approach him with any words other than the obvious, "May I help you?"

For instance, after you give him a warm reassuring hello and a smile, you could ask—"Are you looking for equipment for home or business use?" "Is this for a new business or existing business?" "What equipment if any do you have now?" "What have you been considering?"

You actually preplan the types of questions to ask your customers depending on who they are. Sometimes the questions will be the same; other times they will be quite different. All of the questions are designed to show customers that you care about them and above all, you want to help them. You get valuable information by asking the right questions. You get the specifics you need to help your client. You want to get as much specific information as early as possible. Remember too, by asking the right questions, you not only get more customers to buy, but each customer buys more.

It is possible that your customer may view you as being intrusive, almost as if you are the enemy if you repeatedly fire questions at them. If the customer feels that way, they will certainly tell you those two dreaded words at any moment: "Just looking."

You may want to consider repeating the questions that your customer or clients ask you. Doing this allows you to have a few extra seconds to think about what you want your response to be. This will also allow you to rephrase it, taking it in the direction you feel the question should be taken.

At those moments, it is your job and your place to let them know that you understand how they feel because other customers have felt like browsing for a while too. But, in the end, customers have found that they can save a lot of time and money by talking with you. I call these the Three F's of communication— Feel, Felt, Found. The Three F's can be used in a variety of ways. They work wonderfully when it comes to price resistance (or any other objection) and closing a sale. It is imperative not to overuse the Three F's and to choose very carefully when and where to use them. Most customers will be unaware of you using them in conversation if you use them only once or twice.

Here's an example of how to use the Three F's when it's time to

ACCOMPLISHMENT SHEET
Selling Through Questioning

What makes you interested in this product or service now?
When do you need it?

What/who have you used in the past?

How did you hear about us?

Who will be using our product or service at your company/firm/
association?

Tell me more about your company. How did you get involved with them?

Do you want to use our easy credit payment plan or is there
another source of financing you prefer to use?

List some of your own questions:

Practice using The Three F's for different objections that may
come up with your customers. List three likely objections you
have heard or may hear from your customers. Write down how
you will use Feel, Felt, and Found. You may need to alter the
following sentences depending upon how you want to say them:

1.

2.

3.

       I can understand how you *feel*....

       Others have *felt* that way too....

       But, here's what they have *found*.

close a sale. Only use information in your Three F scenarios that are based on fact. You never want to lie.

In the case of closing Joe Sampson—you have learned much about him and you want him to know that you understand his needs and concerns— "Joe, I can understand how you must be feeling, wanting to buy that dream mobile and needing the fastest and most up-to-date computer equipment. I just had a customer the other day who must have felt pretty much the same way. He needed equipment similar to what you've been looking at and he also decided to buy the building he is in instead of just renting it. He found he didn't feel so financially strapped anymore when he took advantage of our easy payment plan. Nobody can get a better payment plan any place else. May I tell you about it?"

The Three F's are virtually fail-proof. But, you must practice using them and your example that will accompany Feel, Felt and Found.

4. Targeting the need

Three main ingredients go into targeting your customer's need: 1.) What makes them feel good; how can you enhance their joy with your product or service? 2.) What brings them pain; how does what you offer fix their angst? 3.) What can you do to help them; how can you best serve them to find solutions to make their life easier?

You are the specialist in a very strong sense. You are who your customer needs to make them feel better and to reassure them by delivering the best product or service you have available. Truly, the only way you can help them is to find out as much about them as you can before you begin telling what you can do for them. Why is targeting your customer's needs so important? Can it really make that much of a difference? You can bet your success that it does!

Imagine this...you have an awful toothache. You have been putting up with excruciating pain for over a week. You can't eat. You can't sleep. You can't concentrate. Reluctantly, you go to the dentist.

As you drive to the dentist's office you remember that for the past several years you have avoided going in for your routine six-month teeth cleaning and check-up. Upon entering the office, the sound of the dentist's drill wafts through the air. The distinctive smell of dental hygiene is everywhere. You are led from the waiting room into the dental chair. The dentist comes in to greet you. Imagine this...the dentist says... "You have a toothache. Let me guess where it is!!!"

Sure, the dentist could guess. But your dentist could find out valuable information and possibly pinpoint where your exact pain is by simply asking you the right questions. The questions might simply be: Where is your pain? Is it on the right side or left side? Upper or lower? You get the idea.

Sometimes you may need to point out to the person you're helping the need they have. I heard of a savvy and helpful gardener who carefully listened to Jackie, who he hoped would become a new customer. Jackie had wanted him to cut the grass around the home. As the gardener and Jackie walked the grounds, the gardener noticed that there were some unruly hedges surrounding the property. At that point, the gardener commented that keeping-up on yard work could be like dealing with a jungle. The gardener further mentioned he knew his customers often didn't have the time to take care of their properties the way they would like to. The gardener went on to say he liked the idea of being able to give back the precious commodity of time to his customers, plus he enjoyed the challenge of restoring the order to his customers' homes that he knew they liked! The gardener asked, "Do you want me to help you out the same way?" Jackie said, "You know, I usually trim the bushes, but it really takes so much of my time. Would you mind trimming them for me?" The gardener didn't mind at all.

The bottom line here is to totally understand and know what is motivating your clients' or customers' need.

5. Using your signature stories

A large part of your success as a salesperson will depend on your ability to comfortably weave into your conversations stories of how you have successfully helped others. Such stories are called Signature Stories. Just as no one has the exact same experiences you have had, no one will have a Signature Story quite like yours. These experiences become your Signature Stories. I first became aware of these stories years ago when I became a professional speaker. (A professional speaker is someone who speaks for a living, just as a professional boxer is someone who boxes for a living.)

For instance, in one of my talks called Delighting the Customer, I tell the "Boot" story. When I was a teenager, I worked at a high-end women's shoe store where I made a 30 percent commission on everything I sold. Everyone made the same commission whether they were a part-time or full-time employee. Depending upon the day, I made double to quadruple the minimum wage. Even Mr. Hay, the store's top producer, often stood in amazement as the "kid," as he called me, made as much if not more than he did!

ACCOMPLISHMENT SHEET
Targeting the Need

What makes your customer feel good?

How can you enhance your customer's joy with your product or service?

What causes your client pain?

How does what you do fix their pain or angst?

What can you do to help your customer?

How can you best serve as someone who can partner with them to find solutions to make their life easier?

One day, Fran came in to buy a pair of boots. We went to school together. I learned Fran didn't like wearing boots. They never quite fit comfortably on her calf. In general, she found boots and shoes uncomfortable. I brought out the perfect boots and a pair of shoes I knew fit extraordinarily well. "Yes!" to the shoes. "No!" to the boots. I told Fran I honestly didn't know what I could do to make the boot more comfortable for her nor was I aware of a boot that would work as well. She had a suggestion—take them in the back and see if there was something I could do—maybe stretch them.

I hadn't a clue as to what to do in this instance. I asked my boss. Mr. Hay joined in on the consultation and so did two other salesmen. I stood as a member of the huddle which had gathered. My boss handed the right boot to Mr. Hay. Mr. Hay held up the boot to the light and blew on the leather which would soon hug Fran's calf. He then passed the boot around the huddle and told us all to do the same. We did. Next, Mr. Hay took the boot and pounded the heel against a wall in the back room. He smiled and said, "Try this boot on your customer now." I looked at him in disbelief and said, "But you didn't do anything." He smiled again and said, "Let your customer be the determiner."

As Fran tried the boot on, she said, "I heard you banging around back there. Whatever you did really made a difference." I assured her that I really hadn't done anything... there was really nothing that could be done. I then told her the process the boot underwent in the back. This time she smiled and said,

"Who knows, maybe the banging or something made a difference." She asked me to do the same thing to the other boot and so I took both of the boots back with me.

We all huddled together there in the back room. The left boot was blown upon and banged. I didn't feel right about this. I decided to use my bare hands in an attempt to stretch the leather at the top which was sewn together with tiny elastic inserts to allow comfort as needed. Mr. Hay laughed and said, "Kid, that won't do anything. But kid, the customer thinks there's this great mystique in the back room and that you can fix things here. This is part of the job—making the customer comfortable and happy in their selection."

Fran left happy. She knew we hadn't really done anything— except listen to her and show her we understood her concern, plus I sold her the best possible shoes available on the market! Mr. Hay taught me a meaningful lesson—it is important to work with the customer to make them comfortable.

As a professional speaker, I always say I must constantly think of what I can do to meet the needs of my audience and take them to the next level. As a salesperson, you must take your customer to the next level they wish to attain through the knowledge you have about the products and/or services you offer.

Sometimes, bear with me here for a moment, you may feel like you're barking up the wrong tree with a particular customer. You may be unless you start talking their language and take the time to consider who they are. For this Signature Story, we will travel to the beautiful Caribbean island of St. Martin where I had an opportunity to jog along one of the island's most magnificent beaches. I put my Walkman on, blasted it on high, and jogged along to a sixties tune called "Set Me Free."

After a while, I noticed I had gone way past the resort area and had only seen tiny shanties and shacks for the past several minutes. I decided to turn around. The warmth of the sun felt delightful. The waves gently moved to and from the shore. As I blissfully sang the words to "Set Me Free," I heard sounds above the din of the music and my voice. I looked behind me. My life flashed before my eyes as I saw an angry pack of dogs racing toward me. At first there were just a few. Then, as the pack passed by each shanty, another dog or two would join the already-established group. They were gaining on me. I turned my jog into a run. I didn't stand a chance. There were too many and they were too fast. In the seconds until they caught up to me, I remembered the dogs I had as pets. I remembered I could calm them down if I spoke to them in a friendly voice. These dogs coming after me were obviously domesticated I thought. Their owners must use friendly voices with them. I stopped running and turned around dead in my tracks to meet them head on. With my most friendly, most inviting voice I said..."Yes, hello, how are you, good dogs, come-on, let's run together." The barks almost instantaneously turned to sighs of affection.

Had I not addressed my audience as I did, had I acted with terror and started to lash out, had I not spoken the language as I did, I shudder to think of what my fate would have been on the shores of St. Martin. Know your audience—or you'll be eaten alive!

Signature Stories are meant to be memorable and make a point. If you don't speak the language of your customer, odds are you won't have a customer. What are your Signature Stories and how can you weave them into your sales conversations? You'll have a chance on the worksheet to think your response through regarding this extremely relevant question.

Here is one final example. In addition to being a professional speaker, I coach executives who must make critically important presentations. I once had a potential client from a Fortune 500 company say to me, "How can you help me make my technical talk more interesting?"

I shared with him the story of Mark George, a vice president of an environmental company, who had to give a presentation about a new industry innovation. Mark was having a difficult time trying to figure out how to sell his soon-to-be audience of CEO's and presidents on how exciting this innovation would be to the industry and its customers. I suggested to Mark that we put his talk aside for a moment and just chat about what was going on in his life. He gave me an odd look asking "Why?" I replied with, "I have an idea. Do you mind if I ask you some questions?" He said "No." And so I asked!

"What's new with you and your wife?" He told me they had recently moved. His wife was busy with her job, didn't like the shopping mall near the new house, but they loved their new home. Mark said he had spent a fair amount of time at the dentist's office lately as he took care of an abscessed tooth. "Oh, speaking of doctors, I just had a baby granddaughter." He smiled, but I detected a bit of concern in his eyes.

I offered my congratulations and asked how his granddaughter was. "Fine now, but she had a rough time in the beginning. They were able to keep her alive with breathing tubes and it seemed like they used every type of tube imaginable. Just a few years ago, she wouldn't have made it. Today, medical science is incredible and my granddaughter is beautiful."

BINGO!!! I found what I needed. A story belonging to Mark that everyone in the audience could relate to, find interesting, and could make the point of how technical know-how could save a life. Plus, this story showed how innovations could be life-saving and how the environmental industry's life could depend upon the use of the new technological innovation Mark was introducing. Mark won the critical support of the audience he needed. The example he used of his granddaughter sent a powerful message.

See what experiences from your life you can use to identify signature stories to make your points to help and sell your customers. Never use someone else's Signature Story unless you have their approval to do so.

In addition to using Signature Stories, you can use testimonials. You might want to show a complimentary letter someone has written to you. Or, you can refer to how you were able to help someone reach tremendous success because of your valuable input.

ACCOMPLISHMENT SHEET
Using Your Signature Stories

Identify personal experiences you can use as Signature Stories. Also identify the point that story will make when being used with your customer:

Story	Point

If you are not already doing so, keep a list of Signature Stories you find interesting as well as testimonials. Review your lists from time to time. You will find a use for many of your collectibles from your list.

6. Dressing to sell

I am often asked, "Does it really matter what I wear?" The answer is simple. It only matters if it matters to your client or impacts the way you feel! You should know your client better than anyone else. If you don't, you better learn who they are pretty quickly if you want to be as successful as you possibly can be.

Remember, you are always selling product, concept, service or self. Whether you are selling services to corporations, appliances in a store, or something else, people have a strong tendency to judge you by the way you are dressed and how you carry yourself. People want to affiliate with people who know what they are talking about and who represent the image of knowledge and success. An elusive part of success is the impression you make on people, including the clothes you wear.

I have found that many people don't like this simple answer. They want hard and fast rules for what they should and shouldn't do for every situation. I contend it is virtually impossible to predict every situation. But yet, you the reader, are my audience and I want to address your every concern about this issue.

Yes. It matters what you wear. I advise clients to dress up for business situations. This means a suit and tie for men in the corporate world. For women, a business-skirt suit, not a pants suit. However, business casual continues to grow in popularity. . . Fridays are casual days at many companies. If you make sales quotas, you are allowed to wear jeans. So, you see it matters, but you must make a judgement call for each situation.

I remember one time someone came to me quite frustrated. This person was unable to secure a position as a professor at a local university in the eastern U.S. city where he lived. I looked at him. Designer Armani suit accompanied by what he called his "colorful California tie." An Alpha Romeo sports car. Elegant eel skin brief case. I asked him who his audience was. He replied that they were college students. I felt the students were his ultimate audience not his initial audience. I asked who his initial audience was at the university. He told me the Dean and some other important administrators. When I asked him how they dressed, he replied, "Sports coats, khakis or jeans, no ties, older model hi-mileage cars, and well-worn brief cases."

Well, our professor, on the exterior, didn't fit the mold. Having missed out on the opportunity to teach at what we will call University A, he met with the powers-to-be at University B shortly after our discussion. He drove his wife's well-used station wagon to the interview. He carried his old, tired and truly expandable brief case. He wore slacks and a sports coat. He went without his "colorful California tie." He got the job!

A few paragraphs ago, I said you should dress up when in doubt as opposed to dressing down. Yet, I say consider the audience. When I was working with a group of speakers from a city's transit authority, one of the men in the session, who we will call Jack, was an undercover officer. Everyone in the session, including Jack, spoke to civic organizations in the community about how the authority was there to help whenever possible. Jack was the only individual who I actually suggested to dress as he did when he was on the job—scuzzy, worn jeans, dirty-looking. He told me he always wore a suit when he did his public speaking engagements. When he began dressing in his usual undercover garb, people began to ask him more questions and appreciate the authority's ingenuity and much more!

Just the other day, the marketing manager from a payroll services company, which does four million dollars in business annually, called me. Jenine desperately wanted to find the following words in print somewhere: *What you wear, matters.* She said of the 14 people in their shop, two were men, the rest women. The men always wore suits to work. The women would wear matching skirt outfits or pants on their sales calls. Jenine said her sales staff thinks she's old fashioned. Dress shouldn't matter. So, here it is in writing again. *What you wear, matters!* Once the relationship is established, use your judgement to determine if it's appropriate to change your dress for the occasion.

7. Being specific

In this segment, we're going to talk about substance with style. You absolutely must know what you are talking about. Know your product line or lines. Know who your competition is. Know who your customer is. But, even if you know all this, and are incredibly knowledgeable....watch out....you better say whatever it is you have to say not only with the right amount of empathy and appeal, but also with the right amount of detail.

Colleen, my new office manager, once told me about a call she received from Karen, an administrative assistant to Brad who has been my client for over six years. Karen explained to Colleen that Brad **NEEDED** me to fly in to help him prepare for a tough annual shareholders meeting that was to take place within two weeks. Karen offered three dates. One was the day before the annual meeting, which Brad didn't really want because it was so close to the actual meeting. The other two dates were within the next ten days. Colleen told Karen I had

ACCOMPLISHMENT SHEET
Dressing to Sell

Describe the selling situation, customer, and what is most appropriate to wear.

Selling Situation	Customer	Appropriate Attire

meetings on both of those days,and she didn't feel comfortable saying that I could or couldn't fly in to help Brad. Colleen further informed Karen that I was out of the office at an economic summit and might not return until the morning.

When I got back to the office that afternoon around 5:00 P.M., I immediately called Karen. She was gone until 7:30 A.M. the next morning. Brad was not in the office either. Based upon what Colleen told me of the conversation she had with Karen, I had an uneasy feeling that my client was left in limbo not knowing if I would be able to meet his needs. Not good.

My suspicion was confirmed when I spoke with Karen early the next morning. Karen said that when Colleen talked about my schedule, Brad began to think of how to make it work for both of our schedules. He was even willing to fly into Pittsburgh to see me if there was a convenient time. As Karen and I chatted, I let her know that Brad wouldn't need to fly to me unless he absolutely wanted to do so. I explained that I would be glad to move my meetings around to accommodate his needs. As we continued talking, we actually found a fourth date on which Brad and I were able to clear our schedules and meet.

When I shared the above conversation with Colleen, she looked sad and very unhappy with herself because of how her words were interpreted by Karen. Colleen in the initial conversation, left Karen feeling uncertain about how we would accommodate Brad. Colleen asked what she should have done differently.

Changing around a few words and adding some here and there is all that was necessary. Colleen could have said, "I know Linda will do everything she can to rearrange her schedule to fly in and see Brad. Linda might not be back in the office today, but I can get a message to her this evening. So, if she doesn't call before you leave work, she can call you at home tonight or first thing in the morning. Which will be best for you?" In this instance, Karen is left knowing her boss's needs will be met and we will bend over backwards to get back to her. Essential elements for good solid selling and on-going relationship building.

Are there instances when you should have rephrased what you were saying? Keep track of those times and think of rephrases. Also keep track of when you have artfully met the needs of your customer or client and remember to do it that way again.

How often have you heard somebody say to you, "I'm not angry for what you said to me but for how you said it!" The way you talk to people, including your customers, has a great impact on them. Also remember, sometimes what you don't say can have a dramatic impact too. One of the best examples of this has to do with Tim and Mary, who were getting ready to go on a trip to Holland. Mary decided that she wanted her parents to go along. She asked her husband, "Tim, is it okay if they come along with us?," and he said, "Sure, I like your parents. Let's all go to Holland together." So they left the States, flew to Holland and they got to this quaint little inn. When they were leaving the inn, they were carrying luggage down. Mary was huffing and puffing, and as she met up with Tim on the landing, dropped the luggage and said, "I'm done." He said "OK" and he picked up the luggage, brought it downstairs, put it in the trunk, closed it and they all drove off. They got to the next location, Mary opened up the trunk and said, "Tim, where's Mom and Dad's luggage?" Tim replied, "I don't know. Mary, you told me you were done. I thought that was it. I thought that was the end of the luggage. "They had some words together and he drove back to pick up the rest of the luggage.

What went wrong in this communication? Assumptions—you're not supposed to assume. Assuming incorrectly in personal and selling relationships can be deadly to the life of the relationship. One time an audience member yelled out to me, "You know what Tim did wrong? He shouldn't have taken the in-laws along." I get some of my best material from my audience and customers. That's another great reason to talk with those you help. You get great information and great lines to help drive points home and to provide humor.

What could Tim or Mary have done differently in this situation? Well, at the point Tim and Mary met on the landing, for good solid communication, they should have been specific with one another. "Gee Mary, you're done. Does that mean that there's no more luggage upstairs?" Or, "Gee Tom, I'm exhausted. I really don't want to get the rest of the luggage. Let's go together and get it or would you please go get it." Be specific with everybody. It helps to deal with assumptions.

A wise high school teacher of mine had an interesting way of driving this point home. He used to write B.S. over my papers. He would write the same on many of my classmates' papers too! I can still picture the scene in my mind's eye. Whenever a student would turn in a paper that was not specific enough or to the point, he would write in bright red marker over the entire paper in huge letters those two mentioned letters. He told us that B.S. means—Be Specific. Over the years, I have learned that the more specific you are, the more understandable you are. The more specific you are, the more time you'll save. And that means, the more time you will have to help people and be an incredibly effective salesperson.

ACCOMPLISHMENT SHEET
Being Specific

Please use this page to begin cataloging situations you have
experienced when being more specific would have created better
understanding between you and your customer. You may also
like to keep track of situations involving other salespeople as
well. Decide how you could have recognized the fact that one of
you wasn't being specific enough.

Situation	False Assumptions	Warning Signs

8. Learning the signs of body language

Understanding your customer's body language is a critical part of selling. There are three concepts we'll look at. First, look for gesture clusters. Secondly, look at the way your customer's body is positioned in relation to you. And, lastly, look at how your customer moves his or her hands to see if the hand movements support the words being spoken.

Here's what I mean by gesture clusters. A lot of times we hear people say, "OK, your arms are folded. That means that you must be on the defensive." Not necessarily. Some people are just comfortable with their arms folded. When I was in the ninth month of my pregnancy with Felise, my second child, I tipped the scale at about 200 pounds. Now, I can honestly say to you that a pregnant woman in the ninth month has no place to put her arms. The arms either have to be out to the side or folded on top of the stomach. So, it doesn't necessarily mean you're defensive if you do cross your arms. But if you're talking to a customer who has their arms folded and suddenly, almost simultaneously, they cross over at another point on their body—this is a clue. If they begin to dig into the fleshy part of their body—this is another clue. If their hands suddenly form a fist, guess what?—a clue. This gesture cluster tells you that they are on the defensive.

Besides gesture clusters, look at the way your customer's body is positioned in relationship to you. If you are talking to a person about selling a particular product and suddenly they shift their attention to a window or door, this is a pretty solid indication they are not comfortable with what is being said. Use this as an opportunity to ask them what they're thinking so you can squelch their objection before it begins to grow.

Hand movements are also a key to what people are really thinking. Here's an example: It was in 1983 when I was privy to what I call a "hallway conversation." I'm sure some of you have heard or seen something as you were walking down a hall, something that you really weren't supposed to see or hear. I saw the president of QUBE Cable, owned and operated by Warner Communications, talking to somebody from a major lending institution.At that time, I was doing a business talk show for QUBE Cable. Also at that time, money was at the highest interest rate it has ever been the United States; the prime rate was at a whopping 21 percent.

Here's exactly what I saw and heard—The president of my company was saying to the man from the lending institution, "Everything here is under control. I'm really glad you stopped by." As the president said 'everything is under control,' his hands were going around in circles. I went home that night and said to my husband, "I'm going to lose my job." He said, "What did you do? What did you say?" I told him that I saw a hallway conversation and described the details. My husband replied, "Linda, you just put too much stock into this stuff about body language." Well, I hoped he was right, but then came the Black Friday. They lined up everyone in my programming department and called us in one by one. They did not call me in until the very end. I thought that I probably read that body language wrong, but then again I knew I couldn't have. When they finally called me in, I kept thinking to myself that I knew they were going to keep me around to continue doing my show. I was convinced. You know what?—I was wrong. I walked out of there being a part of a redesign and reorganization before it was even popular.

I stood on the unemployment line in my early thirties for the first and only time in my life. I didn't like it. I didn't want to be there. So I did what every entrepreneur-at-heart does when they're in the unemployment line—start my own business, and that's what I've been doing ever since.

The moral of the story is to make sure that you look for people's gestures in clusters, watch body-positioning, and note if hand movements support the words being spoken. In order to be successful, I have watched the body language closely of each person I have helped. Plus, I treat every customer and audience with the utmost care and respect.

ACCOMPLISHMENT SHEET
Learning the Signs of Body Language

Take notice of your customer's body language as well as yours. Monitor what you observe in your next several sales calls. After you write down what you see, think of when and why it occurred and what the body language was saying.

You will get to the point where you will automatically begin to read this helpful language. Some people like to keep track of what they see on each call. You'll be able to use this information to better understand your customers and clients.

Body Language	When/Why
Gesture Clusters Observed	
Body Positioning	
Hand Movement versus Words	

9. Establishing the qualities of a loving relationship

What are the qualities of a loving relationship? Hmmm....So, I suspect you want to know why I'm asking you this question. Fair enough. But, before I tell you why, let's explore the answers. As we do so, I invite you to join in on a presentation I gave to an audience regarding this question...

Me: *What are the qualities of a loving relationship?*

Audience: *Trust.*

Me: *Do you think trust has any place in your business and when you talk to people? Trust. Yes, what else?*

Audience: *Commitment and dedication.*

Me: *So if you have commitment and dedication when you help your customers, will it make a difference?*

Audience: *YES!!! (A collective and resounding "YES!!!" was accompanied by total excitement along with nods of approval)*

Me: *This technique of Presentational Selling is yet one more golden nugget to help you help your customer which will help you increase your sales. Any other qualities come to mind?*

Audience: *Honesty. Patience. Respect.*

Me: *All of these qualities, they will help you. The qualities of a loving relationship...*

Audience: *Acceptance and humor.*

Me: *Sure if there's something that you can talk about that's funny—use it. Acceptance. You want people to accept your knowledge, your products, your services and you as being the best person to lead them to make the right choices. So if you have love, and you have compassion surrounding your job—it's going to matter.*

I'm asking you to bring passion to your job, not that you don't, but with everything that you do. I want you to have a passionate commitment to helping the people you talk to every day.

One of the best parts of a truly loving relationship is there's an intimacy where you can talk to each other about absolutely anything. That's a deep relationship. Now, I'm not telling you to get so deep with everyone you talk to.

But, if you can have a level of intimacy that lets them want to talk with you—you're going to be able to help them. The person will feel like they're being heard by you. Above all, you want to make sure your customer, client and audience hears you, and that you hear them.

Now what are the qualities of a loving relationship? What do those qualities have to do with you and Presentational Selling? These qualities mold the type of relationship and the level of understanding and commitment you are willing to give to your job and customer!

(Sometimes, I find fate amazingly uncanny. As I was writing this segment for you, I took a few minutes off to eat some Chinese food for lunch. My fortune cookie's wisdom read: Love is the glue that holds together everything in the world!) This is the glue that holds you and your customer together.

10. Identifying the adjectives that best describe you

One time a vice president of a company called me up and said, "Linda we have a problem. We have to go in front of the government and talk about something that our company did drastically wrong. There is only one man, Martin, we can send in to talk to the government. Martin is technically brilliant, but he's arrogant. Linda, can you make him not arrogant?" I was foolish enough to say, "Sure, I can do that."

I went in and I worked with this man and it became apparent to me in the first few minutes, I could not help. I was really convinced that the man was not capable of listening to anybody or anything. I suggested we break early for lunch—about 10:30 A.M. I said, "Why don't we just go over to the restaurant and start on lunch a little bit early? I'm hungry and we have both been up since early this morning."

At lunch, as I began to look for divine intervention, I heard myself utter, "You know, tell me four adjectives that best describe you." He said to me, "Cut and dry, condescending, nervous, and humorous."

ACCOMPLISHMENT SHEET
Establishing the Qualities of a Loving Relationship

Think about the qualities that are important to you in a loving relationship. Write the qualities down in the space provided here.

Look at your responses. Select only those qualities from what you've said that will help you in a selling relationship and write those down under the column called "Qualities." In the column called "Results," write down the benefit of exhibiting that quality when you are Presentational Selling.

Qualities	Results

I didn't think these were the four best qualities to go up in front of the government with. Out of all the adjectives he mentioned, I thought it was best to focus on "cut and dry." I asked him "Well, where does this cut and dry quality come from?

He retorted, "I really don't like to talk about it, but, I was in Vietnam."

I said, "OK, don't talk about it."

"Don't ask me to talk about it, I won't even talk to my wife about it."

I told him fine and that I would no longer talk to him about it at all.

The more I said not to talk to me about the subject, he opened up. He told me that he was a photoanalyst in Vietnam. He would look at those pictures; he would decide where the bombs would drop, where they wouldn't. Who would die, who would live. Cut and dry, black and white, thirty years ago he was in Vietnam.

What is wrong with this picture? It's the nineties now and he's still reacting like he was living in the sixties and seventies! It's a different audience. You have to change what you're doing to address the needs of your audience.

Martin realized that the adjectives he used to describe himself, especially cut and dry, prevented him from moving forward the way he wanted. Plus, he realized that his "cut and dry" attitude revealed arrogance. With these realizations, Martin was able to woo the government to see things his way. Today, he continues to be successful and gets along much better with people.

Here's a closer look at how Martin's adjectives are likely to be interpreted by those whom he will be speaking to:

ADJECTIVE	INTERPRETATION
Cut and dry	*Cut and dry could be interpreted as being inflexible. This is okay if that's the desired outcome.*
Humorous	*Being humorous is an excellent quality when it is properly placed.*
Condescending	*Condescending often translates to an audience as being a combination of arrogant, superior and patronizing.*
Nervous	*Coming across as being nervous may make your audience feel that you're not telling the truth or may be uncertain of what you are saying.*

ACCOMPLISHMENT SHEET
Identifying the Adjectives that Best Describe You

Write the four adjectives which describe how you see yourself as you sell your product, concept or service. Then, objectively write down the quality(s) of how that adjective affects your client or customer. For instance, if you are understanding. . . what emotions might that elicit? If you are fast-talking, think of how your customer will know and perceive you. Your visualization of yourself will have a direct impact upon the person you are helping.

	Adjective	Interpretation
1.		
2.		
3.		
4.		

11. Building and keeping the relationship

Once you have helped someone, by not only selling to them, but by value-adding every step of the way—you have a satisfied customer. You have planted a foundation for a wonderful relationship. Relationship? Yes, of course. You don't want them to buy from you just once do you? You want them to come back to you as often as possible. Plus, you want them to refer people to you as new customers, right? So, build, build, build on to what you have already done.

If you want to be successful today, you must consider the Three P's—Passion. Partnering. Possibilities.

Please have passion for all that you do in life. Even your job! Truly, you've got to like and love what you do if you are serious about succeeding. Wake up every morning and be thankful that you have the opportunity to make a difference in people's lives by selling them what you have to offer. Think about how nobody can quite offer what you have to sell in quite the way that you can. Be excited to make a difference in people's lives.

On partnering, I am reminded of a bank and its relationship managers (RM's). It was the job of the RM's to respond to the current needs of the bank's best customers, to anticipate their future wants, and to let the customer know they are important and valued. At this bank, a special data base was designed to identify the products each customer used, future wants, likes and dislikes, you name it. The RM found it out. The customer's banking needs were met and the customers felt special in receiving tickets to events they enjoyed attending. Building the relationship—one of the best ways to secure your selling future. Even send birthday and anniversary cards!

The possibilities are endless for your success if you partner and have passion regarding the products and services that you sell. Imagine what might happen if you go back to a satisfied customer who you have built a relationship with. You might say something like, "Hi! just calling to touch base with you to see how that new computer is working." You would also want to talk with them about other information you had learned from them during your various conversations. You should keep notes not only on the needs and wants of your clients, but also personal items they may have mentioned. Perhaps they talked to you about how their daughter had hurt her arm when she slipped after making the winning basket. Ask them how their daughter's arm is doing. You might even go on to say you'd love to be able to help their friends, colleagues or others at their company. Ask them for some recommendations. Will everyone refer someone to you? No. However, a high percentage of satisfied customers will be willing to refer other people to you. My research reveals that five out of ten clients will give referrals, sometimes more than one referral at a time. But, you must ask!

ACCOMPLISHMENT SHEET
Building and Keeping the Relationship

Partnering
How do you partner with your clients?

How can you partner with your clients?

Passion for Your Job
What do you love about your job?

Describe the feelings you have once you have a satisfied customer:

Possibilities
What should you continue to do that's working in cultivating your customer relationships

What should you do to begin cultivating or to further cultivate your customer relationships?

---

12. Bonus items

Four final items for you to consider to round out your Presentational Selling™: Eye contact, Fillers, Visual Aids and Props, Minimizers.

Eye Contact —Good eye contact is imperative in all selling and presentational situations. Here's the mandatory rule: Always maintain eye contact whether you are selling or presenting to one person, two, ten, or any size audience. Maintain that eye contact with the person you are talking to or listening to. When you are speaking to an audience, select one person at a time and talk directly to that person. Then, shift your eye contact to another person and so on through your entire presentation. However, there's an exception—When you are speaking and an audience member asks you a question, this is what to do: Look at the questioner when he or she is asking the question. Then, repeat or rephrase the question.

Sometimes, it is necessary to rephrase a question. At this point, break eye contact with that individual as you rephrase. As you begin your response, address your answer to the entire audience and follow the mandatory rule. To enhance your eye contact, here's an exercise for you:

Look at objects in a room and practice talking to one or more of those objects.

Have a friend help you practice keeping eye contact. Look at your friend as you talk about whatever you feel like; have that person let you know if you look away from them or roll your eyes.

Practice these exercises for three to five minutes a day for three to six months.

Fillers—Fillers are sounds like uh, um, er, well, that fill up your flow of speech when you may be uncertain of exactly what you want to say. I have heard salespeople use as many as thirty in a minute. Each filler lasts about a second. If you need help in getting rid of fillers, do the following:

Record your voice into an audio recorder as you talk about any subject you feel like. Each time you use a filler, stop the recorder. Go back and listen to what you recorded. Now, go back and say what you were saying before. This time, instead of using an uh, pause. Your speech pattern may sound a little choppy at first, but soon these pauses will replace your filler and the pauses will come across as being quite natural.

Visual Aids and Props —Whenever possible, use visual aids and props to enhance your selling. You might want to use written examples of how your customer can save money with your product and have them fill in the numbers you need as you work out the figures for their particular situation. You could have them try the product they are considering purchasing. Begin thinking about what you can do in this area.

Minimizers —Lastly in this segment, please refrain from using what I call minimizers. Minimizers are words that water down the importance of what you are about to say. Some actual examples of minimizers that I hear people use on a regular basis are italicized below:

> Do you have *just* a minute?
> I talked *a little bit* about the variable pay objective setting.
> *I think* you have a problem!

What you have to say is very important not only to yourself but to your clients. Don't minimize your words, say them with utmost conviction. Make your audience want to listen to you. This way, you will be happy and they will be too!

You've done it!

Congratulations! You have just brought out the natural salesperson in you by having completed reading The Hottest New Results-Producing Way to Sell: Presentational Selling™!!! You will accomplish much more than you ever thought possible.

If you ever have any questions or comments, call me, fax me, write me, e-mail me! Thank you for letting me share my secrets of how to best present yourself and dramatically multiply sales. All the best to you!

"...everything you do and say is for the benefit of your audience. Through your ability to help your client or customer you automatically and continually skyrocket your career..."

-Linda Blackman
The Image Guru ®

About Linda Blackman

Linda Blackman strongly believes "you must not only bring passion to your job, but to everything you do...make a passionate commitment to helping each person you talk to every day."

Linda has been in the public spotlight for more than twenty years and has touched the hearts of all. After graduating from Northwestern University with a B.S. in Radio, Television and Film Production, Linda, for a decade, was a highly acclaimed coast-to-coast television news anchor, reporter and talk show host. In Philadelphia, she earned the prestigious Mayoral Award for Excellence in Broadcast Journalism. Immediately following her broadcasting years, she founded The Executive Image, Inc. and became a sought after speaker, trainer and consultant.

Successful Women Magazine featured Linda as a charismatic speaker with a "genuinely enthusiastic" attitude and a "relentless work ethic" who helps people communicate their message effectively. *Pittsburgh Style Magazine* dubbed Linda one of the top 100 people in Pittsburgh with Style! Linda's articles and inspirational stories have appeared in many publications. Linda is a featured author in *Chicken Soup for the Surviving Soul* and *Chocolate for a Woman's Soul*. She is currently working on several new books.

Linda helps Fortune 500 companies, associations, businesses, executives, salespeople — even politicians and sports stars. Linda's dynamic talks and programs on sales, presentation skills and how to deal with the media, arm her audiences with everything they need to know to get what they want from a given situation.

Linda lives in Pittsburgh with her family.

For more information about Linda Blackman, contact her at:

5020 Castleman Street, Pittsburgh, PA 15232
phone (412) 682-2200; fax (412) 621-6218
E-Mail: MsBlackman@aol.com
The World Wide Web:
http://www.ibp.com/pit/executive

Company Profile

Did you ever see an audience rise and applaud at the end of a speaker's presentation? That's what happens whenever Linda Blackman, President of The Executive Image, Inc., gives a presentation. At last, an exciting speaker and author who motivates, inspires and teaches while she speaks. Best of all, her audiences have fun while they learn! Linda took her impressive ten year background as a broadcast journalist and founded The Executive Image, Inc. in 1983. Through her talks and her company you will —

- **Enhance your bottom line**
- **Strengthen your leadership skills and relationships**
- **Reach your utmost success**

Linda shows you how to achieve personal and professional greatness as she shares her proven techniques.

With that in mind, Linda has developed blockbuster keynotes and workshops. Her most requested programs include:

- **Presentational Selling™**
- **Power Presenting**
- **Media Savvy**
- **Delighting the Customer**
- **The Thirteen Secrets of Assertiveness**
- **Crisis Communication**

Linda also provides private, one-on-one and small group coaching sessions.

To better serve her audiences' needs, Linda developed a number of products you can get to continue incorporating her results-producing nuggets into your life. Her audio tapes include *Power Presenting, Media Savvy,* and *Seventeen Steps to Skyrocket Your Success.*

Just for asking, Linda will send you her video brochure titled *"Linda Blackman —Your Connection to Generating Dollars and Sense,"* plus information on the programs offered by her company.

Whether you are in sales, a corporate employee, an executive, or a member of an association, you need the right skills to take you to your highest level of performance. Linda Blackman **will** take you there for the sale you need to close, the audience you must face and the client you must reach!

Chapter 2

Time Management:
A Strategy for Personal Sales Success

By
Joe Killian

Your greatest, long-term success will come as a result of employing the principles of time management only after you've discovered what truly motivates you and why.

—Joe Killian

Success is a journey

*A journey of a thousand miles must begin with a
single step.*

—*Lao Tzu*

D
o you know what it takes for you to be successful? Are you as
successful as you want to be? Are you as successful as you are
capable of being?

A growing number of companies promise success as a result of
using their time management systems. You've seen the products — a
handsome, zippered leather binder with a shoulder strap that holds a
calendar through the year 2040, yearly, monthly, weekly and daily
planners, a phone directory, business card file, legal pad, calculator, pens
and pencils, all for the price of $129.95. These "time management
experts" suggest that by following prescribed techniques, you'll learn to
manage your time more efficiently, gain control of your life, reduce
stress, improve relationships, lead a more balanced existence, and
ultimately, be a happier, more successful person. Sounds great. Everyone
would agree that these are desirable outcomes. And most people would
admit they could use their time more wisely.

Unfortunately it's not that simple. Efficiency does not equal
effectiveness. Author Peter Drucker put it succinctly: "Efficiency is doing
the thing right, but effectiveness is doing the right thing." This is not to
suggest that techniques and tools that help you manage your time more
efficiently are not valuable. They are. In fact, later in this chapter I will
present some which are quite helpful and that I strongly recommend you
use. But, if everyone could become more fulfilled simply by using a
leather-bound time management system, I suspect we'd all be successful.
The fact is, they're just one part of the solution.

Perhaps the first person to recognize that something important
was missing from conventional approaches to time management was
Stephen R. Covey, author, teacher and founder of the Covey Leadership
Center. As a result, Covey is credited with a breakthrough in time
management. In his book *First Things First*, Covey and co-authors

A. Roger Merrill and Rebecca R. Merrill offer the premise that we must focus on what's important to us—put "first things first"—if we are to be truly effective. Rather than focus on time and things, they emphasize relationships and results, effectiveness over efficiency. Covey was right when he observed that "Doing more things faster is no substitute for doing the right things."

No doubt you should understand what's important to you before you try to manage your time. Otherwise, you may spend a great deal of time and energy on what is essentially "busy work." But I'm convinced from my experience, both personal and in consulting with people from executives to salespeople to educators, that there's more to it than that.

What's missing from other approaches to time management is this: your greatest, long-term success will come as a result of employing the principles of time management only after you've discovered what truly motivates you and why. First you've got to make time to honestly reflect upon what motivates you, what drives you. Once you understand who you are and what you need, you can move forward and set the right goals and apply the right time management techniques. You'll then reach the success and fulfillment you seek, success that will satisfy your most important needs.

In this chapter, I'll take you through a process I call "Looking Inside and Out." This process is made up of four steps that should be followed in the order they are presented. You may be tempted to jump in somewhere in the middle or go out of order, but I strongly advise that you do not. You wouldn't start cooking in the middle of a recipe and expect your meal to turn out well. Be patient with the process; complete each exercise as you go along. Take your time in answering the questions within each exercise, just like the good chef who carefully prepares a gourmet meal. By mastering each step, you will learn more about yourself on your journey to your ultimate success.

Here's how it works. In Step One, you'll begin by looking "inside" with an introspective look and analysis of what drives you internally. You'll identify your "success factors." In Step Two, you'll then take what you've learned about your motivation and apply your insights to creating your personal vision of success and developing a personal mission statement. Because you will have already determined your success factors, you'll be better able to define your success. In Step Three, you'll begin looking "outside" and planning for your success. In Step Four, you'll apply the knowledge you've acquired, along with some basic time management techniques, to implement a unique personal success strategy that works best for you.

Step 1. What makes you successful?

Tell me what you pay attention to and I will tell you who you are.

—*Jose Ortega y Gasset*

My client, Bill, has reached his goal. Over the past 20 years, he has ascended the ranks in his financial services company, from agent to district manager, and ultimately to agency manager. Now the highest ranking person in his office, Bill is responsible for 100 employees who generate millions of dollars in sales annually. He is described by the people he works with as achieving most of his success through hard work and perseverance. As a result, he has done what he wanted most— in his words "provide for my family." Bill, his wife and daughter live in a home valued at well over half a million dollars, own a vacation home, and drive expensive cars. They contribute a great deal of money to charities. Bill is especially proud of the fact that he's been able to pay for his daughter to attend an Ivy League college. And, he's accomplished it all by the age of 45.

By many people's standards, Bill is a success. But Bill is in trouble. A former college athlete, he is overweight, overworked, in financial difficulty and in danger of losing his job.

There's more to achieving success than just having a clear goal. Bill's goal was certainly clear—to become manager of his company. There's more to it than talent. Bill was not the best or brightest agent when he began his career. There's more to it than perseverance. On his way up the ladder, Bill's typical work week was six or seven days, 10 to 12 hours a day. There's also more to it than having a noble motivation. Bill's motivation has always been to provide for his family.

There's more to it... and it begins by looking inside yourself.

Personal discovery

Unfortunately, Bill's situation is not that uncommon. Many people pursue a goal only to find that they do not feel the satisfaction and fulfillment they anticipated when they reach their goal.

Everyone has his or her share of success and failure in life. But few of us take the time to analyze why we were successful in some situations and not in others. Understanding what makes us successful is not easy, and yet, if we take the time to understand our own unique needs and talents, we'll dramatically improve our opportunities for success.

The following exercise is designed to help you to better understand yourself and your motivations. Think for a moment about your greatest personal accomplishment. Perhaps it was graduating from college or running a marathon. Maybe it was designing your own home. With this in mind, answer the following questions. Your answers will provide important clues about how your unique needs improve your opportunities for success.

Describe your greatest personal accomplishment.

a. What was the easiest aspect of accomplishing it?

b. What was the most difficult aspect of this accomplishment?

Now, answer the following questions, this time with your greatest professional accomplishment in mind. Perhaps you landed an important account after others had tried and failed. Or, maybe you were named salesperson of the year.

Describe your greatest professional accomplishment.

a. What was the easiest aspect of this accomplishment?

b. What was the most difficult aspect of this accomplishment?

Now think about some of the more difficult times in your life and answer the following.

Describe your most difficult personal experience.

a. What helped you to persevere through this experience?

b. What caused your difficulty?

Describe your most difficult professional experience.

a. What helped you to persevere through this experience?

b. What caused your difficulty?

Look at your responses to the easiest and hardest aspects of your personal and professional accomplishments. Compare those to your answers regarding difficult personal and professional experiences. Do you see any patterns or consistencies? Even if you don't immediately, this exercise should shed some light on your motivations, needs and talents. Take a few minutes to write down what you have learned as a result of completing the exercise. You will use this knowledge as you continue the "Inside-Out" process.

Finding your success zone

My greatest professional challenge occurred in a territory sales position selling training services. I spent a great deal of my time traveling alone. The job was very cold call intensive. My prospective clients were typically unresponsive and often defensive as I applied my hard selling, hard closing sales techniques. The additional responsibilities of the job required me to act as the sole administrator of all of the training programs in my territory.

In the first couple of months on the job, I did very well. In fact, I was on track to be among the best in the world in this multi-million dollar, 2000-person sales force. Everything was going great. But as time wore on, I became increasingly ineffective. Despite working excessive hours, my numbers continued to drop. I found myself desperately hoping that the next call would make my month, even though that seldom, if ever, happened. After struggling for several more months, I finally, with a heavy heart, quit my job. Despite my efforts, I had gone from the heights of possibility to the depths of despair.

I consider this experience to be one of my greatest professional challenges. Put simply, I had failed. I also consider it to be one of the greatest learning experiences of my life. The understanding that I painfully gained in that job has shaped everything I have done since, including writing this chapter.

To better understand what happened to me and help you avoid a similar fate, let's consider two key concepts: "Preferred Thought Process" and "Preferred Surroundings." These concepts are at the core of who you are and why you behave the way you do.

The first concept, Preferred Thought Process, includes how you think and how you approach goals, problems and day-to-day activities. Read the following descriptions and note which one defines you better.

Flexible: Adaptable to change, spontaneous, quickly tires of routine activities, enjoys thinking about the "big picture," pursues creative endeavors, is impulsive, imaginative, original, quick to make decisions.

Structured: Organized, resistant to change, comfortable with routine activities, enjoys thinking about details, pursues logical endeavors, analytical, reasonable, careful in making decisions, talks about facts.

One of these categories may describe you perfectly, or it may only describe you somewhat. In choosing, recognize that every person is unique and there is no right or wrong answer. Based on the descriptions, circle the letter on the scale below that best describes your Preferred Thought Process. Be as honest with yourself as you possibly can.

Preferred Thought Process

Flexible

A | **Very Flexible**

B | **Somewhat Flexible**

Somewhat Structured | C

Very Structured | D

Structured

The second concept to consider is your Preferred Surroundings. This describes the external environment that you enjoy, your relationships and how you interact with others.

Involved: Adaptable to others, preferred being included, enjoys and thrives on being with others, values making and having friends, is supportive of others, needs to belong, prefers group activities, is a team player, feelings are important, susceptible to peer pressure, needs to be liked, fears rejection.

Independent: Self-reliant, not influenced by others, objective, individual, needs to be alone, doesn't care what others think, not susceptible to peer pressure.

Based on the descriptions of Preferred Surroundings, circle the number that best describes you on the scale below. Be honest with yourself. Don't choose based on your current situation; instead describe your ideal situation.

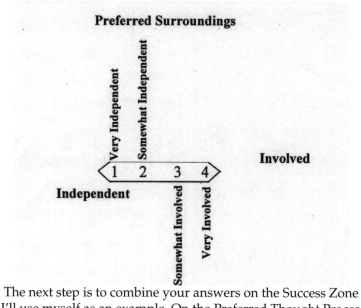

Preferred Surroundings

The next step is to combine your answers on the Success Zone Model. I'll use myself as an example. On the Preferred Thought Process scale, I'm a "B" and on the Preferred Surroundings scale, I'm a "4." I'll shade the area where they intersect. This area is my "Success Zone."

Refer back to your preferences. Circle your letter and number on the model below. Shade the square that defines your Success Zone.

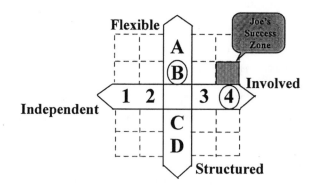

Your Success Zone is the area in which you are most comfortable and most productive. Activities that come most naturally for you are

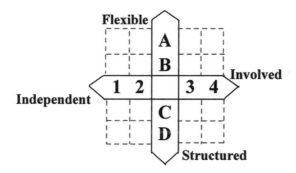

located in this area, and you tend to perform them well. When you're in your zone, you have the greatest potential to be your best. You're motivated, energized and excited about what you're doing. You are most likely to succeed while doing activities in your Success Zone.

On the other hand, when you're outside your Success Zone, you're less comfortable. You're likely to find activities in this area more challenging and less enjoyable. Your energy level tends to drop when you spend time in this area. You may procrastinate and avoid activities outside your Success Zone. It is important to note that being outside of your Success Zone is not an excuse for failure. You must adjust your approach to these activities in order to avoid burnout and to increase your opportunities for success.

Today, when I think back to my territory sales position, I realize that most of my difficulties existed because of a misalignment between my job responsibilities and my Success Zone. Many of those responsibilities were very solitary activities. The travel, the cold calls, the hard sell and hard close approach to the business all required me to be independent. I am highly involved and find these activities very draining. My administrative duties required me to be structured and organized. Because I'm flexible, these activities were also more difficult for me to perform. The net result was that most of the time I was outside of my Success Zone. No matter how much time I put into the job, it got increasingly more difficult for me to succeed. My energy was drained. Ultimately I burned out.

Two additional points of interest in my story: First, I started out very well, and then experienced an accelerating downward spiral. My fast start can be attributed to my enthusiasm and desire to be successful.

It was easier for me to ignore the discomfort that I was experiencing outside of my Success Zone. But as time wore on, it became increasingly difficult for me to keep my self-esteem up and to perform well.

The second point worth noting is that I did enjoy one part of my job–teaching. Occasionally I would find myself in front of an audience. After speaking to a group, I drove home energized and excited. I looked forward to my next speaking opportunity. When I left that job, I realized that I should be spending more time as a speaker and trainer.

Bill's experience was similar. The further he rose in his organization, the more his job responsibilities forced him outside of his Success Zone. Bill is a "4" on the "Preferred Surrounding" scale. He has difficulty making the tough decisions that affect the people in his organization because he is so involved with them. On the "Preferred Thought Process" scale he's an "A." He's so flexible that his two full-time secretaries have difficulty keeping him organized. Without an awareness of his Success Zone and the ability to adjust accordingly, Bill will continue to struggle.

In order to avoid your own struggle, look back to the exercise on "Personal Discovery." The aspects you identified as easiest about your greatest achievements are probably activities that are in or near your Success Zone. Likewise, the most difficult aspects probably are further away from your zone. As you review the most difficult times you identified in that exercise, you may find you were operating outside of your Success Zone.

It's not unusual for people to be hard on themselves for not being able to do certain things as easily as they can do other tasks. In reality, the reason these tasks may be difficult is because they are outside of your Success Zone. So instead of wasting time and energy on brow-beating yourself, accept yourself. Accept that some things come more naturally than others. In Step 4, we'll talk more about using your Success Zone to your advantage.

Influences, expectations and the perfect job

It's easy to take all the credit when we succeed and blame others when we fail. The fact is, most success comes from within. Yet we can't discount our environment. Factors like our upbringing, our work and home environment and accepted social morays all influence our opportunities for success.

Upbringing and parental influences can have a tremendous impact on your level of success. For example, were you raised in a loving, supportive environment where you were able to develop a positive self-image, or were you constantly berated, controlled and made to feel that nothing you did was good enough? Many studies have been done regarding the impact of upbringing and how the way we're treated as children affects us later in life. Most experts agree that there is an important connection. (For those interested in pursuing this further, there is an extensive amount of material available.)

If your work environment is closely aligned with your Success Zone, your chances for success are improved. But when it doesn't, using excuses like, "I didn't get the information I needed from the other department on time," "I had no idea someone else was pitching the account," "There's so much paperwork, it's practically impossible to close a sale!" don't justify failure.

On the home front, people who have children are very aware of the impact a newborn baby has on a good night's sleep and what we consider to be most important in our lives.

Environmental influences can be positive, as in the case of a mentor who recognizes a young person's skills, interests and talents and guides her at a time when she most needs it. Or, you may be steered in the wrong direction. How many students have chosen their college majors based on the advice of well-meaning parents, teachers, and guidance counselors only to realize that the chosen field was not at all right for them? I started college as a computer science major because everyone convinced me I'd have a lot of job opportunities upon graduation. They were probably right, but I quickly discovered that a computer career was not right for me. Before the end of the first semester, I changed my major to business administration/human resources and continue to have a successful career in that field today.

Social, moral and business standards also play a role. People may find themselves caught up in a lifestyle because it's considered not only desirable but also necessary by coworkers, friends or family.

Sarah is a friend of mine who worked as a sales representative for a profitable, well-known national corporation. Salespeople in her organization had high income potential and most enjoyed a high standard of living. Sarah worked very hard to fit in. She quickly discovered, however, that the expenses associated with maintaining this lifestyle were costly, in more ways than one. A townhouse mortgage, a big car payment and an expensive designer wardrobe put Sarah in debt. As a result, she was forced to work much harder to continually produce a certain level of sales. Paying her bills had become her primary motivation; a powerful one at that. The stress of the debt, compounded with the stress of the job, caused Sarah to quickly burn out.

Success comes easier when you get what you need both from the job itself and from people around you. The bad news is that most of us will never find a job that is an absolutely perfect fit, that always meets our needs, where we can be successful 100 percent of the time. The good news is, once you've clearly identified what you need, you will be better able to seek out and recognize a good fit. You'll also be better equipped to adjust when your needs are not being completely met.

In the sales job I quit, I had to make cold calls, an independent, structured activity. If I had recognized I was far out of my zone, I could have better prepared myself for the difficulties I would face. One way would have been to break up a full day of cold calls with activities more in line with my Success Zone. For example, I could have taken some time during the day to brainstorm, in a creative, open-minded way, about upcoming speaking engagements. These "Success Zone Breaks" can energize us to higher levels of productivity and can make those activities outside of your zone more tolerable.

List your current job responsibilities. Identify where you are operating on the Success Zone Model when performing each of those activities. This process of aligning job responsibilities with your Success Zone improves your understanding of how you operate. By going through this process with all your responsibilities, you can identify where potential difficulties lie and deal with them before they become major problems.

Understanding all of the influences on our lives ensures an enlightened journey toward success.

Smoothing life's ride

> *Perpetual devotion to what a man calls his business, is only to be sustained by perpetual neglect of many other things.*
> —*Robert Louis Stevenson*

We often get caught up in pursuing our dream career only to find that our single-minded pursuit leads us to the wrong destination. When we arrive, any satisfaction we feel about our accomplishment is overshadowed by the problems that our neglect has created. In our own way, Sarah, Bill and I each believed that hard work was the key to our success. In reality, we were in jobs that constantly forced us outside of our Success Zone. As a result, working harder only served to drain our energy and cause more stress and frustration. The excessive time we spent trying to succeed threw our lives out of balance.

There are many parts that make up a whole, balanced life. I call these "Personal Priority Areas." They include: your family life, financial security, career, mental health, physical health, spiritual well-being, friends/social life and community involvement.

Family—Parents, spouse/significant other, children, listening ability, forgiveness, time together (quality and quantity), support system, respect, love and compassion
Physical—Exercise, conditioning, appearance, weight control, nutrition, general wellness, prevention and treatment
Mental—Imagination, general attitude, reading, stimulation, continuing education, curiosity, vocabulary
Spiritual—Inner peace, sense of purpose, prayer, meditation, religious study, belief in higher being, congregational involvement
Social—Friends, sense of humor, self confidence, manners, caring/empathy, avocational pursuits, hobbies, communication/listening skills
Career—Alignment with success zone, job satisfaction, effectiveness, training, understanding, purpose, competence, professional associations
Financial—Earnings, savings, investments, budget, insurance, debt, net worth
Community—Financial contributions, volunteer work, service organizations, civic office or committee, PTA involvement, youth projects

Taken together, these components make up your "Life's Wheel."

Life's Wheel

Evaluate your current level of satisfaction with the quality of time you spend in each of theseareas. Using the wheel and definitions above, make a dot on each line, with the intersection of the line and the outer circle meaning "100% completely satisfied" and the center or hub of the wheel being "0% completely dissatisfied." Once you have marked each line, then connect the dots as in the example below.

Life's Wheel

The ideal shape of any wheel is round. Look at the shape of your wheel. By focusing on those areas you rated lowest, you can begin to pay more attention to them and "balance" your Life's Wheel. If it's constantly out of balance and you're spending too much time in one or two areas, your journey to success will be a bumpy one. You could very well end up in situations like Sarah, Bill and me. The most important thing to be cognizant of is the fact that there's more to a balanced, successful life than just one or two areas.

It is important to recognize that there may be times when important and urgent situations demand you focus on one area. This might happen when you take over a new sales territory or when you first start working with a new client. In fact, long-term balance in life requires periods of short-term imbalance. But, as a rule, you will best maintain your course in life by keeping your wheel round.

Step 2: Envisioning success: seeing is believing

> *Many persons have a wrong idea of what constitutes true happiness. It is not attained through self-gratification, but through fidelity to a worthy purpose.*
> —*Helen Keller*

Emmit Smith, running back for the Dallas Cowboys and four-time NFL rushing champion, tells the story of determining his definition of success. When he was a senior in high school, Smith was named the Gatorade High School Player of the Year. For this honor, he won a trip to the Super Bowl at the Rose Bowl in Pasadena, California. As he walked on the field to accept his award, Smith resolved that he would return to play in a Super Bowl. Smith ultimately played with the Cowboys in the Super Bowl, not once but three times. Each time they were world champions.

A long car ride

Clarity of purpose is vital to achieving success. With a clear vision and commitment to that vision, you can reach the goals you set. Smith had a clear vision of what success meant to him. His vision kept him focused and drove him to accomplish it, despite the fact that many people felt that Smith was too small to play professional football.

As I struggled through my territory sales job, my sales manager used to "come along for the ride" every once in a while and grill me about my progress. I remember one rather long and punishing ride when Tom asked me, "What's behind your visor?" I flipped down my visor and replied, "Nothing. Why?" Tom said, "That's your problem." He then went on to explain that, when he had been in my position, he taped a photo of his dream yacht to the back of the visor in his car. "That's what kept me motivated to do the things I had to do to be successful."

Imagine the warmth of the sun on your face as you lounge on the deck of Tom's yacht, sip a cool drink and listen to the lapping ocean waves. Imagine the sights, sounds, and sensations of scoring the winning touchdown in the Super Bowl with Smith. When you can visualize your success that clearly, you dramatically improve your opportunities for achieving that success. Significant studies, especially in sports, have shown the positive impact of visualization on performance.

In sales workshops, I ask people to go through an envisioning process. One very descriptive example was given to me by a successful sales professional named Dave. He closed his eyes and described his vision out loud: "I'm sitting alone on top of a mountain. I can feel a cool breeze on my face, I can smell the pine. Except for the whistle of the wind through the trees, it is very quiet, peaceful, and serene. All I can see is forest, mountains and some occasional wildlife."

Dave envisions success as having the freedom to do whatever he wants. One important thing to understand about Dave is that he is a "1" on the preferred surroundings scale, meaning he is very independent. I still remember his "independent" words, "I want to get there on my own and be alone when I get there." He aligned his vision with his Success Zone.

Visions of success are unique and personal. For Smith it was playing in the Super Bowl. For Tom, it was owning a luxury yacht. For another one of my clients who's a financial planner, it's "when I have 1,000 satisfied clients and don't have to make marketing calls anymore." How do you envision success?

To begin the process of clarifying your vision, complete the following sentences:

I most enjoy doing . . .

I get excited about . . .

My passion is . . .

Reflect on what you want to accomplish in life. Review your answers to the previous questions. Now, complete the following sentence. Be as descriptive as possible and remember to involve all your senses.

I'll know I'm a success when . . .

Close your eyes. Describe what your success looks like. What do you see around you? How does it feel? How does it sound? What do you hear? You should get very excited about your vision of success, especially when you involve all of your senses.

Since your vision is a long-term goal you'll need to set intermediate and short-term goals to achieve it. Make sure you set "SMART" goals that are:

Specific— Clearly defined and detailed.
Measurable—You can track progress and completion.
Actionable—Break them down into steps you can act upon.
Realistic—They are achievable.
Time-Frame—Set deadlines.

A note of caution: if you make a conscious decision to reach your goal at all costs, you may pay a price. Remember your Life's Wheel. Too narrow a focus will throw it out of balance. If your focus is one-dimensional, e.g., making enough money to own a yacht or becoming the youngest vice president of sales for your company, you may very well achieve it. But what if you spend so much time working that you ignore your health and become physically ill? You would have achieved your goal, but would you be successful? Is it enough to just own the yacht if you can't make time to enjoy it? Only you can determine how much you're willing to invest in achieving your vision of success. Only you can determine how much and for how long you can go along with your wheel out of balance.

Smith got his Super Bowl rings. Tom got his yacht. I quit that job. So what's behind your visor?

What matters most

Occasionally, life's wheel is out of balance. It's easy to get caught up in our busy, sometimes hectic lives and find that we haven't been paying enough attention to some very important areas.

Take Bill for example. His pursuit of his career goals caused him to miss many of his daughter's experiences as she was growing up. Although he has provided for her financially, he was often an absentee father, spending long days at the office and late night meetings with his clients. Without anything to give him direction as to where he was spending his time, Bill got caught in a cycle that flattened some very important parts of his Life's Wheel.

Now it is time to define what is most important in your life. Return to your Life's Wheel and write a value statement about each of your personal priority areas. Describe what you value about your family, your career, your social life, and so on. Take your time in doing this exercise. It is critical that you look deep within yourself to define what is truly important to you. To help you get started, here are a few basic value statements:

Family: I value a family environment that is loving and supportive.
Career: Satisfying my clients is my first priority in business.
Social: Having close friends is important to me.

Is there a gap between your actions and words? More than likely there is. Are you spending enough time on those areas you consider priorities? If not, one reason may be that your journey lacks direction.

Unfolding your road map

You've defined your values. Next you'll use that information to develop a mission statement. In the same way a company's mission outlines their way of doing business, your mission helps keep you on the right path and directs you toward your vision. It is your unique road map to success.

Write down phrases, sentences or paragraphs that make your value statements actionaable. The form of your mission is not important, the content is. I've included my mission statement as an example:

Joseph Michael Killian
Mission Statement

My personal mission is:
- To continually strive for a better understanding of and commitment to God.
- To enjoy and appreciate life.
- To continually expand my personal horizons both physically and mentally.
- To nurture a loving and giving relationship with my wife.
- To instill in my children, the virtues of integrity, honesty, compassion, and diligence.
- To stay in close contact with my friends.

- To continuously improve our home.
- To travel the world with my family.

My professional mission is:
- To assist individuals and organizations in the pursuit of their potential.
- To far exceed the expectations of my customers.
- To continually develop my professional skills and abilities.
- To be recognized as an expert and a leader in the training and consulting field.
- To develop and deliver high impact, content rich training programs and materials.
- To develop open, supportive and rewarding professional relationships.
- To offer my services, expertise and time to the community.

The day I first created my mission, I immediately began to notice a difference. It was easier to make decisions and be confident that I was right. I no longer felt guilty about spending time at work or at play. Perhaps most importantly, with my mission as my road map, I take steps every day toward my vision.

Your mission should be a living document, not something you write and put away in a desk drawer. Since I first developed my mission statement, I have updated it on several occasions. Read your mission frequently; refine or revise it when necessary.

Put your mission "behind your visor."

Earlier in this section, you defined success. Review your definition again. Does it include what you value most? Is it consistent with your mission? Does it reflect a well-balanced wheel? You now have the tools to reevaluate your definition of success. Think back to your Success Zone. Consider more than what you think you want or should have. Consider what you need. If necessary, refine or rewrite it.

Now you've got the "right idea" of what constitutes true happiness. It's time to make it happen.

Step 3. Planning for personal sales success

> *You will never 'find' time for anything. If you want time, you must make it.*
> —*Charles Burton*

Does this sound familiar? With the best of intentions, you sit down to "plan." You start by making a list of all of the things that you need to accomplish in a certain time frame. Once the list is finished, you begin by working on those things you think are most important, only to find that you're forced to start working on another task on the list or on something not even on the original list. The list grows longer as time goes by. Many of the things that seemed to be important at the beginning of your planning session fall farther and farther down the list, only to show up as crises later on. All of this causes more stress and frustration and you throw the list away.

There is a better way!

Armed with your new-found knowledge of your Success Zone, your Life's Wheel, your vision and your mission, you're ready to look "outside yourself." The planning process is made up of eight steps that will ensure that you achieve your success.

To illustrate this process, we'll use the example of Kim, a real estate sales professional. Kim's professional vision is to be able to make enough money in the next 10 to 12 years so that she can leave real estate full-time to open and operate a Bed and Breakfast in New England.

Step 1. Start with your vision in mind.

Kim has defined a clear vision and a time by which she wants to accomplish it. She sees herself at the Bed and Breakfast with a full guest register. She can describe the old Victorian house in detail, from the large wrap-around front porch with a wicker swing to the sunny, well-equipped kitchen to the comfortable guest rooms, to the backyard herb and wildflower garden, to the. . . You get the point.

Step 2. Define the key activities necessary to make your vision a reality.

Working backwards, Kim has to consider the activities she needs to accomplish including: determining the total amount of money she will need for her B & B; figuring how much she needs to earn over the next 10 years; setting up an investment program to make her money grow.

Step 3. Break down the key activities into smaller, more manageable tasks.
    Kim sets yearly and monthly sales goals for herself; she determines how many properties she will need to list, etc.

Step 4. Align key activities with your Success Zone.
    Kim lists all of the key activities and then plots them onto her Success Zone Model. She closes her share of sales, but needs advice to make her money grow. She starts by getting referrals on names of financial planners.

Step 5. Develop a time line for all activities and tasks.
    Kim lays out the various activities on a time line that she hangs on the wall beside her desk.

Step 6. Share the plan and time line with those actively involved or affected.
    Kim talks with her family about her plan, about how they feel about relocating, how they can save money, and how they can help her if they choose to do so.

Step 7. Begin to schedule the activities and tasks.
    Kim enters the activities onto a long range calendar. She then schedules some of the more specific tasks onto her monthly and weekly calendars.

Step 8. Track progress; review plan, modify it if needed.
    Kim regularly refers to her time line to see how she's doing.

    Take the time to go through this process with your own vision in mind. Start a planning notebook or use your personal planner. It is important to be structured in your approach to planning. (Especially you flexible types!) There is a great deal of truth to the adage, "Fail to plan, plan to fail," so plan to succeed.

Hang up that firefighters helmet

There cannot be a crisis next week. My schedule is
already full.
　　　　　　　　　　　　　　　　　—Henry Kissinger

Marty, another successful sales professional, talks about being "constantly beat up by the urgencies of his job." He complains that he never has the time to do the activities that are most important to him. He went so far as to say that he found it less than enjoyable to go on vacation because of the intensity of the urgencies that he is faced with before and after he takes time off work.

Are you constantly putting out fires? Dealing with crises? Handling the urgency du jour? Have you ever looked at your vacation as added stress rather than relaxation? Many people get so comfortable with dealing with urgencies that they put their firefighter's helmet on and go looking for fires. Or, they ignore smoldering situations until they catch fire. Have you found yourself saying "That's OK, I work better under pressure." This mentality not only sidetracks you from your vision, it can also be detrimental to your health.

To avoid becoming overwhelmed by urgencies, you must learn to make disciplined decisions. This begins in the earliest planning stages and continues through to the moment when you choose between two activities in the middle of a typical day.

The Priority Matrix below is a tool that you can use to make decisions that will keep you focused on the most important activities in your life. The Priority Matrix is broken down into four quadrants that answer two basic questions about each activity:

1.　　　Is it important?
2.　　　Is it urgent?

Based on importance and urgency, all activities and tasks fit into one of the matrix's four quadrants. Following are descriptions of the quadrants and typical activities that fall within each.

The Priority Matrix

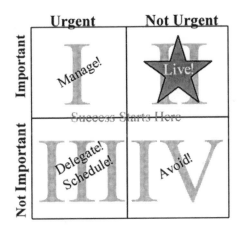

Quadrant I (QI)

Definition: Activities that are both important and urgent.

Typical Activities: Dealing with customer issues and complaints, important meetings, projects critical to your job/organization, your boss' latest priority, sales calls and presentations.

Opportunities/Problems: Because these activities are important and urgent it is easier to pay attention to them. They often have deadlines attached to them which puts them foremost in your mind. At the same time they can overwhelm you. If you have ever been frustrated by preparing quarterly reports when you are trying to close an important deal, you know what I mean.

Actions: QI activities have to be managed closely.

Quadrant II (QII)

Definition: Activities that are important but not urgent.

Typical Activities: Mission statement activities!

Opportunities/Problems: These activities make up the most important areas of your life. Completion of QII activities is often the most satisfying because of their importance. They typically require an amount of discipline to be completed while dealing with distractions, interruptions and urgencies. Because they have no deadlines attached to them, we may tend to put QII activities off while we deal with urgencies.

Actions: As the star denotes, strive to live your QII activities as much as possible. In order to reach your ultimate definition of success, spend as much time as possible working on QII activities. By doing so you maximize your productivity as you move toward your success.

Quadrant III (QIII)

Definition: Activities that are urgent but not important.

Typical Activities: Other people's urgencies, interruptions, some meetings, paperwork.

Opportunities/Problems: Often these activities are urgent to others and that urgency is forced onto you. Many of these activities are necessary but are not important.

Actions: Schedule or delegate these activities. Do not accept other's urgencies if they are not important to you. Schedule blocks of time when you can return phone calls or when you can complete routine paperwork. Delegate any activities that can be handled by others.

Quadrant IV (QIV)

Definition: Activities that are not important and not urgent.

Typical Activities: The unimportant things you do while you are procrastinating, reading junk mail, excessive socialization, some phone calls, some meetings

Opportunities/Problems: Typically these activities are very easy and enjoyable. In the end, however, these activities are tremendous time wasters, especially when you spend too much time doing them.

Actions: Avoid these activities!

As you become more comfortable with identifying each of the quadrants and their activities, you can more effectively make plans and decisions. The Priority Matrix will help you identify where you spend your time, keep you focused on what's important and maximize your productivity.

Your goal is to maximize the time you spend above the Success Line, specifically, doing QI and QII activities. Most importantly, the Priority Matrix provides a model to ensure that you act on QII items. We will continue to use the Priority Matrix as we move forward.

Sales calls, birthday parties and forced urgency

A good friend of mine has mastered the use of the Priority Matrix. This allows him to be highly effective in his software systems sales job and to balance a very busy life. Bob juggles his full-time sales job with two entrepreneurial ventures, along with his roles as husband and father of five children, ages one to ten years old, and little league coach.

I asked Bob how he handles so many responsibilities so well. His answer was simple. He plans as much urgency into his days as possible. He forces urgency on activities which are important to him but not urgent. He gave me a recent example to illustrate.

Bob knew that an upcoming week was going to be particularly busy. His son's sixth birthday was on Thursday of that week, the same day that he had four appointments with different customers at various locations throughout his territory. Knowing this, he planned his week in a way that forced urgency on multiple activities. He made sure that he was ready for his appointments by scheduling time on his calendar early in the week for preparation. This helped ensure that the meetings went smoothly and that he would have ample time to set up for his son's party.

Bob's approach to planning urgency allows him to maximize his use of work time and still allows him to pay the right amount of attention to his most important priority, his family. In his weekly planning, Bob looks at his scheduled appointments and deliverables (things due to others), looks at what needs to be prepared in advance of those appointments and schedules time for that preparation. Bob is also capitalizing on his Success Zone. He is a "C" on the structure scale and a "3" on the involved scale. His ability to plan and organize, coupled with his ease in working with others, combine for a successful sales career. Those same skills also help him to keep his Life's Wheel balanced.

When faced with a busy week, people often make the excuse that they don't have time to plan. The result is that they are controlled by the immediate urgencies of doing everything at the last minute. You can help avoid this by planning correctly. Your short-term plans should take into consideration all of the things we have discussed up to this point: your Success Zone, your vision and mission, your Life's Wheel and your long-term goals.

Weekly planning is important because it is the link between your long-term goals and daily activities. It helps you to keep the "big picture" in mind while dealing with the daily demands on your time. Make time to focus on the upcoming week. Commit to doing those activities that move you closer to your vision and long-term goals.

Before the week begins, look at all of your pre-scheduled activities. Identify the time periods where you are free to work on non-scheduled tasks. Plan blocks of time for the QII activities that need to be done consistently like prospecting, sales calls and follow-up.

Begin your daily planning process in your weekly planning session. Structure each day to accomplish the most important activities. Acknowledge that some days will be more hectic than others. By anticipating these days, you are better equipped to accomplish those ever important QII activities.

The planning process must be handled systematically. If you have a structured thought process like Bob, that's good news. If on the other hand you are more flexible, planning may be more challenging for you. If that is the case you need to find ways to be more structured. I am flexible and I have learned to plan frequently. I don't do it at the same time and place every day, but I do it consistently. Sometimes I do it while sitting in bumper-to-bumper traffic or while I'm waiting in the lobby to see a client. This is a good use of otherwise wasted time and it makes a good impression on my clients.

Planner mania

In the introduction to this chapter, I made light of companies that promise success as a result of using their time management systems. Actually, many of my customers report a greater sense of control and improved productivity as a result of using them. The busier I get, the more I need my planner. If you don't already have a planner or the one you have isn't working for you, look into what's available. Since there are so many products available, figuring out which one is right for you can be confusing. The most important thing is not which system or planner you use but that you use something and you use it consistently. Your planner doesn't have to be extravagant but it must be functional.

Once you recognize the importance of planning and begin to do it on a regular basis, you will begin to take more control of your career and your life.

Step 4. Implementing your personal sales success

> *Nothing contributes so much to tranquilize the mind as*
> *a steady purpose - a point on which the soul may fix its*
> *intellectual eye.*
> —*Mary Wollstonecraft Shelley*

The key to Bob's success is that he implements his plans with a purpose. Once you make your plans, convert them into action. As elementary as it may seem, developing lists that guide you through your daily activities is essential to your success. However, you can't expect to be highly effective by just making lists. Purposeful lists are the blueprints for the implementation of your plans.

Elementary school revisited

In order to give purpose to our lists, I recommend that you think back to elementary school. Use your ABC's and 123's. The following steps will give the activities on your list purpose. Begin by making a list of all the activities that you have to accomplish for the day. Second, use the Priority Matrix to answer the important and urgent questions for each activity. Then identify the quadrant that each activity belongs in.

For example, consider these activities:

- Complete proposal due to client today—Important/Urgent—QI

- Plan for next week's sales presentation—Important/Not Urgent—QII

Using the quadrant for each activity, put an "A" beside anything that must be done today. Your A's should always consist of items you define as important (those in quadrants I and II). Be realistic, because by definition, you cannot go home until they are finished.

Next, put a "B" beside anything that should be done today. Although important, these tasks can wait until tomorrow if you can't get to them today. Finally, mark any of the remaining items as "C," which identifies them as things you would like to get done today. Typically, these items end up on tomorrow's list.

- Complete proposal due to client today—Important/Urgent—QI—A

- Plan for next week's sales presentation—Important/Not Urgent—QII —B

You have now added value to your list. Next, put the tasks in proper order. Return to your "A" items and identify the one that you must complete first and then mark it as your A-1 item. This is critically important. Putting your activities in order can be difficult. It is important that your keep your vision, mission and values in mind when doing so. Be careful to resist the urge to make your most urgent item your "A-1" In fact, doing a QII activity first gives you a sense of momentum and satisfaction. It also helps keep that activity from being pushed further down the list by unavoidable interruptions.

Mark the next item as A-2 and so on through the rest of the A's. Do the same to the B's and the C's. Now your list has purpose.

Ideally, I like to go through this process at the end of each day. It gives me peace of mind and the ability to start the next day quickly and effectively. Many of my clients are surprised to discover how much more productive they are when they first apply this technique. Take a few minutes to record the activities that you have planned for tomorrow on the worksheet below. By combining the Priority Matrix with purposeful lists, you give yourself a much greater opportunity to be successful.

Activity	Important	Urgent	Quadrant	Value	Order	Completed
———	———	———	———	———	———	———
———	———	———	———	———	———	———
———	———	———	———	———	———	———
———	———	———	———	———	———	———
———	———	———	———	———	———	———
———	———	———	———	———	———	———
———	———	———	———	———	———	———

It should be obvious by now that the first thing you are going to work on tomorrow is your A-1 item. In the best case scenario you will be able to complete the A-1 and then move on to your A-2. However if you happen to be interrupted in the middle of your A-1 by phone calls, drop-in visitors, crisis or any other catastrophe, you can immediately return to that task as soon as you have dealt with the interruption. This should hold true for every planned activity that you do.

The last (and my personal favorite) step in this process is to check off each item when you have completed it. Sometimes at the completion of very important and difficult tasks I have made these check marks with such fervor that I have ripped the paper in my planner. I really do enjoy it! Actually there is a reason for the intensity of my check mark ritual. That reason can be summed up in one word—endorphins. Endorphins are the result of a chemical reaction triggered in the brain. It's commonly referred to as the "runner's high." The euphoric sensation can be triggered by the completion of a strenuous exercise. I like to call it a legal and totally healthy drug that I take every chance I get.

Check it off, cross it out, or highlight it; it doesn't matter which you do as long as you complete it and reward yourself with that little endorphin injection.

Keeping "Mr. have ya gotta minute?" at bay

The man who is tenacious of purpose in a rightful cause is not shaken from his firm resolve by the frenzy of his fellow citizens clamoring for what is wrong, or by the tyrant's threatening countenance.

—Horace

A purposeful priority list can help you fend off everybody from "Mr. Have Ya Gotta Minute?" and his close cousin "Ms. Just a Quick Question," to your boss (a.k.a. tyrant) with the latest pressing project. How? Throughout an average day, you may be bombarded by a myriad of interruptions and time wasters. The best defense against this seemingly never-ending onslaught of time wasters is a good offense. Your offensive weapons include your focus on your vision, your understanding of your Success Zone, the priority matrix and your purposeful planning. If you are disciplined in your approach to these steps, I guarantee that you will be better prepared to handle just about any situation.

Time wasters: the scourge of productivity

A lack of planning on your part, does not constitute an
emergency for me.

—Anonymous

Time wasters. They're the enemy. Yet most people let themselves be ambushed by them daily. They're handy rationalizations like: "Every time I sat down to write the proposal I was interrupted by phone calls from clients."

What you may fail to recognize is that you do have control over many time wasters. Let's take a look at some of the biggest time wasters. Check those that plague you.

	attempting too much		inability to say "no"
	personal disorganization		incomplete information
	inadequate planning		leaving tasks unfinished
	meetings		management by crisis
	procrastination		paperwork
	lack of self-discipline		socializing
	interruptions		ineffective delegation
	poor communication		inadequate staff
	confused responsibility or authority		progress reports
	drop-in visitors		travel

Because the list is so long, I'll recommend solutions to some of the most common problems. Ultimately, the answer to most time wasters is the development of an effective personal time management system that incorporates the Priority Matrix.

Time wasters like procrastination, lack of self-discipline, and leaving tasks unfinished are all ones you have a great deal of control over. Many of these should be eliminated as you become more effective using the concepts we've discussed so far, like thoughtful planning with your mission statement and purposeful list development.

Specifically, to overcome procrastination and lack of self-discipline, think back to your Success Zone. The activities that you routinely procrastinate on are most likely outside of your zone. For large "procrastination" projects, break them down into their smallest components. Then tackle the smaller activities one at a time. Occasionally, you may find it helpful to "cheat" a little bit. Plan to do a small activity within your Success Zone to get you started. Then as you check off the completed task, let your endorphins carry you over to those tasks outside your Success Zone. Finally, you sometimes have to give yourself a kick in the seat of the pants and do the things that you don't like to do. As Albert E. N. Gray found in his studies of successful salespeople in the insurance industry:

> *"The secret of success of every man who has been successful—*
> *lies in the fact that he forms the habits of doing things that*
> *failures don't like to do."*

You have somewhat less control over time wasters like paperwork and travel. It will take a little more work to eliminate or minimize them, but you can make a difference. Try to minimize paperwork by delegating or developing templates that reduce the time to complete your paperwork. Make better use of your travel time. When traveling by air, use the time to complete paperwork, make purposeful lists, or catch up on your reading (about your competition or the latest in technology). When traveling by car, use your cellular phone to contact clients, use a tape recorder to dictate letters to clients or plan your strategy for your next sales call, or listen to educational or motivational tapes to get you pumped up for your next big presentation.

Finally, there are time wasters over which you have even less control. Interruptions, poor communication and drop-in visitors fall into this category. These can be the most difficult, because they involve other people. It's difficult if not impossible to change other people, especially when those people are your clients or your superiors. You can, however, change your behavior. For example, is it really necessary to answer your phone every time it rings? With secretaries, voice mail, or whatever systems you have in place to cover when you're not available, let these systems work for you while you complete your important "A-1" activities.

Learning how to say "no" can be a powerful tool in eliminating unwanted interruptions. When you are interrupted, consciously define the interruption using the priority matrix. If it is more important than the activity that you are currently working on, handle it and then return to the original activity. If it is less important than the activity you are currently working on, explain to the person who has interrupted you that you are in the middle of something very important, and that you will get back to them when you are finished. Schedule a follow up meeting or phone call and assure them you'll give them your undivided attention. Most people respond very well to this approach and if you keep your promise to get back to them, they begin to monitor their interruptions without your input.

The key to avoiding time wasters is to make the decision consciously. If you don't, you end up wearing your firefighter's helmet. My friend Bob typically doesn't have to worry about time wasters because he has become disciplined in his approach to time management. His forced urgency allows him to say "no" without guilt. He's able to say "no" to people and to the wasteful habits that fritter away the valuable minutes that make up his day.

In today's fast-paced, highly competitive world, we can't expect to eliminate all time wasters but we can take control of them and minimize the impact that they have on us.

Developing long-term habits for success

Take what you've learned about yourself from this chapter and apply it daily. You will be able to capitalize on what you do best, and be better equipped to deal with those things that you are not as comfortable with. You'll begin to see results almost immediately. Your vision of success is much clearer now. Your mission will guide you along the way. Approach everything you do with your Success Zone in mind. You have the knowledge and tools to plan your journey. Use the Priority Matrix to keep you focused on the activities that will move you closer toward your vision. Use all of these tools to navigate around any roadblocks that the many time wasters may throw in front of you.

As you proceed on your journey, keep in mind that you may occasionally hit a bump in the road. Other times you may find it difficult to stay on course. Don't be discouraged by temporary setbacks. Be patient with yourself. Remember, you are developing new habits and discarding old ones. As Mark Twain said:

> *Habit is habit, and not to be flung out the window by any man, but coaxed downstairs a step at a time.*

Good luck and enjoy the ride!

"Only you can determine how much you're willing to invest in achieving your vision of success."
-Joe Killian

About Joe Killian

Described by audiences as one of the best speakers that they have had, Joe Killian's dynamic style and versatile approach to tailoring programs provide participants with the skills and techniques that allow them to be their best!

Joe is president and founder of Priority Training. He has developed and delivered training programs for all organizational levels and for a wide variety of audiences in diverse industries. A partial list of his sales training clients include Xerox, The Equitable, Century 21, Caterpillar, Royal Insurance and SmithKline Beecham.

Joe is a member of the National Speakers Association and is listed in the *Who's Who in Professional Speaking*. He has over 11 years of sales, training and consulting experience while working for companies such as Electronic Data Systems (EDS) and the Dale Carnegie courses. Joe has an MBA from the Katz Graduate School of Business at the University of Pittsburgh.

Priority Training

746 Thirteenth Street
Oakmont, PA 15139
412-828-0725

Company Profile

Program Descriptions

Joe's dynamic style and versatility can be experienced in each of the following programs:

Workshops

Be Your Best

A unique and enlightening approach to understanding what makes each of us successful. Using Joe's proven techniques, participants will better understand, define, plan and implement strategies and skills that produce sales success.

Time Management Success

Participants in this program will learn the concepts and skills which are essential for regaining control of their busy lives. Participants achieve success by developing a personalized time and life management system that works best for them.

Presentation Success

Participants develop the skills necessary to confidently and effectively prepare and deliver professional presentations in any selling environment.

Presentations

A Boy and His Baseball Glove

Joe takes the audience back with a refreshing look at childhood to identify what truly motivates us and why. This self-understanding is used to develop a vision of personal success. Joe then provides a proven approach to achieving success in your sales career and beyond.

Juggling Responsibilities and Relationships

Participants learn to put things into perspective and take control of their increasingly hectic and often mismanaged careers and lives. Yes, Joe juggles and teaches others to do so, literally and figuratively.

The Physical Antics of Presentation

This humorous presentation lets the audience see what not to do when presenting. Some basic pointers enable participants to strengthen presentation skills.

Chapter 3

Goal Setting or
How Did I Get to Where I am Today?

by
Steve Richards

*"Would you tell me please, which
way I ought to go from here?"
"That depends a good deal on where
you want to get to."*

—Lewis Carrol
Alice in Wonderland

T he intent of this chapter is to create action. *Learning to set goals is the single most important skill that you can learn and perfect.* I've diligently and intently left out the psycho babble Only real world, real doable stuff, if you will. Reading this chapter and not taking any action is a waste of your time. If you don't intend on taking action, skip this chapter. The action I ask you take is simple and will not take much time. Its impact, however, will change your life. After all, how much more can you learn about goal setting? And, if you are making $250,000, why bother? On the other hand, if you want to chance creating a more productive life, please answer a couple of questions for yourself.

QUESTIONS

Are you presently selling for a living or do you plan on selling for a living?

While you were in school, did you intend on selling for a living? If not, what did you want to be when you grew up?

Here is an interesting and telling list. SurveyWorks, Ltd., a leading market research company, conducted a survey of American workers. When interviewed and asked the question, "Did you want to be a (insert career here)_ growing up?" Here are the responses given by the various professionals.

Of professional athletes–97% said professional athlete.
Of doctors–88% said doctor.
Of attorneys–79% said attorney.
Of models–67% said model.
Of farmers–56% said farmer.
Of nurses–49% said nurse.
Of teachers–47% said teacher.
Of accountants–41% said accountant.
Of factory workers–40% said factory worker.
Of sales people–5% said sales person!

Think of it! only 5% of the 15 million people selling for a living had any intention of "selling for a living"! What does that tell us? A lot. First of all, most people never intended on selling in the first place. Second, selling is the most competitive profession on earth—more competitive than any of the other above mentioned professions. Yet selling skills are practiced and studied less than any of the above professions. Why? Too many sales people are *trying* sales until something *better* comes along. People *trying* sales make significantly less money than people who have committed themselves to the sales profession.

Committed sales people practice their profession for the same reasons that Joe Montana showed up for pre-season practice each year, including, after each of his Super Bowl championships. He also practiced each week during the season. Why? He wasn't just *trying* football; he was committed to football.

The same can be said for doctors, attorneys, accountants, and most other professionals. They practice, study, and make learning a continuos behavior, not a sometimes behavior. Think about yourself. Do you practice, study, and intensely seek new information about selling? One goal you must set for yourself, a goal that when achieved will dramatically increase your earning power is this: ***Quit trying sales. Commit yourself to the sales profession. Decide you are a salesperson.*** If you do that and discover selling is not for you, you will never have any regrets. Chances are though that you will find challenge and satisfaction and that you will never leave the sales profession.

> *One person with a commitment is worth more than one hundred (100) people who have only an interest.*
> —Mary Crowley, noted speaker, author, and sales manager.

Once you commit to the profession, it's time to set goals and take action.

In order for you to be committed, you must become competent at goal setting. When that happens, great opportunities will open for you. So what is the great news? You are in a highly competitive arena with millions of other people, the vast majority of whom don't set goals or practice their profession. You are a step or two away from separating yourself from the pack. Separating yourself from the pack means increasing your income via superior performance. But you must take some ACTION!

It appears that one of the fundamental problems is that the vast majority of sales people didn't set a goal to become a sales person. So, is it fair to say that if you didn't mean to be a sales person, you might be lacking some essential goal setting techniques?

The rest of this chapter is a track to crawl, walk, run, then sprint. Do the exercises, study this chapter more intensely than anything you've ever studied before, and your return on invested time will be massive and quick. Most importantly, take some ACTION! The more ACTION you take, the better and sooner the results.

Most people don't consistently set goals—that is a known fact. Yet virtually all people have at least one aspect of their lives that they would like to change. How about you?

Changing your life, yourself, your job performance or anything else you desire to change is not a case of ability, nor is it a case of motivation. *It is a matter of will.* You must have the willingness to do what you know to be the right or most productive thing.

How many people who would take the time to read this book have not heard that it's wise to set goals or objectives? How many have not read somewhere that to change or create a habit it takes 21 days of altered behavior? How many have not heard, read about, or seen someone who owes his or her life changes to the fact that they decided to set goals? Chances are you, yes you, know all of the above.

Chances are that 97% of you reading this right now cannot reach into your pocket and find an index card, look at your planner or your electronic organizer or computer and find an updated version of your personal or professional goals, *that you have viewed every day for the past two weeks.* Even if you have those goals written, how often do you review them? Not concentrated on, visualized, meditated upon, but just *viewed* everyday for the past two weeks.

Failure is most often simply a failure to execute. Some people do not have enough time to set goals. Some people are going to set goals tomorrow. Some people think a "to do" list will suffice. Some people do not believe in setting goals. Some people just have their goals in their head? Here is a wake up call. You are an adult, somewhat more motivated than most because you have picked up this publication, but possibly still making far less than someone with the same abilities who has learned to set and review goals consistently. To set goals or objectives creates purpose for your life, instead of living an *aimless* life (if you don't possess written goals, your life is *aimless*, but, not worthless!). If that hurts, so be it. My aim is not to please you or be good to you. My aim is to be *good* for you.

What follows is not going to be a "cookie cutter" discussion of goal setting. There is plenty of good information published elsewhere on this topic. What follows is an opportunity for self analysis, designed to give you a better look at yourself! We'll begin with a questionnaire.

Goal Setting

Answer each question honestly and then give some thought to your response.

NO   YES

I know what a short, mid, or long term goal is.

I have short term goals–written down.

I have mid-term goals– written down.

I have long term goals–written down.

I have financial goals–written down.

I have personal goals–written down.

I have professional goals–written down.

I have health goals–written down.

I have fun goals–written down.

I have family goals–written down.

I review my goals consistently.

I revise my goals on a regular basis.

I discuss my goals with others, family, supervisors, etc.

I cross off goals which have been attained or are no longer important.

I have "dates to be accomplished" written with each goal.

I believe goal setting to be a productivity increasing endeavor.

Grade yourself. If you checked 10–16 yes blanks, you are a well disciplined, objective, organized, rich, and highly productive member of society.

If you checked 5–9 yes blanks you are well above average in your ability to focus on an end objective.

If you checked 1–4 yes blanks you are at least cognizant of the importance that goal setting can have in improving the quality of your life.

If you checked 0 yes blanks and you are willing to continue reading this chapter, you have the greatest opportunity of all to dramatically impact the productivity and quality of your life.

Brian Tracy, noted speaker and sales trainer, writing for *Insight* magazine, lists five primary reasons people don't set goals. The three that I especially like are:

1) Most people are simply not serious about setting goals—until you get serious about setting goals, nothing will happen.
2) Most people do not understand the importance of setting goals. Most people did not come from families who were goal oriented. Goal setting is not taught in schools. Most people do not understand that goal setting should be a part of normal existence. Try this one–If you don't have written goals, you are abnormal! (and who wants to be ab-anything?)
3) Most people do not know how to set goals. Goal setting is not taught in school, yet learning to set goals properly is the single most important skill human beings need to realize their potential.

The other two reasons are *fear of rejection* and *fear of failure*. I will address these two shortly.

The keys to personal achievement–seven action steps

1. Think!

One of the hardest, yet most rewarding things we can do, is think. Yes, think. Now, I know what most of you are thinking. "He's crazy, I think all the time." Wrong! Most people actually think very little. Most people, in fact, let others do the thinking for them. The human mind isn't used because we take it for granted.

We must and can control our thinking. What gives you the ability to create success, wealth, happiness, and everything you ever dreamed of, can also lead you to the unemployment line. The mind isn't much different than the earth in this respect. To think is to take the first step in effectively setting goals. The earth is neutral. If you plant food crops, cultivate, and care for them—the earth will return a bountiful harvest. If you plant poison weeds (weeds don't need as much care or cultivation) or if you leave the land alone—the earth will return to you a bountiful crop of weeds. The earth doesn't care what you plantóneither does your mind. If you leave your mind alone, it will produce nothing of any consequence. If you plant the right seeds, it will return to you anything you truly want.

The challenge is that most people want so many different things, they're unable to focus their efforts, minds, and hearts on anything specific. Objective or goal setting is the absolute, 100% of the time, cure for this common malady.

Let's use a ship to draw a telling analogy. What happens if a ship is tied to a dock for a lengthy period of time, never moved, and barely maintained? The ship would fall apart from rust and disuse. Your mind is the same way. The less you use it, the less use it is to you. If the person who owns the ship doesn't have a destination in mind, the ship doesn't leave the dock. The ship rusts away, just like your mind will if it is not used.

Think about the captain of this ship who begins a trip from Miami to the Bahamas. It is a thrill to start the engines and begin a course to a destination that cannot be seen for 99% of the journey. However, it is only a thrill if the captain has been diligent in charting the course. To take off for the Bahamas without a well thought out and written plan of action is dangerous, reckless, a waste of fuel and technology. Your mind is a much more powerful engine than any power plant that drives a ship. Yet the analogy works. Most of our wants, needs, and desires cannot be "seen" until just before we have them. Just like the captain of the ship, you have to determine your destination, chart the course, and then start the engine. Defining the objective is the most important step towards achieving it. Otherwise, you waste your life and the lives of those you care for. Can you think of anything more precious than those lives? Is it worth taking some action to prevent such a waste? Setting goals is like having a built in GPS (Global Positioning System). It keeps you on track on life's journey.

What to do?

You must make time to *think*.

You must make time to *think* on a consistent basis.

You must realize that to *think* is one of the most difficult tasks a human being can undertake.

You must realize that to discipline yourself to *think* leads to the next element of successful goal setting—*desire*.

2. Create the desire!

If you can clearly envision how it will feel to satisfy your *desire*, then it can be yours. That is a fact. Vague wishing or hoping for some undefined feeling or result does not create drive. A burning, *ardent* desire for something for which you can create a mental picture—one you can hear, taste, feel, smell, and see—creates the energy to go for it.

This is a vital exercise: do this right now.

List some items you desire very much, but don't have.

1.

2.

3.

4.

5.

6.

7.

8.

Now ask yourself why you've failed to achieve them. Chances are you have not tried as hard as you might of. The first rule is—a human being must have something worthwhile toward which he or she is working. The key here is 'worthwhile'. Further defined it means that if creating a net worth of $500,000 is your goal, robbing a bank is not a worthwhile action plan!

The source of drive and energy in humans comes from motivating desires. Desire is the key to a long and interesting life. We all have desires, many of them similar. Good health, good love, financial independence, and eternal life—virtually every person reading this has these desires. From the deepest part of Africa to the sands of the Middle East right back to the United States and Canada, people have the same wants and desires. Why then, do so few achieve even the simplest of wants? It's our inane ability to determine exactly what we want. It's our failure to chart the course required to obtain what we want. Take the time and make the effort to think and create a true desire.

- You must decide what you really desire out of life.
- You must decide what you really desire in all phases of your life.
- You must create a burning desire for what you want.
- Once you decide what you desire you must take the next step and write it down.

3. Write them down!

Things seen are mightier than things heard.
　　　　　　—Alfred Lord Tennyson

Things thought about, desired, written down, and then seen consistently are the mightiest of all.
　　　　　　—Steve Richards

Let's address the next aspect of goal setting. The written aspect. Why write it down? There are several important reasons.

- Written goals are a higher form of commitment than just imagined goals.
- Written goals are easier to remember than imagined goals.
- Once your goals are written, you can cross them off when accomplished giving yourself a terrific sense of self satisfaction.
- Reviewing goals that are not written down is virtually impossible.
- Revising goals that are not written down is difficult.

You are significantly more likely to attain a goal if you write it down. We don't know why, or maybe we do subconsciously, but regardless, if a goal is worth achieving, it is worth writing down. If you want it to happen, WRITE IT DOWN NOW!.

4. Date them!

Why *date* a goal?

- **With a date, it's a goal. Without a date, it's a dream.**
- *Date* your goals for a realistic completion.
  You must add a time variable to create the proper framework in which to obtain what you want out of life.
- Life is short, you must create an inner sense of urgency.
- *Dating* your goals will help you accomplish many more of them than if there are not specific time parameters.
- *Dating* your goals will help you stay on track and make progress.

5. Review them!

Circumstances change, desires change, consequently, your goals will change. A navigational system on an airplane is constantly and continuously making adjustments as the aircraft makes its way to its destination. The navigational system is constantly accessing or reviewing where the aircraft is relative to where its destination is positioned. You must do the same with your goals.

- *Review* your goals constantly and consistently. Every day is not too often.
- *Reviewing* your goals every evening and every morning is not a good idea, IT'S A GREAT IDEA! At the very least, review your goals several times a week.
- Carry your goals with you everywhere. Whether the goals are on a 3 X 5 index card, an electronic organizer, or a computer really doesn't matter. To effectively and consistently review your goals you must carry them with you. Dan O'Brien is the 1996 Olympic Decathlon Gold Medal winner and the "world's greatest athlete." During post Gold Medal competition interviews, he attributed much of his success to the fact that he not only learned to set goals, but learned to carry his goals with him so he could review them everywhere and anytime.

6. Revise them!

Once you begin to think about what you want, your wants and desires are going to change. As you begin accomplishing your initial goals, your other objectives will start to grow in complexity and scope. Just like the navigational system in the airplane analogy above, adjustments will have to be made along the way.

- *Revise* your goals anytime your circumstances change—personally, professionally, financially, or in any other area of your life.
- *Revise* your goals when you have reached or accomplished a goal. Another goal must be set immediately.
- *Revise* your goals when you miss a "date to be accomplished."
- *Revise* your goals when a new desire is developed.

7. Share them with those who can help and support you!

Share your goals with others, why?
- *Sharing* your goals leads to a higher level of commitment.
- Not all goals need to be shared with all people. Certainly your family should be privy to most of your goals. They can, if you allow them, be a great 'productivity' support group.
- To *share* your professional goals with your manager or supervisor makes sense. One of two things will happen when you share your professional goals with your company. Either they will support you and give you needed feedback or they will pay scant attention. If the former occurs you work for the right group; if the latter occurs you work for the wrong group.
- *Share* the appropriate goals with the appropriate people or support group.
- To *share* your financial goals with a financial planner, stock broker, insurance agent, or your banker helps them help you

So there you have it—the 'Richards formula' for goal setting success. Simple. If you want to be more successful in any phase of your life—here is the formula.

- *Think about what you really want.*
- *Define your desire, a passion if you will.*
- *Write your goals down.*
- *Date your goals for completion.*
- *Review your goals frequently.*
- *Revise your goals as your circumstances dictate.*
- *Share your goals with the appropriate people.*

Fear

Why do only three percent (3%) of the people follow and adhere to the formula?

Fear is often labeled as the sales person's greatest hurdle. It should be listed as a human being's greatest hurdle. Fear of what? Failure? We've all heard that before and you probably thought to yourself, as did I, "that's foolish"! Who's afraid of being rich, powerful, or successful? Not I, and probably not you. So fear of failure does not fly with me.

Fear of commitment? This may be closer to the truth. However, this is a hollow fear. To sit down and write down your goals is probably one of the safest things a person can do. No, I do not believe people fail to set goals out of fear. I think there is another, easier to understand reason.

Laziness

I have a deep seeded belief that all too often the word fear is substituted for the word lazy. Sales people who don't make enough sales calls use the word "fear" during their therapy sessions, when the more appropriate word is lazy. Those who don't write down their goals, do not take the time to consider them, do not take the three to five minutes a day to review them, are lazy. They are simply cheating themselves. Read the word again—LAZY! If it hurts to come to this realization, good, you are paying attention. There are so many aspects of life we can't control, so why not control the things and the effort we can put into something?

Why do people with goals succeed in life and people without them fail? There is a fundamental truth, written about by many, that a person is what that person thinks about. Intellects through the ages have found little upon which to agree, but this is one concept that seems to be universally accepted. A person can become what they choose to think about. Want better luck? Set some objectives. You cannot buy good luck, it is free. But you have to make the effort, you cannot be lazy.

Earl Nightingale, maybe the most famous self-help writer and speaker of our generation, said "we need reminding as much as we need educating." Earl Nightingale spent his entire life writing and speaking about the importance of goal setting.

There has not been any huge revelations in this chapter so far but, by simply reminding you and jogging your memory, hopefully this will motivate you to take action. Anthony Robbins, motivational speaker and writer (Unlimited Power and Awaken the Giant Within), astutely pointed out to me years ago that "knowledge is not power, action is power." If you finish this chapter and leave with nothing more than a 'warm and fuzzy' feeling, than neither of us have achieved our short term objective of making you more successful in goal setting.

Free

Have you ever thought about the fact that most of what we have that is worthwhile is free. Minds, souls, bodies, hopes, dreams, ambitions, intelligence, love of family, children, friends, and country—all are priceless and free. The things money can buy are replaceable. A person can be wiped out in terms of material belongings, but make another fortune based solely on what he or she has inside them. History is full of stories about people who "had it," "lost it," and "made it back!"

More questions

Do you appreciate the life you have fashioned for yourself? It is the only one you're going to have. Life is not a rehearsal, THIS IS IT!. Appreciate life itself first; then learn to fashion your life in a manner which will make you happy. Develop a burning, ardent desire for what you want. Then enthusiastically pursue it.

When was the last time you assessed your long-term goals? If you haven't written them down, you can't have truly assessed them. How about your mid-term goals? DITTO

Short-term goals? DITTO

Are you prepared to create new goals after you have accomplished your current goals? If they aren't written, dated, shared and reviewed now, how can you create new ones?

The only thing you need to do now...

Do yourself, your business, your company, and your family a favor. Write down one goal right now, that can be accomplished in a day. Date it for tomorrow. Then, take action on that goal. Look at it tomorrow. It's accomplished. Write another one day goal down again. Date it for the following day. Take action on that goal. Look at it again. It's accomplished.

Keep it up. This one simple exercise WILL DRAMATICALLY CHANGE THE BOUNTY YOU RECEIVE FROM YOUR LIFE.

I'll help. I'll give you the one, seven part goal you need to set. This should be the only goal you allow anyone else to give to you. Your goals must be your own. Read this, then write it down where you'll be sure to see it again, and again. Here is your first goal:

#1 I will think. I will define my desires. I will write my goals. I will date them. I will review them. I will revise them. And I will share them.

That is it. I've given you the first step, the most difficult step. If you think, define, write, date, review, revise, and share this first goal, the rest will come naturally. You will start to see immediate results. Things you have only wished for or dreamed about will become a reality. Do it now! You won't need good luck, but you will have it.

About Steve Richards

Steve Richards, motivational speaker, sales trainer and management consultant believes "you are responsible for your own success and failure, and only you!" The first step to success is admitting this. Steve gets a standing ovation every time he speaks. But that's not all - he gets his participates to take action which impacts their lives!

Steve learned the fundamentals of training while working for IBM during graduate school in the mid 70's. Observing the amount of time and money invested in employees by IBM created the dogmatic approach to the sale of training that Steve brings to the market today.

In 1978, after graduate school, Steve went to work in the automobile industry. Finding a shortage of quality in this, the largest industry on earth, planted the seed for what he does today. After a 12 year tenure with the Ryan Group, a Chicago based automotive consulting firm, Steve left to form his own company in 1992.

Today, working with his three partners, the Dealer Advantage Group trains about 8,000 sales people and sales managers a year. Steve trains sales people in the importance of taking responsibility for their own development, the necessity of the "fun" factor in selling, and the critical nature of goal setting. If you do not leave one of his seminars recommitted or committed to the sales profession, chances are you have decided sales is not for you.

Steve resides in Marietta, Georgia with his wife.

Dealer Advantage Group
2619 Sandy Plains Road, Suite 208
Marietta, GA 30066
Phone: 770-565-1900
Fax: 770-509-1333
E-mail: auto rich@aol.com.Symbol

Company profile

The Dealer Advantage Group was founded in 1992 by Steve Richards. The principals are Steve, his two brothers, Bob and Pete, and Susan Hutto. All four left very successful jobs in the automobile industry to form an alliance dedicated to providing quality and affordable training to any company whose revenues are driven by sales. Whether it is their sales fundamentals taught to entry level sales people or their leadership training for sales managers, the seminars are widely acclaimed to be the most exciting and practically applicable available.

The most popular training seminars are:

Leadership Skills for Sales Managers
Understand the difference between management and leadership and start your journey toward leading!

The Communication Advantage
Understand the key human behaviors and how they effect communication as well as the work and sales environment!

Power Networking
It's all in who you know. Find out how to know the right and where to find them.

Powerful Sales Presentations
Enthusiasm sells! Learn to sizzle in your sales presentations!

Dealer Advantage Group boasts some of the finest sales organizations in the country as clients. To reach the Dealer Advantage Group call, write, or e-mail them at:

Chapter 4

How to Market Yourself

by
Mary Maloney Cronin

*The most effective marketing tool
you can use is YOU.*

—Mary Maloney Cronin

In the mainstream business world, you and your sales manager likely reviewed your methods of marketing such as advertising, direct mail, publication design, public relations, special events, telemarketing, market research, the Internet, and video/audio production. However, many sales managers fail to mention the underlying values associated with each of these tools—the real keys to making your marketing efforts a huge success. Anyone can hire an agency to place ads, to develop a marketing plan, to get free publicity. But not everyone understands the secret to making marketing efforts work for the long run. The secret lies in more intangible tactics, in using subtle ways to get your message across, and most importantly being consistent, focused and totally convincing. It lies in the personal touch, which in reality is the fundamental principle of marketing.

I am frequently asked to define the theory of marketing. The explanation is very simply—**marketing is the process of getting noticed so that people buy from you.** Many tools can be used in that process, both paid and unpaid. The key word in that definition is "noticed." There are many other ways of getting noticed besides the traditional marketing methods. The bottom line in my marketing philosophy is that marketing works best when people notice YOU as an individual. Let's face it, it's really up to you to get the word out.

If given a blueprint, just about anyone could go through the motions of placing an ad, designing a direct mail piece, writing a press release. But it's the exemplary salesperson who adds that extra something to make it extraordinary and memorable. In this chapter, you'll learn what the "extra" ingredients are that will put your marketing efforts over the top. I'll share them with you as they were shared with me through one of my mentors. Once I started implementing these extras on a daily basis, my notoriety and my business really took off.

Take these ideas to heart. I didn't at first. I thought they were a waste of billable hours. Trust me, they're not. Don't repeat my mistakes. These ideas will take you further and faster than you ever imagined because these marketing techniques will affect every other area of your business—guaranteed.

In this chapter you will find yourself having "eurekas." That is, you may not be introduced to anything "new", but you will begin to understand the information in a totally new light. Therefore you may be saying to yourself, "I knew that all along, but now I've finally got it! It finally makes sense!" That's the goal of this chapter, for you to have "eurekas" and begin to implement those ideas immediately.

The first step is to start by clearing up some misconceptions you may have about marketing. Then we'll move on to the 7 Secret Questions you must answer before you can go any further. It's recommended to spend some quality time answering these questions. You may not have been asked questions like this before. You may even want to think about your answers, write them down, then revisit them a day or two later so the concepts really sink into your brain. The answers to these questions will get you moving further along than your peers who aren't employing this strategy. The idea is to get focused, in order to get moving!

Your answers to the 7 Secret Questions you ask yourself about marketing will serve as a foundation for you to get started in a positive and exciting direction. Keep the answers to these questions close by where you can refer to them often. They may change as you change, and that's O.K. It means you're evolving and you may need to think of new angles in terms of marketing. Remember that marketing is never stagnant. The best salespeople are those who are always on the move using new ideas they've learned. You'll be anxious to test out the tips and techniques described in this chapter as soon as you can! For example, you'll develop a 30-second commercial for yourself that you will use and be remembered for wherever you go. You'll start using people's names in every conversation. You'll understand the power of enthusiasm; realize how critical it is to make a good first impression; learn to identify personality styles and much more. All this serves as the underlying means to making your marketing efforts an enviable success. These are the extras! Use them and more people will remember you. People who remember you will ultimately buy from you!

A chapter on marketing would not be complete without mentioning the traditional, and important tools used in business today to get the word out. However, in this information, you'll be pleasantly surprised at the "twist." The twist is that we emphasize how to market on a shoestring, introducing creative and proven methods that you can design on your own. You'll wish there were more hours in a day when you start putting these methods into action! It's not recommended to read this part of the book if you're trying to go to sleep. Most people get so energized, they can't wait to get started!

Speaking of getting started, have you ever mapped out your marketing efforts on a daily, weekly, monthly, even yearly calendar? Most of us in sales use a time management system—a Franklin planner,

Day-timer, etc. to manage our time and perhaps map out our goals in a systematic format. If you are using a day planner, great. You're off to a positive start. And, it will be easy for you to work your marketing goals into your daily routine using the approach outlined in this part of the chapter. If you're serious about yourself then you need to pay attention to this approach. It will get you closer to your goals much faster and with half the learning curve.

The final section of this chapter will expand from the specific to the broad as a stepping stone to your profitable future. One step on those stones is developing a mission statement. In fact, it's the most crucial component of your marketing efforts. Whether you own a small business, a home-based business, run a Fortune 500 company or are employed by a company, you must have a mission statement. This mission will drive your business, particularly your marketing efforts. It will appear either directly or indirectly in everything you do. In many cases, it becomes a part of you. It will even get you out of bed on those mornings when it seems tough. But most of all, it will keep you thinking about marketing every day in everything you do.

Getting unstuck

Let's clear up some serious misconceptions about marketing before we get started. For example,

Myth #1: Good marketing costs a fortune.

Not true if you really understand how marketing works from a grassroots level. Sure an expensive advertising and public relations campaign can do wonders for any salesperson or business. However, truly good marketing doesn't have to cost you a king's ransom. It's all about presentation. Presenting yourself. That's what we're going to emphasize—making those extras work for you. The extras are about being dependable, being willing to assume responsibilities, always being on hand, being loyal, being courteous, being willing to help others get ahead, and knowing exactly what you want. Coupled with traditional methods, that's when your marketing will really take off.

Myth #2: Marketing on a shoestring means "cheap" or "poor quality."

Not true at all. Good marketing takes ingenuity, not necessarily deep pockets. This chapter will focus mostly on the "other side of marketing." It's the concept side. It's about communicating a consistent, confident message about yourself and your capabilities. People will step up and notice if you're diligent about it.

Myth #3: I can do all of my marketing for free.

If this were true, I'd be out of business. You must make some type of financial and time commitment up front before you can ever expect results. There's no such thing as a free lunch, and it's so true in terms of marketing. If you can't invest the time or the money, then don't expect to reach your goals. However, don't be discouraged by finances. Keep in mind Myth #1. Although it will cost something, it doesn't have to cost a fortune. Marketing doesn't just happen which leads to our next myth...

Myth #4: My product and/or service is so good (or so unique) that people will be calling me for it.

We all wish this was true. The bottom line is that you could have the best product or service, but if no one knows about it through marketing, then you will never be profitable.

Let me illustrate the power of marketing. You could have a borderline product or service, yet if you aggressively market, you can be outrageously profitable. Take the product Gatorade for instance. Here is an ordinary product that is perceived as extraordinary. The next time you are in the grocery store, make sure you read the contents on the label of Gatorade. You will find it consists of water, sodium chloride and color. Colored salt water! We must all commend Gatorade on their tremendous marketing efforts. Gatorade is a multi-million dollar business. They've enlisted endorsements from famous athletes, run a nationwide TV and radio campaign, not to mention special coupons and discounts to get people to try it. As a result they created a nationwide word-of-mouth craze! They've positioned the product to be used by athletes and active individuals. You see the bright orange barrels on the sidelines of every NFL game. They've targeted the baby boomer generation and they've done very well. Who would have ever thought colored salt water would become a commodity? Remember, you could have the best product or service, but if no one knows about it, then you'll never see results.

Not necessarily, because if you truly believe in your business, then the best person to market yourself is you. You have to be marketing yourself all the time. It's a constant and never-ending process. You may want to hire a company to handle the implementation of the "traditional tools" of marketing like placing ads, designing publications or launching a PR campaign. That will give you a short-term boost, a shot in the arm. But good marketing starts and ends with YOU! You must always be marketing if you want to be a successful salesperson! No one understands your business better than you!

Before you start reading the rest of this section, find a pen and a tablet of paper. You're going to keep the information you write down using the guidelines that follow which are 7 Secret Questions you need to answer before you start marketing yourself like crazy. Think about your answers, write them down, and then come back to it at a later date. Then do some polishing, editing and refining and EUREKA! you've got it. Make sure you date your answers. You'll find yourself reading them again in another year or so and be astounded at how much you've changed, grown and accomplished.

Have you ever had the experience of being shown how to do something yet no one ever explained to you why you were doing it? Then sometime down the road, some good soul takes the time to explain, and the entire process takes on more meaning and has more influence on you? That's what these questions are all about. They're a starting point, to get you linked to the big picture. You're not marketing yourself for sport, and you certainly don't want to just go through the motions without a purpose. You have to have a goal or goals to reach and you have to have a "why" underlying those goals. If you have a purpose and a very strong "why" then there's no stopping you in terms of marketing yourself. Let's get to the heart of "why" you want to market yourself like crazy.....

Question #1. Why are you marketing yourself?

Don't you just hate those obvious questions? Most people respond with, "Well why do you think? To make money!" This is true. But I challenge you to really think about this question. I guarantee you'll get bored with just making money after a while (ask the most financially successful people you know!). You have to have a purpose attached to it. Maybe you're a small business owner and you're marketing yourself so you never have to go back to work in the corporate sector. Maybe you're a super sales person who has reached a plateau and you want to market yourself so you can get that much deserved promotion. Perhaps it's something bigger than yourself like raising money to start a foundation to increase self esteem in children. You should start by writing down everything that comes to mind, including the surface level goals like earning more money, increasing sales by 15% this year, developing notoriety in the community. Then spend some time searching deeper. For example, if you do earn more money, does that mean you will ultimately have more time for yourself—to lead a more balanced life? If you do increase your sales by 15% this year, does that mean you can then start that other company you've been wanting to start? If you do become well known in the community, does that mean you can start a community advisory committee for safe neighborhoods? What ever it is—write it down. Examine this question closely—why are you doing this? What's the ultimate goal? Do you have a mission?

Question #2: Who is your target market?

You'd be amazed at how many people say, "anyone who wants to buy from me." Well tell me—who exactly is that? Be as specific as possible. For a sales person in the healthcare industry, they may say the purchasing manager of hospitals in rural areas or they may say they market only to cardiologists who are members of a group practice affiliated with major metropolitan hospitals in a specific state. A professional speaker may say their audience is meeting planners who cater to the insurance industry or meeting planners who book keynote speeches for conventions held in Florida. Know exactly who it is you are marketing to so you are prepared when someone asks, "What would be an ideal lead for you." If you don't stumble, your chances of getting a referral through your marketing efforts increase dramatically because you'll sound like someone who has it all figured out. People will respond to your confidence.

Question #3: What's the benefit for my prospect?

The major mistake that is made in business today is that salespeople talk more about what they can do, rather than ask their prospect what they want. For example, when people are asked what they do, they respond by saying something like "I'm an attorney. I graduated from Cornell with honors. I'm with a major law firm downtown." (In other words—"I am this and I am that.) This is O.K. However, this is what most people say, and in terms of effective marketing you want to be different. People want to know "what's in it for them" so I suggest you give it to them as short, succinctly and consistently as possible. For example, the attorney may want to say, "I'm an attorney. I help individuals win cases in wrongful employment lawsuits." The benefit here (what's in it for them) is "win cases." If you can give your prospect a benefit statement every time, they'll start to seek you out. And I hate to say this, but many people don't really care if you graduated from Cornell with honors. That's more of a bonus. What they really care about is winning their case. So think about it—what's in your marketing for your prospect? What can you really do for them that will make a difference, keep them coming back and get you more referrals?

Question #4: What do I want my prospect to do as a result of my marketing?

Here's another one of those obvious questions. Most people say, "Well what do you think? I want them to buy!" This is true. But there may be more to it, particularly if you are using many different marketing methods. For instance, you may be marketing to position yourself as the leader in a particular industry. A sales rep for the salon industry once said, "I want my prospect to know that I am the primary resource for supplying products to color the hair." He would tell everyone he met exactly that. And suddenly, he became recognized as the "go-to guy" in the beauty salon industry. What is it that you really want your prospect to do? Do you want your prospect to recognize you as a primary resource? Is it to buy from you, then tell two friends? Is it to understand your business more thoroughly? Make sure you write everything down because what comes to mind is probably the right thing to do.

Question #5: What specifically are you selling through your marketing efforts?

Is it a product? A service? Both? Define the product specifically —maybe it's a mouse trap that traps mice without causing any pain to the animal. Therefore, in addition to a product, you may be selling your commitment to animal rights activism. Are you developing marketing plans for women-owned businesses? Therefore you may be selling a dedication to women in business. Is it a toy for toddlers? Then maybe you're selling your dedication to educating our youth. Don't you know more people interested in talking about educating our youth rather than a new toy?

Question #6: What reason do you give your prospect to act now?

In terms of marketing, you almost always want your prospect to pick up that phone and act now. Not tomorrow, not next month. Now. Are you offering your clients and prospects something they just can't refuse? Maybe it's a money-back guarantee or a discount before a certain date. Or maybe you have a handle on what your customer really needs and you can point it out to them directly, that if they don't act now, they may regret it for a long time or be in a lot of pain down the road. Create urgency. Get people excited about you and your line of business. No matter what you sell, there is a way to get people excited enough to make an immediate buying decision.

Question #7: Overall, what is the image you want to project?

Jot down some words that come to mind....classic, sophisticated, high-tech, breakthrough information, timeless, rich in how-to, a mover and a shaker, intelligent, committed, results on a deep level. After you get at least 10 words down, pick three. Pick the three that mean the most to you. Pick the three that you feel most comfortable with. Pick the three that indicate how you would like other people to describe you if you weren't in the room. Anchor that image in everything you do. You'll be pleasantly surprised at how fast you start to get exactly what you want.

Exhausted? I'll bet you are. Most people never spend time on questions like these when they launch a marketing program. Be proud of yourself. By finishing these questions, you are far ahead of the game...

Getting started

Now it's time to get energized! What I'm about to share with you are just some of the tips and techniques that were shared with me by one of my mentors, Harvey. He believed in fundamentals, not whiz-bang marketing techniques. He believed that marketing is actually a simple process, but people make it hard. He insisted that the focal point of all good marketing is you and how you present yourself. He also believed that you have to work at it, consistently and with passion in order to be great. I didn't believe him at first, but I believe him now. Implement these ideas throughout your daily activities and you'll be astounded at the results as well as the compliments!

Marketing tip #1: Always use a 30-second commercial.

Let's start with the 30-second commercial. Have you ever had the experience of being at a luncheon or at a networking function where you have the opportunity to stand up and tell the group a little about yourself, and you found yourself nervous about what you're going to say? Or worse yet, you get your moment in the spotlight and after you sit down, you think of all the things you wish you had said (or hadn't said)?

I conducted a marketing program for about one hundred CPA's. One of the questions asked was, "What do I say when I'm in front of a group and I have the chance to market myself?" Most accountants in the workshop agreed that they simply said their name, then mentioned that they were a certified public accountant and may have said the company they were with. That's O.K. Yet, what impression does that leave you? Less than compelling, perhaps. An introduction like that certainly does not set you apart from the competition and if you want your marketing to work for you, you have to be different. It all starts with a 30-second commercial.

The formula for a 30-second commercial is simple. Tell people who you are, what you do and give them a strong, memorable benefit. For example, one of my CPA's used to say he's an accountant who handles bankruptcies. People used to approach him and say "Oh what a depressing line of work," or "it must be a difficult job for you." When in fact he felt a great pride when helping people through difficult times. He rarely got referrals when he introduced himself to a group. Now that he developed a 30-second commercial, he says, "I'm Greg Mooney. I'm a CPA who helps people turn their businesses around, particularly after bankruptcy." He uses this simple yet powerful marketing technique wherever he goes. He says the same thing every single time people ask him what he does for a living. It's short. It's simple. It's memorable and therefore powerful. I received a card from him not too long after that seminar and he said he's getting referrals like he never got before. And, the referrals are for financial planning, developing business plans—things that people perceive as helping them "turn their business around." He did plenty of financial planning and business plans when he handled bankruptcies, yet it never occurred to him to market those components individually. People now know Mr. Mooney as the CPA who can help you turn your business around! The formula again is simple. Tell people who you are, what you do and always, always, always, supply a benefit. Take a few minutes right now to write down your own 30-second commercial. Test it out on colleagues and friends. Then test it out on people you would like to influence and assess their reaction. The more you use it, the more power it holds. The secret is that people only want to know what's in it for them. Give it to them, and they'll reward you.

Now that you have a 30-second commercial, you will no longer have to worry again about having fear of introducing yourself to a group. Remember that there is genius in simplicity and that less is more. It's true in this case. Start using your 30-second commercial today! Use it on your marketing literature—flyers, brochures, fax cover sheets, wherever people will make the connection between you and what you do. You can even use it as your outgoing voice mail message so every time someone gets your machine or answering system, your message will be reinforced!

Marketing tip #2: Always use a prospect's name.

There's something magical about using a person's name. Try it. It makes people feel special. It allows you to keep control of the conversation. And most importantly, if you're marketing yourself to this person, using their name allows you to emphasize a point (particularly your benefit to your prospect!) This marketing tip is so easy, however, you would be surprised at how few salespeople take advantage of it. Moreover, most people forget the person's name within just a few minutes of meeting them for the first time. Are you the type of person that says, "I'm terrible at remembering names." How would you like to remember the name of everyone you meet? Would you be impressed if I met you for five minutes, then we bumped into each other again six months from now and I remembered your name? I can't tell you how powerful this can be for you in terms of marketing. Most people are so shocked and impressed when someone remembers their name that it translates to other areas of the business. For example, people who remember names are perceived as highly intelligent, focused, totally reliable and impressive. Wouldn't you want to be described that way? Remembering names could potentially be one of the simplest and most powerful marketing tools in your personal marketing arsenal.

There are only three things you need to remember anything: 1) A place in your mind to put the information; 2) a vivid picture of what you want to remember; and 3) Action! combining the first two steps in picture form in your mind.

Most people remember faces but don't remember names. There's only one reason for this: paying attention. By saying "paying attention" I mean this very literally. Very few people were ever formally taught how to "pay attention" to remembering names. By putting in a little extra effort, you are sure to set yourself apart from your competition which is the best of marketing tools. Here's how remembering names works:

When you meet someone, you must "pay attention" to their face to find a "place to put the information" in your mind. In other words, you want to pick the first thing that strikes you about a person. It could be permanent, like their eyes, ears, nose, lips, hair, beauty marks; or it could be temporary like a scarf, unusual earrings, a bow in the hair, eyeglasses. Whatever it is, pick just one thing. Then exaggerate that picture in your mind. Give yourself permission to be creative and to use your imagination! The bigger the better. The funnier the better. Action is the key. For example, if you met Bill Clinton for the first time, you may choose his silver hair as being striking. Then exaggerate the picture of his hair to become something like silver bells hanging on the ends of his hair! Sound crazy? You haven't even started.

Now that you have a place to put the information. You need a vivid picture of what you want to remember, which is his name, Bill. Use that creativity again to come up with a picture symbol for the name, Bill. Maybe it's a $100 bill. Maybe it's the bill on Daffy Duck. Again, whatever it is, pick one thing and be creative!

The last step is to combine the two pictures, meaning the place to put the information and the picture symbol for his name. You may see silver bells clanging in a tornado of $100 bills! The more imaginative the better. The more action the better. Give yourself permission to let go and be creative for it will help you be creative in your other marketing effors.

Here's how it works. The next time you see Bill Clinton, you'll ask yourself, "what was the first thing that struck me about him?" And if you concentrated enough, you'll automatically remember his silver hair. And if you paid attention long enough, you would immediately remember those silver bells. Then all of a sudden, you would recall those silver bells clanging in a severe windstorm where $100 bills were swirling all around you. And you would say to yourself, "Bills?" Your name must be Bill. I know it's hard to believe for a beginner, but this whole process takes less than seconds, once you get good at it. Challenge yourself to learn one new person a day using this fun technique. It will go a long way in your marketing efforts.

Marketing tip #3: Enthusiasm is the source of achievement.
One of the great men of the 20th century, Henry Ford said this,

> *You can do anything with enthusiasm. Enthusiasm is the yeast that makes your hope rise to the stars. Enthusiasm is the sparkle in your eyes, it's the swing in your gait, the grip of your hand, the irresistible surge of your will and your energy to execute your ideas. Enthusiasts are fighters. They have fortitude. They have staying qualities. Enthusiasm is at the bottom of all progress. With it, there is accomplishment. Without it, there are only alibis.*

Remember, true genius in marketing starts with you. A positive, optimistic, cooperative and enthusiastic individual will ultimately earn more money, win more respect and achieve more success than a negative, pessimistic, uncooperative and indifferent person with a lot of money to spend on marketing.

As an example, a notable hospital in Pennsylvania was coming up on their centennial celebration. They wanted to hire a marketing and communications company to handle all aspects of their anniversary. This would include developing concepts, implementing the ideas and following through on a campaign that would last 1-2 years once the preparation time and the follow up time was factored in. Several companies were interviewed and it finally came down to two. The first company had offices downtown with lots of staff. They had an enviable portfolio of past successes. They brought samples of other centennials they had planned. And they had a 20-year reputation of excellence to boot. Not to mention, one of the principals of the company was a golfing buddy of the Chairman of the Board of the hospital. Let's face it, they appeared to be a shoe-in for the job.

Then there was another little company—the Cinderella company if you will. Been in business for only about a year. Had a strong referral list, many from physicians who were affiliated with the hospital. Known to go the extra mile and demonstrated impeccable quality. Had never managed a centennial celebration before. Very creative. Enthusiastic about their work. The Board believed that both companies were capable.

The question was, who could do it better—with flair? Now the President of the Hospital had both proposals copied and submitted to the Board members for review. However, he asked to take the names of the companies off the proposals so the Board had no idea which company submitted which proposal. Both proposals were good, but one clearly stood out. It was the one that communicated enthusiasm and energy and fresh ideas. It was the Cinderella company. (It was my company!) Enthusiasm ultimately enabled us to land a major account. We proposed ideas that were new, big, that would set the hospital apart from the competition, which is what the Board wanted most of all. We even admitted we couldn't do it on our own so we proposed to form a committee from the hospital and the community. The other company submitted a proposal that looked very similar to those they had proposed to other companies before. No new ideas. No big ideas. We later made a presentation to the Board that closed the deal. The Cinderella company launched an effort the hospital will never forget, thanks to our committee, and thanks to enthusiasm.

Did you know that Henry Ford never made it past the first grade? Did you know that Henry Ford was illiterate? Yet look at what he accomplished! He revolutionized the world through his invention. He has said that the core of getting his idea across was enthusiasm. His sole marketing strategy was enthusiasm!

Marketing tip #4: Always make a good first impression.

Whether it's in person or on the phone, it is absolutely critical to make a good first impression if you want your marketing efforts to succeed. You could have gorgeous billboards, clever ads, lots of stories in the paper, but if a prospect picks up the phone to call you and they get an indifferent or even rude person on the other end of the line, then your marketing efforts were all for nothing. As my mentor always insisted, the focal point of all marketing efforts ultimately is you!

There's an easy trick to always making a good first impression. Pretend that every new person you meet in person or talk to on the phone is Bill Gates! For those of you who don't know who Bill Gates is— he is the founder of Microsoft and his net worth is measured in the billions. Do you know the difference between a million and a billion? Let me put it in perspective for you. A vice president for a bank told me that if you started counting today from one to 1 million it would take you twelve days. If you started counting right now from one to one billion— guess how long it would take you? Thirty years!!! So do you see the significance of getting a call from or meeting Bill Gates? People who have worked with me tease me relentlessly about how I answer the phone. But I don't care anymore. It's one of my most powerful marketing techniques, thanks to my mentor's insistence. I have actually convinced myself that Bill Gates is on the other end of the line every time I pick up that phone. I am so excited about the possibility that it really may be Bill Gates that every time that phone rings, I run to get to it before the second ring. And as I run to that phone I've smile from ear to ear because I "just know" it's Bill Gates. As I'm running to the phone I say to myself...It's Bill Gates!.....It's Bill Gates!.....and when I get to the phone I pick it up grinning from ear to ear and I say with positive anticipation, "Hello! This is Mary Cronin speaking!. How can I help you today!" Amazing how people respond. The next time you hear the phone ring, ask yourself, "Who is your Bill Gates?" Try it... I guarantee you'll get unbelievable results.

Marketing tip #5: Look and talk important so you feel important.

If you feel important, other people will automatically perceive you as important. This takes on a lot of forms. Go first class in everything you do. Make sure you're dressed well every time you go out the door of your office—who knows who you're going to meet? Work on the way you speak. Do you have an accent? Do you say YEAH instead of YES? Do you get lazy at the end of sentences and say things like "nothin'" instead of "nothing?" How about the speed and pitch of your speech. Is it too fast—maybe even too slow. Is your voice high pitched? Ask someone on the other end of the phone about your voice pitch. Your voice actually gets higher as it travels along the phone lines. What about posture—take note to how you sit and/or stand in meetings—make sure your back is straight, your chin is up high. Are you taking care of yourself? Eating healthy, exercising, resting are all equivalent to making a good presentation. Everytime you make a good presentation, you're marketing yourself.

Marketing tip #6: Learn to understand your own personality as well as other personalities.

Other than learning how to remember names, this is the single most powerful marketing tool you can use for yourself. Study person-alities. Get a good handle on your own personality. I know it's a humbling experience to have to admit your faults and limitations. But don't think of it as a disadvantage, think of it as being uniquely different from everyone else. Understanding your own personality can allow you the great power of adapting your tendencies to mesh with the personality of others. By the way, this marketing tip is a necessity, not a luxury. Those who can learn to master this technique of identifying and marketing to different personality styles will indeed set themselves apart from the competition.

Take my husband for instance. I love my husband dearly, however the more I think about it the more I think how different we really are. Our closet is a perfect example. When I come home from work after a long day, I take my shoes and I aim from across the room to hit the floor of the closet. If they hit the floor of the closet—great—if not, oh well. And, when I hang things up—I simply hang them up—no order, rhyme or reason. Does anyone else do that?

Now my husband Chris—his shoes are perfectly lined up toe to toe. His white shirts hang together. His blue shirts hang together. All the hangers face the same way. He even has one of those battery operated tieholders that rotates slowly around so he can assess his tie options in the morning. He drives me crazy! And you know something, I drive him crazy too.

Let's take a look at this—even though we're very different, we're still happily married. There is only one overriding reason—we have learned to accept and embrace each others personalities—the good and the bad. There's a tip you can use when marketing yourself. "Embrace your own personality as well as the personalities of others and you can't lose!"

Did you know that just about everyone falls into one of four different personality styles? Keep in mind that there is not a personality style that is better or worse than another, simply different. Ask yourself the next few questions and as you answer them, simple questions, start analyzing yourself. I guarantee some of you may be surprised.....

First question, "What day is today?" How would you answer this? Just think of all the different answers to this very simple question. Ask other people just for fun. Keep in mind there is not a right or wrong answer to this just like there is not a right or wrong personality—only different. Consider your own answer as the four basic personality styles are described.

The first personality style is pragmatic which also could be called a straight shooter. The pragmatic marketer would say that today is "Saturday," no question about it, absolutely, today is Saturday. Pragmatic people are very cut and dry. Everything to them is black and white. They do not beat around the bush. They say exactly what's on their mind and rarely sugar coat an answer. Not very emotional people, they tend to be impatient. But they sure can get things done—they're leaders. Many doctors tend to be straight shooters simply by the nature of their work. When mom takes Johnny in to the emergency room with a broken arm, the doctor may come in, check the arm, check the X-ray, make sure there are no other problems, tell the nurse what to do and out the door he or she goes. Have you ever experienced that behavior? Pragmatics make great leaders because they are so bottom line and task oriented. If you're marketing to a pragmatic person, get right to your point. Although they make good leaders, they're not always the most popular.

The popularity award tends to go to the Flamboyant or Extroverts. You can't help but like an extrovert. You can spot an extrovert 25 miles away. They've got energy galore. They're excited about things. They love to tell stories—many times exaggerated. If you ask them what day it is they say, it's the most beautiful day I've ever experienced in my lifetime! They like to get other people curious and involved in things. However, since they move so fast, they tend not to pay too much attention to details. They'd rather be socializing. . They're contagious people—hopelessly optimistic. They're what I call a fish story teller. For example, when Flamboyant Dad and straight shooter 16-year old Johnny come in from their fishing trip together. Flamboyant Dad may say to his family, "you should have seen the giant fish I caught in the lake—I swear it was the Lock Ness Monster, wasn't it Johnny?" And straight shooter Johnny says, "no it was a lake trout, it was 13 inches in length and it was half dead when you pulled it in the boat Dad." Flamboyant Dad says, "no way. When I hooked that fish, it dragged the boat at least 100 feet! I fought with that fish—it was nasty." Straight shooter Johnny would retort, " After I scooped the fish up with the net, I had to remove the hook because Dad wouldn't touch it and then I put it back in the water because it wasn't big enough to keep." You get the idea. If you're marketing to a flamboyant person, get them excited. You may even start asking questions about them; urge them to tell you a story. They'll love you for it.

Then there's the amiable person. Like Sister Rose Marie—she was my teacher in high school. We called her Sister Salvation because she was someone you always wanted to be around. Very comfortable to talk with. Positive. Accommodating. She had lots of friends. She liked her routine—she never wanted to shake up the status quo. Mild mannered and very easy to get along with. Always doing something for someone else. Amiable personalities are very thoughtful, compassionate people. If you asked Sister Salvation what day it was, she would say, "well honey what day do you want it to be?" If you're marketing to an amiable person, take things slow. Try to bond with them—make a friend. Form a trusting relationship before anything else. Be gentle and they'll thank you for being so patient with them.

And finally, there is my personal favorite, the studious or the analytical person. Analytical people are always analyzing, of course. Love information. Very detail oriented. Precise about information and fanatics about being on time. If you ask them a question, they take the long way out to answer it, explaining every detail and using charts and graphs if you let them. My father is an analytical person. I remember going to Philadelphia where I'm from to speak to an organization. I thought it would be nice to see my family while I was there and my father volunteered to be the one to pick me up at the airport to meet for dinner. He is always on time. Actually, he's always early. But this time, he was late because they had stopped him at the metal detector and made him empty out his pockets. He had nuts and bolts and gadgets, inventions he was working on, all in his pockets. Not to mention the pocket protector that includes a thermometer, a mechanical pencil and other strange things he insists he needs on a daily basis. He's an engineer—need I say more. If you ask him, an analytical person, what day it was, he will respond, " It's Friday, in most parts of the world." Analyticals are great thinkers. They're fascinating people. If you're marketing to an analytical person, make sure you're armed with detailed information and always expect them to ask questions. Analyticals double check everything.

These are the four personality styles: pragmatic—cut and dry; extroverts—the story tellers; amiable—easy going; and analytical—great thinkers. Now that you've heard a little bit about each, do you know where you fall? Right now you may be saying, "I think I may be this one, but I could be that one too." Right? Well, you are right. We can all be anyone one of these personalities at any given moment depending on the situation. But inherently, we are one. Case in point. Did you ever have a very stern, disciplinarian type of boss? Didn't talk much, never showed much emotion. Very cut and dry. Inherently, he/she is a straight shooter. But the minute his/her granddaughter visits the office, hugs and kisses, your boss melts and suddenly becomes the most easy going, amiable person in the world.

And it's good that we can change because that's the key to getting along with other people. One of the keys to successful marketing is adapting our personality style to fit the personality styles of others.

When marketing, keep in mind the underlying principles you must understand about personalities:

1) Personalities make the world go around. You are interacting with personalities all the time. You can't market anything successfully without the cooperation of other people.

2) Everything you want in terms of marketing is owned or controlled by another personality. (for example, the money to buy, the decision to buy)

3) If you can understand personalities, you can begin to predict how people will respond to any given situation and therefore gear your marketing efforts accordingly.

4) To be successful at marketing, whether you're casually at the grocery store or formally conducting business, it's important to understand and embrace not only your personality but other personalities.

When you understand the theory of personalities, there is no limit to what you can accomplish.

Marketing tip #7: Follow up on every meeting, every phone call and every project with thoroughness and flair.

Why wait? Try this today. After your last meeting, go back to the office and immediately fax a short note summarizing what you talked about, what the next steps are, and most of all, mention you enjoyed your conversation. Then when you meet with your client again, do the same thing. Then again, and again. You'll be amazed at the perception the client will develop about you. You'll be seen as efficient, on the ball, assertive—a results oriented person who can get the job done. It only takes a few minutes and a few minutes of your time can earn you a lasting, anchored impression. When you get off the phone with someone and you promise you will do something. DO IT IMMEDIATELY! Don't put it off. Or at least get things in motion. Don't let it wait until the last minute when you have to delegate it to someone else who doesn't fully understand the goals. In terms of marketing, you'll want to factor time to do these extras into each day. After a while, people will appreciate the same level of efficiency and won't question your judgment. They just know you'll get the job done. And if it's the end of the day and you're on deadline and you just know you can't get that letter out A.S.A.P., then tell your customer. Tell them when you'll deliver it to them and make sure you can get it there on time. At the conclusion of a project, take a minute or two to handwrite a thank you letter, expressing specifically what you enjoyed about the project, mention that you would appreciate consideration for the future, and ask for a referral. You'd be surprised at how many people keep these small notes in a file folder and when it comes time to make a decision in the future, that little extra something may get you the job over someone else. Remember, marketing is about getting noticed. The personal touch will get you noticed.

The best marketing tools

A chapter on marketing would not be complete without mentioning the traditional methods that supplement the individual marketing efforts we've already described. They're listed below with some examples of how to add your personality and a benefit to your customer. Remember that 30-second commercial? It's time to fall in love with it. Make sure you have a strong benefit statement that gets you noticed then use that statement in every single one of your marketing tools. You may even start to get sick of seeing it after a while. But that's good. As soon as you get sick of saying it and sick of seeing it in print on everything you send out, is just when people may slowly start to be noticing you. The key is consistency. For example read aloud the following bulleted items:

- Advertising—Use your 30-second commercial.
- Brochures/Publications—Use your 30-second commercial.
- Direct Mail—Use your 30-second commercial.
- Public Relations—Use your 30-second commercial.
- Publishing—Use your 30-second commercial.
- Telemarketing
- Video—Use your 30-second commercial.
- Networking
- Internet—Use your 30-second commercial.
- Signage— Use your 30-second commercial.
- Yellow Pages—Use your 30-second commercial.
- Trade Show/Exhibits—Use your 30-second commercial.
- Promotional Products—Use your 30-second commercial.
- Professional Speaking/seminars—Use your 30-second commercial.

There are no typos here. It is a demonstration of the power of redundancy. It's a proven marketing method. Now that you've seen the "redundancy" element demonstrated above, I guarantee you will always remember to use your thirty second commercial! The key is to drive that concept home to the point where people just can't forget it, even if they tried. Take the following memorable marketing slogans used in **ad campaigns** and fill in the blank:

(sing) Have it your way...have it your way....at _____ (Burger King.)

_____: It's the Real Thing (Coke)

_____really satisfies (Snickers)

MMM..MMM...MMM Good (Campbell Soup)
They're TERRIFIC! (Frosted Flakes)

You've seen these marketing materials so many times in so many places, saying the exact same thing that it's almost next to impossible to forget. Whether it's a small ad in your child's annual high school play program or a regional billboard campaign—use your 30-second commercial as a reinforcement in all your marketing efforts. Make sure you place your ads where you know your prospects will read them. The most popular local magazine may not be the right place for you. Good publications will supply you with demographic information to review.

When using **brochures/publications** now in the age of technology, sometimes less is more. The average person does not take the time to pour through pages of a marketing brochure. The new craze is called a "head sheet" or a "fax sheet."

This is where you succinctly and persuasively produce a one-page flyer that can be faxed at a moments notice. It's called a head sheet when you're selling yourself, therefore you put a head shot (photo) on the flyer. But don't forget to load your flyer with benefits for your customer, rather than information about you. In terms of marketing, publications can also include your stationery package, personalized thank you cards, fax cover sheets—anything that is printed that is relayed to the public.

When using **direct mail**, understand that the average rate of return is about 1% if you're lucky. So if you determine that 10 products sold at $100 per product would earn you a profit after you factored in the cost to do the direct mailing, then you'll need to mail out at least 1000 pieces. Direct mail is very hot these days and has become a science. The theory is that the best direct mailings are multiple mailings (again—they're seeing the same name out there constantly) and/or those that are coupled with a follow up system like a phone call.

We can't ignore the **Internet** which is a fantastic place to start utilizing your 30-second commercial, particularly when you get into chat rooms and are asked to do a profile on yourself. Get involved in as many online networking sessions as you possibly can. Refer them to your web page. There's no limit to where your referrals can come from as long as people are clear on what you can do for them.

My favorite marketing tool is **public relations**, mainly because it's challenging and most importantly because it's free! There are advantages and disadvantages to using PR. The first advantage is that it is cost-effective. If you paid for a front page article in the Sunday paper of your local newspaper, it potentially could cost you thousands of dollars for a one-time placement, particularly if it's in color. On the other hand, if it's written by a reporter, it's free—except for the time you spend in the interview. The second advantage is that it is more credible. Take a random poll of your customers, friends and relatives. Most will probably agree that they will read, believe and act upon an editorial opinion before responding to a paid advertisement. Third, it becomes a ready-made marketing tool! For instance, you can get copies of a story printed (I suggest printing, not photocopying to ensure quality) at minimal cost and you can mail them out to your current and potential client base. You can use the article as part of your proposal package to boost credibility and again, get you noticed. You can use it for emphasis when you're sending that story to a major magazine editor or book publisher. Get the most mileage you can out of PR! (Note: Always get permission in writing to reprint. Some publications sell reprints.)

Even if you say you can't write, you still have a story to tell. If you don't want to write it yourself, find someone to write it for you. Hire someone or give an intern at a local college a shot at putting your ideas on paper. It depends on your budget as well as your goals. An **article published** with your byline (and sometimes your photo) in a major periodical adds tremendous credibility to your area of expertise. It automatically positions you as a leader in your field. Again, buy reprints directly from the publisher or get permission to get it printed to use as a marketing tool. Make it a point to try to get at least one article published per quarter in a magazine or newspaper that pertains to your industry. If you're not sure what magazines may be interested, go to the library and peruse through *Writer's Market*—it lists every major magazine by category and details on how to get published. In some cases, you may even get paid!

Telemarketing takes on many forms. There is a formal process where you hire a telemarketing firm to follow up on a direct mail piece or the firm makes calls to set appointments for you. Make sure they use your 30-second commercial! Or it could be that you personally make 3-5 calls every day to new contacts to secure new business. Whatever it is, maintain consistency and project the proper image.

In the speaking industry, **video production** and **audio tapes** are almost a must if you want to succeed. If you have an office lobby where people may sit and wait, you may want to consider running a continuous tape video that highlights what you can do for your customer. I used this idea for a physician group practice. They produced a video that was used in the lobby while patients waited for their appointments. The result was 1) an education for the doctors. The doctors found people had no idea what the scope of programs and services was offered. They even found they had patients who were afraid to ask questions. 2) They also realized that the video alleviated a lot of fears and 3) ultimately generated a tremendous amount of referrals. These doctors solved a basic need which was to alleviate fear. The video also positioned their practice as the best for high tech treatments in the area. Their 30-second commercial was: We're the Eye Care Associates. We're family-oriented ophthalmologists who can restore your natural vision using the latest in technology.

In the beginning, we talked about using our 30-second commercial at networking events and seminars. **Networking** isn't just formal meetings. It's also about informal meetings like standing in line at the grocery store or waiting at the cash register to pay for lunch. Next time you're in that situation, strike up a conversation. Be brief. But make sure you tell them what you do and get a business card! Send a follow up note. Then call again. Ask to put him/her on your mailing list to receive free information. I had a friend who actually bought "fish bowls." These were the large, clear, glass bowls that many restaurants put in their reception area for people to drop a business card in the hopes of receiving a free meal or a catered party for their company. The idea is never to be stagnant; always try to add more names to your list. Meet more people. Expand your referral base.

If you have the opportunity to put a **sign** outside your place of business, by all means do! Make sure you are in compliance with your local township. There are certain specifications that must be adhered to and if you don't you'll be penalized with some embarrassing hassles. So do your homework about the legalities involved then go to it. But plan carefully. That sign, if done well, could be visible for years. Make sure you're communicating the message you really want to market to your audience. A chiropractor I once worked with had an enviable location with a rather large sign but the sign was boring and, it only included his name. He later changed it to read "G. Chiropractic: Getting you Back to Work Sooner by Alleviating Chronic Pain. By using this slogan in all his marketing materials, he was able to attract a medical doctor to partner with him in practice.

If you're in business, then you need to be in the **yellow pages**. Here's why. People may hear about you on the radio or see an ad or get a letter from you. When the need arises for your services, they're not going to spend time looking for that letter or that brochure or that business card buried in a file. They're going to consult the yellow pages. Not all businesses need a display ad. A line listing may be suitable. For example, car repair shops may want to consider a larger display ad to attract attention to the person who is in a hurry to get their car fixed. The same goes for a rental car company. Dentists may want to utilize a simple line ad with their address unless they offer something different and unique from others practicing in their area.

For some salespeople, **trade show/exhibits** can be very beneficial. In some industries, trade shows and exhibits are the lifeline of a business. For example, a friend of mine is an artist. She sews unusual handmade women's apparel and sells her wears at four shows around the country throughout the year. She spends most of her time preparing for the same four shows every year. She has been marketing herself for years as providing unusual one-of-a kind dresses for the woman with distinctive taste. She communicates this in pre-show promotions, sales at the show and post-show follow up. Thanks to her consistency, she is now sought after from all over the country with phone orders, and pre-set appointments to meet her at an upcoming show. Another example is a Frame & Art Gallery that was once known for doing beautiful residential framework. The owner of the shop is now moving into providing contemporary art for the home as well as framing. Therefore she has "trunk shows" where she invites an artist to come and talk about their work, sign original pieces and take custom orders. Wine and cheese is served. They have been very successful with this approach, and she now markets her store as the only frame and art gallery where you can buy original contemporary art from local artists. People come from all over to meet not only the artist but the owner of the shop, the creator of such a wonderful idea.

We always have to be careful when choosing **promotional products** to market ourselves and our business. Have you ever sat down with an advertising specialties catalog and poured through all the nifty things you could purchase? Did you dog-ear the pages thinking you'll use those items one day? In some cases it may work as an ongoing giveaway. Like a bait and tackle shop that gives away materials to tie your own fly. If you tie the fly and bring it back, it gets hung in a showcase of VIP customers, plus you get a discount on anything you purchase in the store. This is a sensational marketing tactic because it keeps the customer thinking about the bait and tackle shop while they're working on their fly. When they bring the fly in, it makes them feel good that they're being showcased. They get a discount, an added bonus, and they're ultimately put on a mailing list to update them on other specials where they encourage you to bring a fishing partner in to mill around the store.

In other cases, it may backfire. For example, the elegant frame and art gallery would never give away plastic key chains. Although keychains are practical and useful, they just don't communicate the image she's trying to market for herself and her store.

Promotional products are sometimes useful for one-time marketing efforts. For example, my company once marketed a "great baby birthday party." In order to attract the media's attention, we found out the media's birthdays and sent them a tiny birthday cake with an invitation to the special event. It worked beautifully and we even got coverage on a nationally syndicated television show as well as *USA Today*. If it makes sense, use it. If it doesn't, don't (no matter how tempted you are!).

If you have a specific expertise, why not hold a free **seminar**? Give your audience valuable information and demonstrate your knowledge. A successful presentation will take you a good deal of the way to creating new customers. There's no question that an in-person commercial is so much better than a paid commercial. Your prospects get to see for themselves what you're all about. In a short one-hour presentation they can make a determination if they want to work with you, if they feel comfortable with you and if they want to refer business to you. Make sure you include your 30-second commercial in everything you present that day. Professional Speaking/seminars for free are great if you market them well to qualified, good prospects, and then close the sale.

Promise yourself to market consistently

Now the last step is to make a pledge to yourself to do the following things every single day to give your marketing efforts a boost to take you over the top! Here are your pledges, passed on from my mentor, Harvey:

Pledge #1: I will use my 30-second commercial whenever I get the chance.

Pledge #2: I will use my prospect's name whenever the opportunity presents itself, and I will make an effort to remember their name permanently!

Pledge #3: I will demonstrate enthusiasm in all my actions, particularly in the way I present myself and my work!

Pledge #4: I will make a good first impression whether it be on the phone or in person.

Pledge #5: I will look and talk like I'm important so I feel like I'm important.

Pledge #6: I will learn to understand my own personality as well as other's personalities so I can market to their needs and wants.

Pledge #7: I will follow up on every meeting, every phone call and every project with thoroughness and flair.

Marketing your mission

Let's now take a close look at the big picture. Ask yourself the following questions:

WHY AM I REALLY IN THIS PROFESSION?
WHAT DO I REALLY WANT TO GIVE?
HOW CAN I MAKE A DIFFERENCE?

Your answers to these key questions will help you to develop your mission statement. This statement should appear on your business plan, on your marketing plan and should hang somewhere in your office. This is why you get out of bed every morning. It's not about making money. It's about service. If you can provide service with enthusiasm and flair, then the money will come a plenty. Take a few minutes to jot down your mission statement. You will most likely change this many times before you decide it is right. But go with your gut feeling. This could be a personal mission or a company mission.

My business mission is simply to help small businesses market and communicate more effectively. A client who owned a printing company adopted as her mission, "Every project is urgent." What is your mission? If you're having trouble, go back to those three key questions introduced at the beginning of the chapter. When you finally get your mission, hang it up somewhere in your office, in your car, put it in your wallet so you can be reminded of why you're marketing yourself like crazy.

Patience is a virtue

I'd love to be the one to tell you that marketing is a quick fix. I'd love to be the one to tell you that marketing is effortless! If I did, I'd be lying to you. I've worked with enough companies and individuals to know that marketing - good marketing - takes planning, time and a concentrated effort by all parties involved. If you feel you've hit a wall, ask yourself, "Am I really focusing on the prospect and what he or she wants?" "Am I really making it easy for him or her to act?" If your answer is no, then it's time to rework your strategy. Or perhaps it's time you brainstorm with people within your sphere of influence. They say that success comes quickly and surely if you learn how to make use of the education, experience, ability and influence of others. Try your ideas out on someone you've never talked to before. Or better yet, go totally empty handed and ask for fresh ideas or a totally new approach. Question yourself often. Am I providing benefit to my customer? Am I making sure I follow the individual principles of marketing like being consistent in my message, using names, demonstrating enthusiasm, etc.

These solid fundamentals of marketing will always get you through the perceived rough spots. Give it time. And remember, marketing is a constant and never ending process. It's a journey where you're always setting new and higher milestones to measure your success. Don't stop. With a marketing mindset—oh, the places you'll go!

About Mary Maloney Cronin

Mary Maloney Cronin, speaker, author and marketing/communications consultant is President of Cronin Communications, a firm dedicated to helping small businesses market and communicate more effectively through customized consulting and workshops. Recognized as One of the Top 50 Women in Business in the State of Pennsylvania by the Commonwealth of PA, Cronin is also one of Oldsmobile's prestigious National Athena Award recipients for outstanding women in business. Featured in *Successful Women, The Pittsburgh Tribune-Review* and others for her unique, relationship-based approach to doing business, she is the author of *How to be a Top Communicator in a Changing Business World*. Cronin holds a Master's degree from Villanova University, Villanova, PA and a Bachelor's degree from Duquesne University, Pittsburgh, PA.

CRONIN COMMUNICATIONS
707 Tally Drive
Pittsburgh, PA152237
412-366-2187 or toll-free 1-800-798-4702
Fax: 412-36677-2407
E-mail: MMCronin@aol.com

Company profile

Cronin Communications is a unique firm dedicated to helping small businesses market and communicate more effectively by providing customized consulting and workshops. The hallmark of the consulting side of the company is the strategic marketing plan whereby the best combination of marketing tools (public relations, advertising, direct mail, etc.) are determined and implemented in a manageable format that results in increased new business and significant positive awareness for the company. The workshop side of the business includes dynamic keynotes, half-day programs and full day programs to introduce proven marketing and communications techniques that can be used immediately. Topics include: How to be a Top Communicator in a Changing Business World, The Secrets of Small Business Success, and How to Market Yourself Exceptionally. Cronin Communications brings high energy, memorable stories and enthusiasm to all projects. If you're looking for ways to change behavior and are ready to take your business to the next level, call Cronin Communications today.

Chapter 5

Networking: Necessity or Nuisance?

by
Deb Haggerty

*Networking is a state of mind.
Always keep in mind those people you
know to whom you can refer others.
In order to receive the benefits of
networking, you must give first.*

—Deb Haggerty

When deciding that speaking professionally became my most important career goal, I discovered that membership in the National Speakers Association (NSA) was critical to my success. I joined the organization and soon had the opportunity to attend my first national event. Let me share my story and my excitement with you!

Washington, DC. July, 1994. I was finally there—at the NSA National Convention! Everywhere I turned I saw speakers rushing from one place to another, greeting each other enthusiastically, meeting old friends. What an opportunity! I took in absolutely everything! Seminars and general sessions and exhibits—would I ever learn all there was to learn? Would I ever get to know any of these people as friends, mentors? Would I ever feel as if I was a part of this excitement?

This is such a great business—but how can I get more involved in NSA? I don't live near a chapter. I know—ask for advice. I posed the question on-line and got lots of advice: volunteer to help at workshops; contact the people in Pittsburgh or Philadelphia about local chapters; contact National and volunteer to help. Great advice, and such willingness to share!

From another on-line friend, I heard of the National Capitol Speakers' Association in Washington, DC. She invited me to attend one of their meetings. The people were friendly and sharing; the speakers were excellent. Another chapter to visit, to go to hear great speakers, another way to be involved!

What's the point? No matter what organization you are in, no matter where you live, you CAN be a vital part of it. The more you're willing to give to the association, the more you'll receive. An open mind, a positive attitude, and a willingness to try some non-traditional means of networking will help you tremendously! For me, a chance drop-in at a seminar on Cyberspace has led to a multitude of new acquaintances and several lasting friendships. So dare to dream, have the courage to explore, and watch the world of networking open wide to you!

Networking—it opened the world of NSA to me and has enabled me to meet many new friends and contacts that will last a lifetime! The same can be true for you—no matter what organization you join! You just have to plunge in, get involved, and build relationships with the people in the group. As a result, your network will grow by leaps and bounds!

Brian Tracy, noted speaker and author, has been quoted as saying, "Your success is going to largely be due to the number of people who know you favorably." In other words, people like doing business with people they like. How do people get to know us favorably? The answer is *networking*. Networking is a lot more than just meeting people; it requires much more effort. Networking, done properly in an intelligent and methodical fashion, is the key to having large numbers of people "know you favorably" and want to do business with **you**!

What is networking?

What is networking? At its most simplistic, networking is getting to know and make friends with people who directly or indirectly can help you further your business objectives. It's planning and making contacts and sharing information for personal and professional gain. The key words are "planning" and "personal."

Networking doesn't just happen; it must be planned, and there will be no gain from your efforts until you build a relationship of trust, respect and friendship. Networking is also about giving as well as getting—it is mutual sharing of information and business leads. You must be willing to share your information and contacts with others, as well as leads for them, if you ever hope to gain from the experience. Successful networking means giving as much as or more than you take. It means being willing to do someone a favor and looking at favors as investments in developing your relationships.

Success may not come immediately; however, it is critical to always be working at developing your network of contacts—building your support systems—so that they will be up and available when you need them.

Plan of action

In order to benefit from networking, the process must be planned and methodical. You must know why and how and who and where and when you will implement networking.

Set Goals

The first step is to determine goals. **What do you want from the process**? Do you want sales leads? Do you want support? Do you want information sources? **Whom do you want in your network**? Do you want customers? Suppliers? Support people? Friends? **How will you make and stay in contact with them?** Telephone? Face to face? Letters? E-mail? Organizations? **How will you track the contacts you make?** Card file? Contact Manager? Database? **How often will you stay in contact?** Daily? Weekly, Monthly? Quarterly? Yearly?

Goal-setting at the beginning of the process will help you to effectively organize your networking and, more importantly, organize the tremendous amount of information you must manage. Set realistic goals. You cannot expect to go from zero to success immediately. You cannot expect to contact 100 people a day. You cannot expect to instantly gain the respect and trust necessary to maintain and keep a contact. Occasionally, you may need to organize others of like interests in order to have an effective network. This allows you to get to know large numbers of people with whom to establish business and/or personal relationships at one time. The following article illustrates how one group of women of like interests organized to network effectively.

By Shari Hennessy Ferrer
The Miami Herald Knight-Ridder/Tribune Business News.
Apr. 1—Broward County has 18 local chambers of commerce, but until now none of them solely addressed women's business issues.

So Laura Gambino, along with Miramar florist Heidi Richards and Miramar lawyer Judy Dolan, have formed the Women's Chamber of Commerce of Broward County.

"I know there's a strong women's presence in business," said Gambino, who is setting up a sales and marketing firm in Fort Lauderdale. "Women are doing more networking, more business. I saw a niche. I think women are reaching out more and more to business organizations that can guide them through the business world."

Nearly 90 people showed up for the group's inaugural meeting Friday at the Tower Club in Fort Lauderdale.

The Women's Chamber will address such issues as applying for minority status with the county, business financing, writing proposals and running a home-based business. More importantly, Dolan said, the chamber will provide a countywide networking opportunity for Broward's business women.

"I think the time has come for this," said Angela Andreola, who owns ABS Auto Repair in Fort Lauderdale.

"Woman-to-woman support is very important in today's business, especially in my field, where we've experienced oppression. You don't get that here. You don't have to fight and prove yourself."

The Women's Chamber is open to all Broward business people, regardless of gender. Already, one man has joined as a board member. "If men want to join and help us fulfill our mission, why not?" Richards said.

Plan your strategy

How will you accomplish your goals? First of all determine who might be included in your network. Start with people you already know. Consider everyone you know: family, friends, co-workers, business associates, business contacts, clergy, club members, neighbors, school associates, past employees or co-workers, professionals (doctors, lawyers, pharmacists, brokers, bankers, accountants, consultants, real estate agents, financial advisors), suppliers, customers, sales personnel, members of professional organizations. Go through your business card file and list people you haven't contacted recently. Use this as an opportunity to reconnect with people you've not contacted in a while because you really should have been in touch much sooner! List them all. Once you begin the process, you will be amazed at the number of people who are already in your network!

Then begin to add to your network. Don't forget cold calls. There are "stars" in every profession. Who are the stars in your industry? They may be people whom you can contact and build into your network. Perhaps someone has told you about a wonderful author you should read or speaker you should hear. They may be people who can be included in your network, too. Often these people are more approachable or available than you would expect. You'll never know until you contact them! All you need is a strategy to get in touch with those people who are valuable contacts for you. The following story illustrates an initiative one group used to get in touch with "those at the top!"

By Nancy Feigenbaum, The Orlando Sentinel, Fla.
Knight-Ridder/Tribune Business News
Apr. 1—Most weekdays, Katrena Haynes can be found working at her small Orlando printing business, where she stays until midnight to finish print jobs. Thursday, she turned over the office to someone else and headed to Church Street instead—not to party

but to learn.

The subject was loans for businesses owned by minorities and women. More than a half dozen loans and initiatives in Central Florida target "disadvantaged businesses." Dozens more offer help to small-business owners in general.

The free, all-day forum was a chance to get information about all these programs at one sitting. Entrepreneurs such as Haynes seized the opportunity, asking for phone numbers and specifics.

Can a small business bid on a contract without having enough money for all the supplies? Will the airport waive bond requirements for a mom-and-pop business? Will the Walt Disney World Co. lend money to a business owner with bad credit? Whom can a small-business owner call to get help with financial statements?

In most cases, the answers came from the people at the top—the ones running loan programs and minority business offices.

The first-time event was put on by the Minority/Women Business Enterprise Alliance Inc., an Orlando umbrella group for a variety of government agencies and private businesses.

"These are the kind of things we need to hear," Haynes said, as Derryl Benton of the Greater Orlando Aviation Authority explained airport bidding policies. The mission of the forum—and much of the new alliance's work is to provide minorities and women with these inside connections. During breaks, lenders shook hands and exchanged business cards with entrepreneurs.

Haynes and Straughter are familiar with the power of connections. The company is debt-free partly because some suppliers are willing to delay billing when Haynes shows them a purchase order from a big customer.

Leon Watkins, executive director of the alliance, called the forum a good starting point. "You've got to build up things like this," Watkins said.

Establish a timetable

Take action! Plan scheduled activities to achieve your goals. Aim for one lunch, one reconnection, one new or cold call contact a week, then build from there. The point is to get started. An ancient truism states, "The longest journey is begun with just one step." Mary Kay Ash, founder and owner of the number one skin care company in the U.S. and also an expert networker, speaks to the fear of failure or rejection which resides in us all and reminds us, "Failure is the opportunity to begin again more intelligently!" Remember, if you don't try, you'll never succeed. We all make mistakes and blow contacts, but the goal is to keep going! Networking helps develop relationships (and confidence, I might add) in an easy non-threatening manner. For example, you can ask a friend, "Would you introduce me to....?" My father had a saying when walking into an unfamiliar environment, "There certainly are a lot of people in this world who do not have the pleasure of my acquaintance!" So seize the moment and take that first step! Then stick to your schedule. Proper behavior is rewarded!

Establish a specific time to write notes or make telephone calls, for example, every Tuesday and Thursday between 3:00 and 5:00 PM. Determine what networking events you will attend and program them into your calendar. Keep those appointments as religiously as customer or client contacts. If you attend a meeting or special networking function, set a goal to meet "x" new people or collect a certain number of business cards. You can do it! It's never too early (or too late) to start the networking process. The students in the following article have the right idea!

> *By Nancy Feigenbaum, The Orlando Sentinel, Fla.*
> *Knight-Ridder/Tribune Business News*
> *Apr. 1 JUMP START. Hispanic students at the new University of Orlando School of Law have formed their own bar association. The student group will act as a networking and support group, reaching out to the national Hispanic bar and local Hispanic business organizations, said Sid Roman, its president.*
> *Roman said the group was created with the idea that law school students need to start job hunting long before they graduate.*

Track your contacts

Track your contacts

Create a notebook or card file to record whom you've contacted and when. If you have a computer, use a contact manager such as ACT!© or Sharkware© or Day-Timer Organizer©. Quentin Steele, an on-line contact and friend says, "When I think of networking, I always think of techno-networking, i.e., keeping a Mackay 66-type[1] of database of all business contacts, and then remembering their special occasions, preferences, etc." Record where you got their names and what the outcome or response to the contact was. Write down your impressions of the call or meeting and how you might be able to assist that contact. Decide when you will contact them again and put it in a follow-up schedule. Write them a note of appreciation for their time or for the other potential contacts they gave you. Read through your files from time to time—you'll be amazed at the number of people with whom you're connecting!

Determine your networking methodology

One method is telephoning. Remember that the purpose of the call is to make a connection between you and the potential contact. Try to talk with them directly—using the name of the person who referred you to them may help. Be up front with them—let them know that you are building a network of contacts and feel there may be synergies between you. Let them know that you want nothing from the contact but to meet them and that you will respect whatever time constraints they place upon the meeting. Always end the call with a thank-you! If you're calling a person at their place of business, don't forget the other people in the company. Find out the name of the person who answers the telephone—they may know other people in the company who may also be of interest to you. They will appreciate that you don't perceive them as just a "nameless voice" to be circumvented in your quest to reach your contact! In fact, they may become the most valuable contact in that company!

Another method is letter writing—almost a forgotten art in today's society. Jot your contact a brief note stating your intent to build a network of support people and that you feel they could be an important part of it. Tell them a little about yourself and what you are doing. Tell them you will be following up with a telephone call and that you want to insure that the contact is mutually beneficial. Ask them to consider, prior to receiving your call, how they might benefit from the association. Networking always needs to be a two-way street—we must always be willing to give as much as or more than we hope to gain. Then follow up!

In this electronic era, communications and contact by computer is also an avenue through which to build contacts. E-mail is one of the most powerful tools for communications that exists today. Studies have shown that people will answer e-mail before they will return telephone calls or answer letters—perhaps because it is so easy to dash off a short reply after reading the message. Be sure to follow the etiquette of e-mail, however. Make sure your message is brief and to the point. Use only a few short sentences. DO NOT USE ALL CAPITAL LETTERS! It is considered "shouting" in the on-line world. Be sure to let them know how they can respond to you. Include your name, address, and telephone numbers as well as your "screen name." Again, follow up!

Places to network

Associations—Some of the easiest places to make contacts are through Associations. The best place to start is with your local Chamber of Commerce. Join and get involved! They are continually providing opportunities from after hours events specifically designed for networking to small business support groups to economic or government forums. Their directory is a wealth of information on the businesses in the area and offers a variety of people to contact.

Other groups such as Optimists, Rotary, Sertoma, Jaycees, Lions, Make a Wish and other service clubs are great places to meet people and to provide service to the community. Remember, it is important to give as well as seek to gain from your networking endeavors. Someone once said, "They won't care to understand you until they understand you care!"

Specialty associations such as Young President's Organizations, Women's Networks, University Clubs, and Alumni Associations are excellent groups to become involved in. They will help you in your networking if you meet the qualifications for membership. If there isn't a group which piques your interest, follow the example in the article which follows and start your own!

Knight-Ridder/Tribune Business News
Lexington, Ky. Mar. 31. So you think you know how to build a better mousetrap? There's a new group that wants to hear from you.

The Central Kentucky Inventors and Entrepreneurs Council hopes to bring inventors and entrepreneurs together to sell new products and start new businesses.

Mohammed Nasser, a retired IBM engineer, and his partner, Don West, started the organization to take advantage of the many inventors and engineers living in Central

Kentucky.

"I wanted to tap the talent." Nasser said

D. Craig McAnelly, economic development specialist for the Bluegrass Area Development Corp., said the group is "a non-profit networking council founded to help inventors bring their ideas to the marketplace and work with entrepreneurs."

Nasser said he was inspired to start the organization after attending a meeting of the Inventors Council of Dayton,Ohio. At that meeting, inventors discussed ways to market a new air compressor for air conditioning systems.

Nasser was impressed by the members' support of such inventions. The new group will be affiliated with the Dayton council, which is part of a larger network of similar groups in Ohio and Michigan.

Nasser would like to draw from a wide range of people to join the group, including engineers, model makers and patent lawyers. He also hopes to recruit politicians, especially those with engineering backgrounds, to join the group.

He has attracted a "mixed bag" of inventors working on projects in engineering, agriculture and biotechnology.

The Bluegrass Area Development Corp. will provide meeting facilities for the council and has worked with Nasser in recruiting people to join the council.

Business leaders in Central Kentucky applauded the effort.

"We need to do anything to raise awareness of technology-based business opportunities, " said Lee Todd, president and CEO of DataBeam. "In the long run," Todd said, "I hope the council will create jobs through new businesses and keep some of the brighter minds in Kentucky."

Industry associations are another place to look. Every industry has an association and most have local or at least regional chapters. You need to know the people in the industry you serve or wish to serve. Ask a good customer or colleague if you can accompany them to a meeting if you are not a member. Industry associations are recognizing the power of networking as a technique to provide marketing and customer service as the following illustrates:

Networking: Necessity or Nuisance?

Traffic World
Knight-Ridder/Tribune Business News
Atlanta—Apr. 1—The official theme of the '96 International Intermodal Expo here last week was "Networking, Knowledge and Technology." But the underlying current in talk about how shippers, carriers and intermodal marketers can survive in the brutal global market was partnershipping and communication.

In his keynote speech, American President Cos. President and CEO Timothy J. Rhein underscored the advances in intermodalism since he entered the business more than 20 years ago. But he noted the industry today faces a flattening market, an unsettled regulatory environment and uncertainty and anxiety that pervade carriers and customers as cutthroat competition winnows out weak or badly managed players. With customer satisfaction emerging as the make-or-break factor, Rhein pointed out that one-time bitter rivals are forming new alliances, using joint container pools, hammering out standards for electronic data interchange and even turning over their cargo to competitors when it better serves the customer's need. "Who would have imagined," Rhein marveled, "that today over half of APL's freight would be riding on somebody else's ship?"

It shows, said Rhein, "that creative new approaches to partnershipping across modes that have not traditionally cooperated" will be needed to squeeze costs out of the supply chain to meet growing demand for time-sensitive, factory-to-home delivery of products.

The notion of partnership more and more involves the exchange of employees between customer and carrier and sharing sensitive data on orders and business strategies. That level of trust is having an impact on rates, as in the truckload market, where excess capacity and tough-minded sophisticated shippers are in a buyers' paradise but concentrating more and more on the quality of service. The result, said Con-Way Truckload Services President and CEO J. Ronald Linkous, are partnerships in which a carrier like Con-Way will study a customer's business and sometimes "raise a shipper's rates but lower his overall transportation costs" by streamlining the logistics process.

Networking Clubs—Networking clubs have been around for years, and they are gaining popularity as more and more people open their own businesses. Networking clubs are groups of people who meet on a periodic basis to exchange business leads, referrals, find camaraderie and get advice and counsel. How can a networking club improve your business? Margie Haddon, writing for *Home-Office Computing*, says: "From my networking experience, I've seen several ways that a club can help anyone run a better business."

• Obtain other club members as your clients.
• Obtain other members' friends and clients as your clients.
• Find sound business advice.
• Keep yourself motivated.

However, Ms. Haddon cautions, "Belonging to a networking club is not just a matter of making contacts and raking in the dough. Here are two things to watch out for:

> • Building a bad reputation—just as word of mouth can work for you..., it can just as easily work against you when you provide an inferior product or service or fail to follow through on your obligations.

> • Wasting your time. Although networking clubs work well for many people, they can be a waste of time if your business or personality doesn't match the needs of the group. You may also waste your time if you join too many groups."[2]

Check the business listings of your local paper to see if such clubs exist and when they meet. One such club that has been of great benefit to me personally is LeTip International. The LeTip creed reads: *LeTip is a professional organization of men and women dedicated to the highest standards of competence and service. Our purpose is the exchange of business tips. Members will, at all times, maintain the highest professional integrity. Each business category is represented by one member and conflicts of interest are disallowed*[3]. LeTip is an international organization with clubs throughout the country. There are six LeTip Clubs within my region alone. When my family moved to our current community from another state, membership in LeTip helped me to build my business—most of my clients are either LeTip members or came from a referral by a LeTip member.

If there is not such a club in your area, you can call LeTip International (1-800-25-LETIP)to see if they are interested in starting one. You may even desire to start your own group. However, if you do join such a group, remember that the "golden rules" of networking apply!

Do unto others. If you want others to refer business to you, send some business their way.

Acknowledge. If someone uses your services or sends you a client, thank him or her. Build relationships. Make a sincere effort to learn about their businesses.

Don't expect immediate results. It takes time to build strong business relationships.

Ask for what you want.

Do a good job.

Succeed together![4]

On-line Connections—Another great place to network is on the Information Superhighway! Today there are dozens, no hundreds, of forums and chat groups in which to meet new people, gather information, sell your products and services, and find friends as well as clients. The easiest place to get initiated to the Internet is through one of the commercial on-line services such as America Online (AOL), CompuServe (CIS) or Microsoft Network (MSN). All you need is a computer, modem, telephone line, and their software (usually free for the first five hours of use). Then explore! Each of the services has an introductory tour that will get you started. An excellent way to learn all about these providers and groups as well as about the Internet itself, is through an audio tape series by Wally Bock, *Doing Business on the Internet,* produced by National Press Publications.[5] Wally is one of the world's leading experts on how individuals and organizations can use the power of on-line technology to do things better and more profitably.

Putting it into practice

Once you've set your priorities, made your plan, and determined the places you are going to network, you need to put it all into practice! You'll need a few more tools to make it easier.

First of all, you need business cards. Business cards are not an expensive investment. You can have them printed professionally or you can print them yourself using a laser printer and one of the business card paper selections available from companies such as Paper Direct or Beaver Prints. You may want to have different cards for building your personal networks than those you use for professional networking. Chuck Littauer, who is a car collector, has a set of "hobby cards" that he uses when networking at car shows. A good practice is to keep your cards in your right hand pocket and those you collect in the left hand pocket. Keep a pen handy to jot notes on the cards you receive to help you remember that person and your conversation until you have the time to transfer the information into your contact manager. Aldonna Ambler, Ambler Organizational Consultants, Hammonton, NJ, suggests bending the corners of cards (upper left to mean "call," upper right to indicate "send material,") so that you don't lose eye contact and the "connection" by taking the time to write a note.

Secondly, you need what outplacement firm, Lee Hecht Harrison calls your "TMAY." You need a short, less than thirty second description about your business which will allow you to answer the question, "Tell me about yourself?" or "What is it that you do?" I tell people that I'm excited because I get to educate and encourage people to put the power and presence of their personalities into practice in a non-threatening and positive way—if they choose to do so. An associate, Pam Myers, tells people that her company "makes people comfortable saying 'No!'" My friend, Marita Littauer, says her company is the "complete service agency for both the established and aspiring Christian speaker, author and publisher." Remember, *first impressions are critical.* Make sure you convey a professional image in dress and body language and that your enthusiasm is contagious!

Once you have your "TMAY" and your business cards, go to it! Follow the "Three Foot Rule." Anyone within three feet is a possible contact or prospect! Psyche yourself up to meet new people—everywhere! Follow these guidelines at the next event you attend:

- Go up to someone you don't know and introduce yourself. Start a conversation.
- Don't be afraid to ask, "What do you do?"
- If a conversation gets stale, gracefully end it.
- Don't hang out with the people you came with.
- When you meet an old acquaintance, tap into his or her network.
- In a conversation, don't wait for someone to suggest that he or she can do something for you; propose how you might help them.
- Don't do business while networking, instead, make a date to follow-up.
- Act like a host, not a guest. Adele Scheele, author of *Skills for Success*, says guests wait to be introduced. A host introduces him or herself.

Remember that the purpose is to meet new people, build your contact base and make new friends. You never know when a contact will come in handy or when you'll be able to be of service to them. Keep a smile on your face and in your voice and have fun!

Post-networking follow-up

You've made the calls or written the letters or been at a function and gathered business cards. Now what? It is important to document all your activities. If you're using a computer contact manager, enter in the data as you go: when you've called or written, the actions you've promised to take. If you've met new people at a function, enter their information into the contact manager with all the identifying points you noted on their business card at the time. If you are using another type of system, be sure to enter all the pertinent data in a methodical fashion. Then follow-up, follow-up, follow-up! Send a brief, handwritten note to those people you just met at the networking function expressing your pleasure at meeting them. Then post a reminder in your system to follow-up with more formal correspondence later. Send the same kind of note to those contacts you've made by telephone, especially if they're new to you. Keeping in touch with your network of contacts is critical.

After you've been networking for a while and have a database of contacts built, go through the list and prioritize them. Those people who are prime prospects or information sources should be contacted more frequently than those who are casual contacts. Be sure to schedule the contacts and either use the computer's notification system or some sort of tickler file so you don't forget. Track all calls and correspondence with those in both your personal and professional networks.

As you build your database of contacts, begin to gather information about them that is not readily apparent from their business cards or brochures. For example, you might note their birthday, their spouse's name, their anniversary, children's names (if any), hobbies, interests, unusual characteristics, etc. Some may play golf, or like fishing, or be avid sports fans. Others may like to read in specialty areas like non-fiction or mysteries. Others may be members of special interest groups. Tracking this information will help you be of service to them if you find articles of interest or events they may wish to attend. The more you know about an individual, the more easily they will come to mind in the event you need help or can assist them in their endeavors.

Harvey Mackay of Mackay Envelope Corporation is an expert in this area of gathering information. At a recent National Speakers Association Convention where he spoke, he demonstrated this knack to us. He picked one of the people on the program about whom relatively little was known. He then proceeded to tell us all about him, including where he and his wife went to college, what they studied, where they grew up and all sorts of other details. The person who was the subject of the research was amazed and thrilled at the amount of information

Mackay had gathered and that he had gone through the time and effort necessary to gather it. Your contacts will also be pleased that you care enough to find out more about them. This kind of information is invaluable in getting to know those people in your networks so that they become "real" and not just "contacts!"

Keep up-to-date on what your contacts are doing. It is critical to read the local newspapers and news magazines for articles or notices that pertain to your contacts or the companies for which they work. If they've done something notable, a congratulatory note or telephone call is in order. If their company is making changes, you may be able to help them, or there may be opportunities for you there. Read everything! You never know when the information may come in handy. Joe Calloway, nationally known speaker, says: "I read about business constantly. Not books—periodicals. *Business Week, Forbes, Fortune, Wall Street Journal*, etc. If a steel company, for example, calls me—I already know what's going on in the steel industry because I READ READ READ." The more you know about the people in your network and what's going on in their lives and their companies, the more effective you will be.

Success in networking

When I started writing this chapter, I knew that networking success stories would play an important part in the effort. The best way to get success stories—networking! I went to my networks, personal, business and on-line and requested my contacts send me stories of how networking has aided in their success. Many replied. For all of us, networking is an integral part of our lives and our success. We cannot imagine a world where it would not impact our lives greatly.

Earlier this year, I was in Sea Island, Georgia, with my husband. We were attending the President's Roundtable, a consortium of presidents of companies similar to his. Part way through the weekend, I realized that these men were indeed networking, albeit at a more elevated level than one would ordinarily conceive. To put into practice the networking techniques I had been researching, I asked these men to tell me what they thought about it. Is networking a nuisance or a necessity?

Jack Krasula, President, Decision Consultants, Inc., called me a few days later to give me his views. Jack said, "The motto of our company is: This company is its people—the best!" He continued, "In today's world, we've got to find more and more better people—it's networking! It's just networking. This morning I was on a sales call with one of my salespeople. We closed a $750,000 sale with a Fortune 50 customer. It was due to networking!"

"My human resources person just came to me to tell me she had made a job offer to fill a key position. "I was at a 30th birthday party and asked people to send me the ten best people they knew and that's how I found him!" Networking again!" Krasula says, "Today companies don't want to hire a total stranger. They want to hire someone they know or whom someone else they know knows—it's much less of a risk. Networking is when somebody approaches us for a key position and I know they've worked for another company in the industry. I'll pick up the phone and call my counterpart in that company and ask how that person did with them, and he'll tell me. It's the relationships we have!" "Networking is the very essence of business!" emphatically states Krasula.

Bill Gallagher, President of Atlantic Data Services, Inc., and also a member of the President's Roundtable, sent me his philosophy of networking:

> *While networking is an intrinsic behavior of all creatures, it has become even more important as society has evolved, developed, and become more specialized. Networking is now a critical component of human survival and prosperity.*
>
> *As an example, 150 years ago families lived on family farms. Each farmer grew his own crops and may have shared his corn with another farmer who grew wheat. Clearly, during the off season they would discuss what they intended to grow the next year, to insure that not everyone grew the same crop. That was networking. Today, however, farmers are besieged by competing seed companies and fertilizer companies. Each says they have spent millions on research and development to create the best product for the farmer. Clearly the farmer is not able to scientifically differentiate among the multitude of available choices. So he relies on this network for advice, experience and support. His ability to call on his peers to help evaluate his alternatives in areas where he does not have the chemical or scientific background to objectively make choices is critical to his success.*
>
> *In all aspects of life, as specialization and scientific or clinical experience grow by leaps and bounds, we are all becoming less capable of expertly evaluating our alternatives. We evolve our decisions from those of a commodity buyer to a solution buyer. The farmer no longer buys seed based principally on the research and development of the seed*

company, or even the price of the seed. He buys on the recommendation and results achieved by his peers in his network of farmers.

This evolution to buying based on solutions as verified by our personal networks has invaded every aspect of our lives. This is how we pick doctors (not by what medical school they attended, or how they ranked in class), lawyers, accountants, investment advisors, etc. We all affiliate with our unique peer groups and seek their advice and experience on positive solutions or negative experiences they have had in areas of interest to us.

From a personal perspective, this philosophy is very evident in the marketing and selling of technology services. I have informed our sales force that their first responsibility is to develop a personal network with their clients. It is more important to me that they create a strong personal relationship with the client than a strong relationship between the client and our Company. I have told them that they must be of personal value to the client. The client must see them as a friend, a peer. They must represent the interest of their friends back to the Company. I have told them that their personal network should be of more value to them than their relationship with our Company. It should be more important than their job. I have told them that if our Company cannot meet the requirements of their network, they should quit their job and take their network with them. They should find a Company who can meet the needs of their friends and go to work for them.

I obviously get very confused looks when I say this to them, but it makes perfect sense. Our buyers network just like the farmers. They rely on each other for advice and experience. I need the people who represent my Company to be part of that network, not outsiders. I need them to be solution providers not commodity providers. The people who can do this the best realize their relationship with their customer is more important than their relationship with the company they work for. Therefore, I will lose the good people if I do not make sure our Company can meet the needs of their friends on their network. I rely on the value of our sales force's personal network more than only technology or the scientific aspect of our industry.

For both of these men, extremely successful CEO's of information technology companies, networking is not only NOT a nuisance, it is an integral part of their strategies and their business. Both companies depend on networking to keep the relationships with their existing customers strong as well as to build relationships with new clients.

These successful men network **all** the time. While we were at dinner that evening, I was talking with John Fain, President of Metro Information Systems, Virginia Beach, VA. As we were talking, I happened to glance around the room and remarked to John that the gentleman at the table next to ours looked very much like Bill Gates of Microsoft. John looked and agreed. A waitress confirmed to us that it was indeed Bill Gates and his wife. John's company and several of the others' companies are Microsoft partners and John had briefly met Bill Gates at a function Microsoft had sponsored. Because of that previous brief meeting, John went over when the Gates' had finished eating, re-introduced himself and then brought Bill and his wife to our table and introduced him to all of us! Because of networking, we all had the opportunity to meet Bill Gates.

Networking is not only a philosophy and a very successful one, but it can also mean basic survival for your business. Nick Nicholas of ProMax, Inc., Austell, Georgia, shares how networking not only aided him in building his business, it rescued him from sure failure!

> *We started our speaking and training business in 1988 right after I retired from the Army. We worked very hard trying to build up a client base and to find a niche market to work. It all came together in late 1989 and we were on our way marketing customer service and cross-selling training to financial institutions.*
>
> *Everything was going very well and each year we were growing and increasing the number of our clients. And then in 1993 everything changed. In the course of one week, we lost 82% of our booked revenue for the year.*
>
> *Another company that sold other products that financial institutions use was losing its market share to a competitor. Their solution was to offer free customer service and cross-sales training to any client who would use them exclusively as the vendor for other needed products. Their strategy worked well.*
>
> *We were devastated! I told my wife that I was going to quit the speaking and training business and go sort mail at*

the post office. Fortunately she wouldn't hear of it so after three days of holding my own private "Pity Party," we settled down to the task of trying to recover.

We put out feelers to everyone we knew both in our personal network as well as our professional network. In addition to the network, we made calls to as many organizations as we could get to talk to us about training and speaking.

About three months after we began our attempt to recover, we got a call from another trainer with whom we'd worked two years earlier. He said he didn't know if we'd be interested or not but he knew of a company in Detroit, MI that was hiring contract trainers to fulfill a large contract. We took the lead. And we got a contract!

Marita Littauer, Director of Marketing for CLASS Services, Inc., and a speaker and author in her own right relates the following success story:

It took years for me to realize the true value of the networking I had been informally conducting. Because of my experience in teaching and launching speakers, I had been invited to speak at a number of writers' conferences throughout the country to teach the writers how to promote their books through speaking. I accepted these invitations, even though they could not pay my usual speaking fee as I knew that being a part of these programs would be good networking for me—I just didn't know how. At these events, major publishers send their representatives to teach classes and meet with potential authors. Since my business, representing speakers and authors, is interwoven with the publishing industry, I wanted to get better acquainted with the editors from the various publishing houses. As a part of the faculty, I was at dinners with them, chatting with them in the staff lounge and sharing housing with them—we became friends. That in itself felt good! At the industry conventions, I would walk the trade show aisles and see many of these "friends." They'd call to me, we'd say "hello," and chat. I'd become an insider! I didn't ask for anything from them, I just developed a relationship.

Last year I decided to put together an event that would connect the speakers and potential authors who

*attended the seminars I taught with the publishing
professionals who were looking for authors. My concept was
an event that would take place in conjunction with the annual
industry convention. All the publishers would already be
there, I just had to bring in the speaker/writers who were ready
to be published.*

*I started calling the publishing industry friends in
my network. Within a matter of days, I had my entire program
filled! Everyone who was called, assuming they were going to
be attending the convention and still had the space in their
agenda, said "yes!" Operating on the "Field of Dreams"
model (if you build it they will come), I now had built the
event. Next I invited the attendees. Preparations began for this
event in May, and in July we had a successful meeting with 80
attendees and 13 leading industry professionals as presenters.
Several good matches were made between publishers and
attendees for both books and magazine articles.*

*This year preparations were started earlier. More
presenters are willing to be involved than the program has
time to include. Many of the same presenters offered to come
back again and we are expecting several hundred people in
attendance from all over the country! All of this has been made
possible because of some low-key networking done several
years earlier which started, not with requests for their time,
but rather with a relationship built on common interest and
trust.*

My friends say I am a master of networking. I asked one of them
recently why she said that. She said, "You are always at networking
functions; you are always personable, and you're always so willing to
share what you know and who you know with others."

Having others think favorably of you is what Brian Tracy said
leads to success in networking. To ensure that success occurs is a matter
of caring, of paying attention, of keeping in touch with your contacts, of
having the discipline to organize your networking information and to
follow-up on it, of thinking about how those people you know can be of
service to others you know, of doing the activities and behaviors
required. Networking is a state of mind! It is being willing to risk
rejection, to take chances on people. It is realizing that what is most
important in life is not possessions or fame or fortune—it is the people
we know and with whom we have relationships, the people we can
impact and those who have had an impact on us.

Summary

To be a success at networking, you must have a methodical plan, scheduled activities, an out-going and professional manner, meticulous follow-up and documentation, and most of all, you must have fun! Remember what my dad always said when looking at a room full of people he did not know, "There certainly are a lot of people here who do not yet have the pleasure of my acquaintance!" By the end of the night, there would have been no strangers to my father—he would have met them all! You and I can do it, too! Go forth, network, make lots of new and lasting acquaintances, and may they all think favorably of you as you succeed in your endeavors!

FOOTNOTES

[1]The Harvey Mackay Rolodex® Network Builder, Harvey B. Mackay, 1993, Mackay Envelope Corporation.

[2]Margie Haddon, "Build Your Business through a Networking Club," *Home-Office Computing*, December 1991, p. 24-26.

[3]LeTip Creed, LeTip International, 4901 Morena Blvd., Ste. 703, San Diego, CA 92117.

[4]*Op. cit.*

[5]Wally Bock, "Doing Business on the Internet," *National Press Publications*, Shawnee Mission, KS, 1996.

[6]Joe Calloway as quoted in "Professional Competency No. 3", Deb Haggerty, *Penn Speaker* (a publication of the Pennsylvania Speakers Association), February 1996.

About Deb Haggerty

Deb Haggerty is President of The Haggerty Group, a management consulting firm she founded in 1985. While most of her clients are located in her local region, she has served companies from coast to coast. Deb's unique management approach, **P**eople, **O**rganization, and **S**trategy **I**ntegrated **T**ogether **I**n **V**ital **E**nterprise, is known as **POSITIVE**". Prior to forming her own company, Deb was with Southern Bell and AT&T for thirteen years.

Deb holds a BA in English and an MBA in Personnel and Human Resources Management and has earned the designation of Professional Management Consultant. Recognized nationally as a professional speaker, she is a member of staff for Florence Littauer's CLASSeminar and the Personality Plus Training Workshop.

Memberships include the National Association of Women Business Owners, the Institute of Management Consultants, the Consultants Bureau, the American Subcontractors Association, the Pennsylvania Society of Association Executives, Toastmasters International and the National Speakers Association.

POSITIVE CONNECTIONS

PMB #306, 2212 S Chickasaw Trail
Orlando FL 32825 1-888-DebSpkr

· (332-7757)

_om

Company Profile

Deb Haggerty is President of The Haggerty Group, a management consulting firm founded in 1985. Deb's unique management philosophy, People, Organization and Strategy Integrated Together in Vital Enterprise, is known as POSITIVE. Prior to forming her own company, Deb was with Southern Bell and AT&T for thirteen years.

Deb's presentations include:

Help! My Computer is Driving Me Crazy!
What do all those numbers mean? What do I do now? A basic introduction to computers and technology.

The Personality Puzzle
Knowing who you are helps you make sense of others to solve the "puzzle" of personalities.

Preparing a Powerhouse Presentation
Teaches effective communications skills while building confidence in presenting to audiences of any size.

Captivating Customer Service
Learn the concepts of practicing customer servant-hood, not merely providing customer service.

Team-Building for the 21st Century
"No man is an island..."How to function as a team to achieve company goals and objectives.

Strategies for Success
What is success? How do we know when we're successful? A non-traditional look at success.

The Time Game
Prioritizing your time the right way!

Chapter 6

Are You Listening?

by
David Goldman

*When you focus on the other person,
you are naturally being a good
listener, this will make you more
likable, result in better relationships,
and increase your sales.*

—David Goldman

Quick—name the one element critical for success in all the aspects of the selling cycle. This skill is vital to prospecting, making contacts, presenting, closing, getting referrals, and all the steps in between. The answer is, of course, listening.

Understanding the way you normally listen, discussing some of the obstacles that get in the way of good listening, and learning how to listen effectively will help you increase sales, and likely, improve many of your professional and personal relationships. This chapter will show how listening is the key to communication and that better communication leads to increased sales.

In this chapter, you will discover the four deadly mistakes we usually make in how we listen; three critical areas of focus and two additional issues that prevent good listening, along with one sure way to listen more effectively. Along the way, I'll share some secrets.

In my experience as a salesperson and as a coach, I have found that the most profound difference in results comes from the ability to listen. There are many other skills that are important. But listening is key. Effective listening separates the champions from the rest of the field. Listening involves patience, openness, emotional strength and understanding.

The first secret

Listening is not something you do. Listening is a function of who you are. I received a fortune cookie after lunch in a Chinese restaurant and it read. "The secret to having good friendships is to be a good friend."

Notice that the fortune did not list things to do. Rather, it said that the secret is to BE a good friend. Friendship is a function of being. So is listening. The secret to listening effectively is to be a good listener. It begins with being genuinely interested in the other person. More about this later.

The four deadly sins of poor listening

Let's start by identifying the most common mistakes, the first three are in actuality caused by the fourth. To begin to engage in constructive listening, you must first undo your existing bad habits. This will open you up and make you more receptive. The four sins are:

Ignore—The worst way to listen in any circumstance, including a sales setting, is to ignore the other person. Have you ever been in a situation where the salesperson is intent on giving the presentation and it doesn't matter what you say or what questions you have? Let's hope that is not your style.

Pretend—Pretending to listen is similar to ignoring. Perhaps you have been in a room where someone is on the phone and you can only hear their end of the conversation. It sounds something like:

"Uh-huh...mm-hmmm...yeah...yeah...right...uh-huh..." and so forth. The person is pretending to listen and is thinking primarily of his or her own agenda.

Another example would involve the salesperson asking a question (like a technique) and then only pretending to listen to the answer while planning to move on to the next point in the presentation. Ignoring and pretending obviously don't work in sales situations.

Selective—Selective listening is where you get accused of "only hearing what you want to hear." In fact, if you are guilty of selective listening, you may be listening for key words or phrases which support or prove your point. Another form of selective listening happens when one is waiting for a break in the conversation or for the other person to take a breath. In either case, when there is a break or when the key word or phrase is heard, that person jumps right in to make a point.

This behavior devastates the goals of a successful sales contact— understanding and meeting the needs of the client. All of the information offered by the client must be heard not merely the points that the salesperson wants to hear.

Autobiographical—Autobiographical listening occurs when one relates everything to his or her own experience. You probably know someone in your life who can't wait to tell you all about their version of whatever you say. For instance, if you have a broken arm, instead of finding out how you are doing, the autobiographical listener will tell you all about the time he/she hurt his/her arm, detail by detail.

In sales, the autobiographical listener may accidentally uncover a situation that is challenging the prospect. Instead of probing deeper, the salesperson responds, "You think you have a problem, you wouldn't believe what happened to me!" Of course, this is often detrimental to the sale.

Another case of autobiographical listening concerns giving advice. We live in a culture that demands fast answers and quick fixes. No wonder Jeopardy! and Wheel of Fortune are so popular. We seem to thrive on immediate gratification. It is disastrous for the salesperson to give a quick answer and immediate solution to a problem without first exploring what's underneath the problem. What's worse, we give the fast response according to our own experience. In other words, the autobiographical listener processes the information and answers based on how he or she has been affected in the past.

All of these four normal listening patterns (ignoring, pretending, selective and autobiographical listening) have one thing in common. They are all ineffective ways to listen and they undermine the development of long-term and mutually beneficial relationships.

There are other causes of ineffective listening. A major one is poor focus. Let's take a look at this dynamic in depth.

Where do you focus?

First and foremost, focus directs listening. In any situation or endeavor, there are three places where you can focus—yourself, the material or the subject matter, or the other person. Let's examine each area.

Yourself—There are times when it is absolutely appropriate to focus on yourself and primarily be concerned with you. Some examples are when you are looking in the mirror, getting ready for the day, practicing your presentation (you are doing this every day, right?), setting or reviewing goals, doing affirmations, thinking of what you need to do and organizing for the day. Again, it is fine for you to focus on yourself in these situations.

However, in any conversation or meeting, especially where you are selling or wanting to persuade or get results, it is deadly to be focused on yourself. It is the worst place to be focused because it leads you to ignore what's being said. Focusing on yourself in a conversation will lead you back to the four deadly sins.

The material or subject matter—Focusing on the subject matter is slightly better than focusing on yourself. At least the attention is off you and onto something that the other person is likely to find interesting. Are there times when focus on the material is okay? Certainly. When you are learning about your product, developing a presentation or speech, or doing a critique of a performance, you must focus on the subject. Even in a conversation, there are times when focus on the material is necessary. If you are delivering or receiving crucial information, then of course the material itself is important.

Yet, if you are going to make an impact on results through listening and communication, focus on material can lead to ignoring, pretending, or selective listening. When I'm coaching individuals or groups, I find a certain amount of disagreement on this issue. While it seems obvious that focus on the self is harmful to the conversation, focus on material seems crucial. You are trying to convey a lot of information. If you are too focused on the material and not enough on the other person, you will not even know if they are following you. You need to focus on the other person.

The other person—As we established earlier, the key to effective listening is being interested in the other person. During the Nixon administration of the late 1960s and early 1970s, Secretary of State Henry Kissinger was one of the more popular dinner companions in Washington, D.C. In an interview with Barbara Walters, he was asked what made him so interesting. He answered, "It's not that I'm so interesting, Barbara, I'm interested!" Whether he was sitting next to a head of state, the wife of an important diplomat, or a congressional aid, Dr. Kissinger was always interested in the other person.

When you are interested, you focus on the other person. When you focus on the other person, you are naturally being a good listener. This will not only make you more likable, it will result in better relationships, more sales, and often, people will listen to you more closely.

What else gets in the way of listening effectively?

The voice in your ear—There is a voice in your ear which can get in the way of effective listening. For those of you who feel you are unfamiliar with the phenomena, take a few moments to stop and listen. It's the voice that is saying, "What voice in my ear? I don't have a voice in my ear. What is he talking about?" That one! It is a constant voice that is with you for as long as you're awake and for all we know even while you are asleep. It is always there.

Some people may refer to this as your conscience. Others call it your subconscious. Who knows? All we know is that you have a voice that speaks to you from inside. I call it the voice in your ear because you hear it. Anyway, this voice can impede effective listening because it may distract you from the other person.

The voice may have you focused on yourself or your material, or some other topic altogether. Point is, the voice can take you away from the person you're conversing with and keep you from hearing their true thoughts and feelings. It is an exercise in concentration to keep your own voice in the background. Or perhaps you can align your voice in synch with what the other person is saying which may enhance its meaning and understanding.

Lenses and filters—Steven Covey talked about seeing through lenses in *The 7 Habits of Highly Effective People*. One of his major themes is that the way we see a problem actually is the problem. So, if we can change our focus or actually change the lens we see through, we can more easily solve the problem. Likewise, we speak and hear through filters. At times, the filter we use to speak and listen through can be a problem. Allow me to illustrate using colors:

Person "A" is speaking an idea called "BLUE." His filter is also "BLUE." So, it could be said that he is speaking "true BLUE." If, however, person "B" has a filter called "YELLOW," she will hear "GREEN." Therefore, person "A" has spoken "BLUE" and person "B" has heard "GREEN." This happens every day. In fact, you have probably experienced having said something and the other person demonstrates hearing something so totally different that you scratch your head and wonder what happened.

However, filters don't come in colors. They appear as attitudes. As an example, some people have a defensive filter. That is, everything they hear or say is protective. This happens in sales situations. The customer has a resistant filter and is wary of the salesperson. Unfortunately, in most instances, the salesperson tries to break through the resistance filter by speaking more forcefully. Or they try to press harder to make their point. The best way to handle someone with a defensive or a resistant filter is to simply listen to them and respond by demonstrating understanding. Show them that you have truly heard what they are saying without becoming an adversary.

Let's summarize. First, there are the four deadly ways we

normally listen— ignore the other person, pretending to be interested, selectively listening, and autobiographically listening. Then there are four things that get in the way of effective listening— focus on yourself, focus on the material, the voice in your ear, and the filter you speak and listen through. The conclusion is that focusing on the other person is the best strategy for effective listening. Let's look at how you can handle the voice in your ear and overcome the filters people use.

Focus revisited—how to listen more effectively

There is only one way to quiet the voice in your ear and that is to focus on the other person. Look closely at them while they speak and consider each thought they share with you. Ask questions—try to understand how they feel.

Dealing with filters is a little more tricky because there are always at least two filters to deal with— yours and the other person's. It is useful to remember that you have no control over the other person's filters and often, it takes effort to gain some degree of control over your own. You can, however, work on changing your filters. For example, if yours is the defensive filter, you can strive to learn to recognize when you are being defensive, and then work to be more open. Or if your filter is overly sensitive, you can work on building your own self-esteem so that you overcome that filter with confidence.

One of my favorite ways to work on changing the defensive filter is "contribution." That is, everything you say from now on should be designed to contribute positively to someone else. If not, you don't say it. On the listening side, whenever someone speaks to you, you become committed to getting the contribution from the communication. It will take practice and yet, I promise you it is a very powerful way to live.

While you cannot control or change the other person's filter, you can have respect and consideration for their filter. If you notice that they are being defensive, take time to deal with that reality before delivering your communication. By the way, if you are focused only on yourself and the material, you will probably not even notice they are being defensive.

The way to deal with defensiveness is to ask a question and listen. The question should not be, "Why are you so defensive?" Instead you might say, "I notice that you seem uncomfortable with the situation. Is there a better time to talk?" Or, "Is there something else I should know?" At this point, it is critical to listen and not be defensive yourself.

A couple more things about filters. First, defensive and resistant are not the only filters. They are simply common and difficult to overcome. Also, while it is obvious when someone else is defensive, it is harder for us to recognize defensiveness in ourselves. However, there are ways to tell. For example, when someone says something or brings up a point that goes against what you are trying to say or prove and you answer right away, you are probably becoming defensive. The more entrenched you both become, the more defensive.

Second, you have more than one filter. We all have many and they are interchangeable. You have control over which one you use and when you use it. My recommendation as a coach is that when you're in a selling/consulting situation, get rid of the defensive filter. The next section will show you how to do this.

But first it's time for...

The second secret

Humans are not perfect and it is impossible to be a perfect (and effective) listener all of the time. You will sometimes lose your focus on the other person. You will forget to pay attention to filters. When you notice that you are off-track, there is a sure-fire way to get back on track and regain the focus on the other person. You simply ask a question.

Whenever you're in trouble in a sales presentation, ask a question! Caution: Don't ask a question as a technique and then pretend to listen. Ask a question that directs the focus back on the other person. If the two of you have developed a high level of trust, you could even admit, "My mind wandered there for a moment. I'm sorry. Could you please repeat what you said?" This type of honesty can show a high regard for the other person—if it's not done too often!

The sure-fire way to listen effectively

The picture at right shows a full glass of water. Question— how much water can you pour into a full glass of water without spilling any of it? Obviously none! And yet, that's exactly what you try to do when you find a problem someone is having and you immediately offer advice. Before you can pour water into an already full glass, you must do one of two things. Either get a bigger glass or find a way to empty the glass you have. Which do you think is easier?

Get a bigger glass—Enlarging someone else's capacity is hard and, if you were able to accomplish this it would take a great deal of time. But the fact is, you can't change someone else. They have to do it. Therefore, allowing someone to empty their glass is easier.

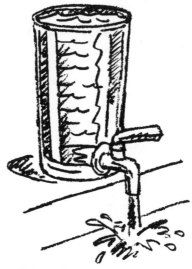

Empty the glass—This is the same glass of water with a spigot at the bottom. The way you allow someone to empty their glass is to ask the right questions. When you ask the right questions, you will be listening for the feelings in addition to content. When you hear the feeling beneath the content, the glass will begin to empty. As this occurs, three things happen which are likely to increase your sales:

1) You will gain more information. In many cases this will challenge the assumptions you were making previously.
2) You will establish a bond with the other person. This bond will clinch more sales than your most persuasive language because the other person will take you into his or her confidence.
3) You will establish yourself as a professional, an expert, and a caring individual. You will automatically differentiate yourself from others in your industry. All of this is based on your ability to ask good questions and listen to the answers.

There are two questions that help you empty the glass. The first is, "How do you mean that, exactly?" I learned this question from one of Brian Tracy's tapes. Brian suggested it as a way to pause and reflect when you aren't sure of an answer to a question asked by a prospect. The question causes people to stop and think. It is grammatically incorrect and that is on purpose. It trips the brain and so people always answer it.

The grammatically correct form, "What do you mean?" is much different. And, in American culture, it invites an argument. This is especially true if said with an assertive tone of voice.

By using the first question, "How do you mean that exactly?" I have found that people respond in a deeper way. They rarely just repeat the previous answer. They add emotion. They more fully express themselves and therefore they release some "water" from their "glass."

You're not finished yet. That's only one question. The second question is "What else?" This question is to be repeated until the other person says, "That's about it." Notice that I did not say "Anything else?" The difference is that "Anything else?" is a conversation ender and "What else?" continues the conversation. Again, allow me to stress the importance of not just asking the questions. You must listen to the responses and, if necessary, take notes. By the way, in a fact-finding interview, these are the notes you want to keep. The "feelings" questions reveal the information you need to establish relationships.

Here is an example of what an "empty the glass" interview would look like:

You: What would you want this program to solve for you?

Other Person

(O.P.): I would like to increase productivity and profits.

You: How do you mean that exactly?

O.P.: I want to make more money from higher sales and save money with less expense.

You: What else?

O.P.: I want my people more conscious of the bottom line.

You: What else?

O.P.: I want everyone to waste less time.

You: What else?

You would continue to ask "What else?" until the other person replies with some form of "That's it." Then you would ask the next question in the interview. This also works for answering objections, customer service complaints, or listening to people in your personal life.

Later I will show you how to use this to get referrals. Let's discuss two important questions that you might have at this point. First, what are the signs that someone has a full glass of water? Second, how do we know when the glass is empty? The answer to the first question is easy. You can assume that everyone is walking around with a full glass. In today's society, people don't have enough opportunity to express themselves. All of us have too few people to confide in, so when we give others the opportunity to open up, we set ourselves apart from other friends or salespeople. If, however, you encounter the rare person who doesn't need to "empty their glass," you have done no harm in asking. Therefore, ask everyone.

How do you know the glass is empty? In a sales situation, the other person will tell you when they answer the last "What else?" with "That's it." In a fact-finding interview, the answer is the same. However, in a complaint or customer service situation, the other person will let you know the glass is empty by giving you a "love" statement. After running through all the complaints which you have drawn out by asking questions, the person will say something nice or good. It will seem to come out of nowhere. Test this by bringing up one of the complaints and if the glass is truly empty, the other person will handle the complaint you just brought up. Then you may proceed to tell the person what you need to tell them.

In summary, if you don't listen first, the other person will not listen to you. Remember, if their glass is still full, they can't even hear you! In other words, as Stephen Covey said in Habit 5 of *The 7 Habits of Highly Effective People,* "Seek first to understand, then to be understood."

Referrals

Question. Why don't you get more referrals? Because you don't ask for them. Okay, why did you stop asking for them? Because you were trained to ask the wrong question. If you are like me, you were trained to ask a question that elicited the response "nobody." The question was, "Who do you know who needs my product?" Now we have gotten smarter over the years and have learned to ask, "Who do you know who needs my service?" Unfortunately, the prospect/client knows that even though you have substituted the word service for product, it is essentially the same question. Therefore, you get the same answer, "Nobody." This is very uncomfortable for the prospect/client who wants to help you and protect his or her relationships.

Since it is very uncomfortable for the other person, it soon becomes uncomfortable for you too. Thus, you stop asking.

If you found a way to change the answer from "Nobody" to "Everybody" would that be significant? The key is listening. You conduct the following survey and then ask for referrals. The entire process takes 20 to 30 minutes and it works. By the way, you will write additional business from the survey and that's good. However, remember, the goal is to obtain referrals.

The David Goldman service survey

Question 1: What is your definition of "good service"?
What does good service mean to you?
The client answers.
Follow-up question: *How do you mean that exactly?*
The client answers.
Follow-up question: *What else?*
The client answers.
Follow up by asking *"What else?"* until the client says some form
of *"That's it."*

Question 2: What do you like about the service you're getting now?
The client answers.
Follow-up question: *How do you mean that exactly?*
The client answers.
Follow-up question: *What else?*
The client answers.
Follow up by asking *"What else?"* until the client says some form
of *"That's it."*

Question 3: What's missing from the service you are getting now?
(Note: the question is not "what's wrong?", but rather "What's
missing?" What is not present that if it were, it would make a
difference?)
The client answers.
Follow-up question: *How do you mean that exactly?*
The client answers.
Follow-up question: *What else?*
The client answers.
Follow up by asking *"What else?"* until the client says some form
of *"That's it."*

After that last "What else?" the client will be at the bottom of the
glass. At this point you are about to make the transition to referrals. First,
as Tom Hopkins says, you must condense the universe for the client.
He/she cannot think of everyone in the world or even everyone in your
town. So, ask the client to think of his or her select circle (business
associates, friends, good buddies, civic group, etc.) of around 25 people.
Then ask:
"Of those people in your group, who believes in service the way

you do?" You will find the answer is "Everybody." Now you qualify the referrals as you normally would. This survey works if you do. If you want a case study proof or if you have any questions when using this, please feel free to write to me or fax your request.

One other thing, as a coach, I just want to say a few words about practice. Vince Lombardi, legendary coach of the Green Bay Packers, had a sign above the locker room door that led to Lambeau Field in Green Bay. It said, "Everyone wants to be a champion; no one wants to practice." The message is clear. In order to be a champion, you have to practice. This brings us to:

The third secret

I remember a client who had a beautifully carved, ornate wooden box that he kept on his desk. On the top was carved, "The Secret to Success." When you opened it, the message inside was, "Work Hard." That takes me back to my favorite Chinese restaurant and my favorite fortune of all time. It said, "None of the secrets of success will work unless you do."

A Story

The big game hunter was on a safari in Africa looking for the elusive tiger. He went out day after day and returned to camp disappointed each night. Toward the end of his trip, he was out one day and he came upon a clearing. There stood the most magnificent tiger he had ever seen. Just as he spied the tiger, the tiger also noticed him. In what seemed like one motion, he shot his rifle as the beast lunged. Fortunately for both, they both missed. The tiger bounded off into the jungle while the hunter dragged himself back to camp.

The next morning, the hunter was up at dawn and took 150 rounds of ammunition with him to practice his short range shooting. He fired round after round and finally stopped for a short break. It was then that he heard a strange noise coming from about 50 yards away. He peered through some bushes to see an amazing sight. The tiger was practicing his short leaps.

Vince Lombardi was right. In order to be a champion, you have to practice. When was the last time you practiced your presentation? If you practice what you have read, it will work for you. Eliminate and stay away from the four sins. Focus on the other person. Pay attention to your own filter while you have respect for the other person's filter. Practice effective listening by allowing the other person to "empty the glass." Your sales will soar. And you will be more effective in many of your professional and personal relationships.

About David Goldman

David Goldman cares about people, the process and results. He has been coaching and consulting since 1989. Before becoming a coach, David spent 13 years in the insurance industry and was a member of the Million Dollar Round Table and a Life Underwriters Training Council Fellow. In addition, David has management and training experience both inside and outside of financial services.

He has worked with 68 companies and well over 100 individuals in the past six years including Cigna Financial, Acacia, Allmerica Financial, PSI, Babst Calland Clements & Zomnir, Cohen & Grigsby, Grossman Yanak & Ford, and Johnson Controls, Inc.

Born in Pittsburgh, PA David continues to live in the Greater Pittsburgh area with his wife, Mary Lou and his children, Hank and Anna. He is a member of the National Speaker's Association. David also is the bass/baritone singer in an "oldies" rock and roll band, "*The Magic Moments*".

David H. Goldman
P.O. Box 15893
Pittsburgh, PA 15244
Phone: 412-771-7447
Fax: 412-771-7443
E-mail: goldman100@aol.com

Company Profile

You will get more of what you want - more time, more money and more energy. Enhance your people skills, life and personal development. If having better communication skills is important to you and your business, Goldman can help you. A coach for sales, leadership and communication as well as a keynote speaker, consultant and facilitator, David brings together a knowledge of people, an insight into what motivates them and the ability to get them into action to produce breakthrough results.

Most Requested Programs

Go for the G.O.L.D.— How to Get the Results You Want
a/k/a The G.O.L.D.Standard—How to Get the Results You Want
What do you want out of life and work? How do you put the goals you set into action—now? How can you turn things around so work and life is the best it can be? Find out the answers to these questions and more. Excellent for a variety of audiences.
Keynotes, 1/2 day to 3 day workshops, coaching, consulting available

How to Apply the 7 Habits of Highly Effective People to Sales and Your Life.
Even if you've read the book, this is a must-have program to cause dramatic changes in your life. You'll get the practical, simplified essence of the 7 habits you need to be effective right now!
Need at least 1/2 day to get optimal results

Stop Look and Listen!—The Key to Effective Communication
Learn how to "listen between the lines" and get others to listen to you. Find out the difference between "what's being said". Learn where to focus your attention when it counts. Maximize your potential for networking relationships. Essential for people who interact with other people.
Keynotes, 1/2 day workshops, coaching, consulting available

Magic Moments— Customer Satisfaction; not Just Service
Who are your customers (inside and outside)? What is service? How do you know and where do you go to find out? Learn how to satisfy your customers and turn complaints and frustrating situations into Magic Moments.
Keynotes, 1/2 day workshops, coaching, consulting available

Chapter 7

Put a Little C.O.L.O.R. in your Selling

by
Jeffrey Tobe

The sole purpose of effective questioning in the sales call should be to uncover basic needs and to then develop them into specific needs.

—Jeffrey Tobe

O ver the past two years, I have traveled with over 150 salespeople and I have had the opportunity to be an impartial observer. Every salesperson should have the same experience. Being able to separate myself from the selling process—like the proverbial "fly on the wall"—has enabled me to make observations about this process that I never could have made when I was directly involved and had something at stake.

This chapter is the result of these years of observing salespeople in several different industries. While the specifics of the product these people were selling are not significant to this chapter, their techniques, their successes and failures and their style are of utmost importance to us. The two skills that I discovered were the absolute keys to the "new way of selling", involved EFFECTIVE QUESTIONING and LISTENING. While the latter is covered at length in another chapter in this book, the former —EFFECTIVE QUESTIONING SKILLS —is the focus of C.O.L.O.R. Selling™

THE OLD WAY OF SELLING

From my observation, I became convinced that the sales process has actually become an easier one than that of its ancestor. The "new wave" of world-class salespeople recognize that their roles have reversed. Instead of being the *giver* of information as they have been in the past, now they must be the *seeker* of information. They understand the importance of networking to the success of their business. They comprehend the new sales process of accumulating and processing information and, finally, they discover that, if they ask the right kinds of questions, the client will actually close the sale for them. It is a much more natural process than that of old. It allows the salesperson to establish the bond they desire with a client to ensure a long-term relationship without the high pressure techniques our sales managers taught us in the seventies and eighties.

C.O.L.O.R Selling™ concentrates on this sequential, probing questioning process. Much of the statistical research on this process was pioneered by Neil Rackham of the Huthwaite Research Institute Corporation, who authored the best seller, *Spin Selling*. In his book he discusses at length the difference between the large sale and small sale. His analysis found that there is a "positive correlation between the use of questions and success in the larger sale."

Being a true salesperson at heart, I did not find it easy to put myself into the analytical research frame of mind that other wonderful authors have been able to accomplish. My own findings were very simple. I observed four basic skills in most world-class salespeople. They were:

1.   Do your homework.
2.   Probe effectively to learn more about your client's preferences and needs.
3.   Uncover, and cater to, the SPECIFIC NEEDS of a prospect/client.
4.   Concentrate on the BENEFIT of your product or service in solving a client's true challenge or need.

The sales call

Almost every sales call goes through four very distinct stages. It is most important that we understand these stages before we can further discuss how the questioning process relates to each of them. This will also help in 'de-mystifying' the sales process and clearing up some of the old myths that still exist from our days in 'Selling 101'. You will also see how it is a good I.D.E.A. to remember these phrases!

Phase 1: Initializing

    Initializing is the first stage of every sales call. In the old model of selling, I have heard it referred to as 'small talk', but in this new model, we must see it for what it really is. Simply put, the Initializing stage is only the launching phase of our call. The sole purpose should be to get the buyer to give us permission to ask questions and get down to business. Think of this in terms of the analogy of a space mission. The Initializing stage would be akin to the blastoff of a rocket. The crew gets the go-ahead to launch and receives the right amount of power to propel it into space where it is set for the next phase. The same is true with initializing. The Initializing stage allows you to get the go-ahead to ask questions and then positions you for the next phase.

    I am certainly not downplaying the need for information gained through 'small talk'. But, consider the amount of time you are spending in this phase and whether or not this is the best use of your time. You see, I believe that in this day of re-engineering, re-staffing, and rebuilding, we are dealing with not only more sophisticated buyers, but buyers who typically do not have as much time to spend with us as they did a decade ago. It is up to us to control the sales situation through every stage.

    There are three keys to the Initializing stage.

Get down to the bottom line quickly

I don't think I have ever heard a buyer complain that a salesperson got down to business too quickly! Be aware of time constraints on the buyer. This is especially true of a new prospect. Salespeople need to be prepared, look professional and get to work. If the prospect is one to socialize or analyze in-depth, then you can back up and provide the time that is needed. If, on the other hand, you begin with a long, arduous initialization, you will lose that buyer who is concerned about time and 'small talk'.

Don't try to solve challenges in this stage

This is one of the most common faults I have observed in selling. Many salespeople tend to talk about their solutions right in the Initializing stage much too early in the sales process. Remember, we are just 'launching' ourselves into our new role as information seekers and we cannot possibly have enough information at this point to make an educated recommendation. As a matter of fact, I believe that this is what differentiates the average salesperson from the world class sales professional. It's the ability to bite our tongues, ask the right questions and develop the client's need for our solution.

Concentrate on questions

Never forget that the Initializing stage is not the most important part of the call. Focus your energy on gathering information. In traveling with a salesperson recently, it struck me how much time she spent before the call worrying about how to open it when she could have used the time far more effectively to plan some effective, probing questions instead.

Phase 2: Digging

Every sale involves asking questions to gather information. The distinction between this stage and the Initializing stage is that it is in this phase of the sales call that we can start to probe for vital information; the information that will help us meet the client's specific needs. The Digging phase is, without a doubt, the most important phase of the sales call, but it is also the least understood and most ignored. The challenge we have stems from the fact that we confuse the Initializing questions with the Digging question. As the C.O.L.O.R. Selling™ model becomes clearer to you, I think you will also get an idea of how both these stages are essential in the sales process and how vitally important Digging questions are to overall sales success.

Phase 3: Effectiveness of your solution

I think we recognize that in this new wave of selling, we are not salespeople as much as we are consultants. In fact, I would put forth that we are no longer selling a product or a service, but we are simply selling solutions to our client's business challenges. In this stage of the sales call, we have to show our customer that we have a solution and that it makes a significant contribution to solving their specific challenge. It's during this stage that we have to concern ourselves with FEATURE vs BENEFIT selling. Anyone who has been through a sales training program in the last 60 years is likely to have been taught the terms FEATURES and BENEFITS. Unfortunately, there are still many salespeople who get them confused. As you will see a little later in this chapter, C.O.L.O.R. Selling™ is more concerned with *where* you offer the benefits—at what point in the sale—versus *why* you should offer benefits. If benefits of your solution become the focal point of your presentation at the proper time in the sales process, you are more likely to succeed in that call.

Phase 4: Attaining the right commitment

The final stage of the successful sales call concentrates on attaining a commitment of some kind from your prospect or client. What you must keep in mind in this new selling environment, is that there may be a whole range of commitments you have to reach prior to securing the order. Your call may just result in the customer agreeing to allow you to make a presentation to his or her committee or to speak to a higher decision-maker. I like to look at this part of the process as a type of 'leap-frogging' toward the final decision. The most successful sales-people I observed understood the difference between leap-frogging and simply zig-zagging.

Too many of us have been happy with a 'zig-zagging' commitment from our clients. In other words, commitments like:

'Quote us on 15,000 widgets and get back to us in two weeks.'

'Write up a proposal and send it to me for my reference.'

'It sounds good. Let me think about it and talk with some of the people around here and I will get back to you later this week.'

I remember some of my salespeople getting excited about this outcome of a sales call because they got to quote some very profitable programs. The challenge, however, is that there is no real commitment on the client's part to take the sales process to the next plateau. Zig-zagging commitments give the impression that the client may do business with you, when they are simply putting you off by getting you to do more, usually unnecessary work.

ZIG-ZAGGING

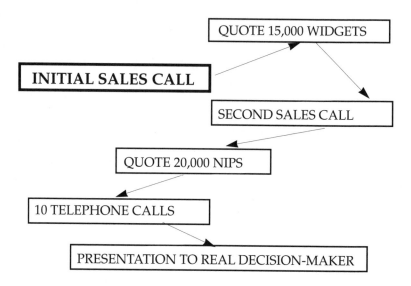

Leap-frogging is completely different. Because of your careful pre-planning of the sales call, you can outline at least one or two different commitments you would settle for prior to even calling on the customer. If during your conversation you discover that it is a committee decision, then perhaps the next logical step is a presentation to the entire panel. If you find out that the Finance Department must approve the budget, then perhaps it is a meeting with them. You can see the need to be flexible in this phase of the sales call and to look for a natural 'leap-frog' to the next plateau. The key is to get the customer to commit to something, even a small step forward.

LEAP FROGGING

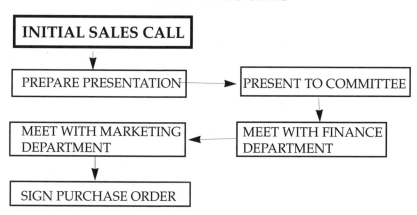

You see, the challenge we have today is that our focus has always been with this last stage: ATTAINING COMMITMENT. Remember the old model of selling? What was the stage on which we were told to concentrate? THE CLOSE! Or, ATTAINING COMMITMENT. We need to take our focus off this stage. Because of the effort we are now going to give in the Digging stage, the final stage does not take on the level of urgency it did when we were required to learn every closing technique under the sun.

What is amazing, however, is the amount of literature that has been written on effective closing techniques. I found a book in my local bookstore entitled, *101 Sure Fire Ways to Irresistibly Close any Sale*. Some of you will remember these.

ASSUMPTIVE: 'Where would you like it delivered?'
ALTERNATIVE: 'Would you prefer one in red or in green?'
STANDING ROOM ONLY: 'If you can't make a decision today, someone else will have the opportunity!'
LAST CHANCE: 'Our suppliers put their new catalogs out with new pricing next month, so unless you act now ...'
DUMB QUESTION: 'What would it take for you to drive home this baby tonight?'

Then I found really exotic closes with names like 'Sharp Angle', 'Ben Franklin', 'Puppy Dog' 'Columbo', and 'Double-Reverse Whammy.' No other area has had more attention paid to it in the sales process than has closing. For many years I bought into this theory. When I was in college, I worked one summer at the Canadian National

Exhibition in Toronto, Canada. Major retailers leased booths in the main pavilions to supposedly offer 'huge discounts' on merchandise one would normally buy in their stores. As a salesperson, I was instructed to 'hook' the customer by getting them on to the booth, looking at specific products and ready to talk price. Then I was to tell them that I needed my 'sales manager' to confirm pricing and I would go off into the back to get one of our 'professional closers'. When I say I am embarrassed at the high pressure techniques this person attempted to use, I mean I was very embarrassed. So, if you happened on to my booth back in 1978, I apologize. Well, I don't want to apologize to my clients today, so I refuse to use any of these so-called 'irresistible' closes on them.

C.O.L.O.R. Selling™ concentrates on the DIGGING phase of the sales process. Simply put, successful calls include questions that leap-frog to sales, not questions that zig-zag. There's no doubt that questions persuade more powerfully than any other form of verbal behavior. So many people in my sales training sessions insist on distinguishing between Open and Closed questions. I stress that these types of questions are both effective, but it certainly is not a new theory. E.K. Strong wrote about these forms of questions as early as 1925. The more I read and the more I observe salespeople, I am less convinced that we should even think about these two types of questions. They both have their place in the selling process, but I would prefer to concentrate on developing questions we need in the Digging phase, questions exploring need.

Needs development

Before we begin delving into our model, I think it is important to take a closer look at needs development and its significance in the new selling environment. Many former sales theories have touched on this area, but we must gain a new understanding of needs development. Needs normally start with minor dissatisfactions and run the gamut to definitive challenges, difficulties and problems. Finally these needs are translated to desires, wants or intentions to act.

I divide needs into two categories. First are BASIC NEEDS. These are simply statements by the customer of problems, difficulties and dissatisfactions. The second type of needs are SPECIFIC NEEDS. Specific needs are not about problems but are statements of wants or desires or intent to take action.

BASIC NEEDS	SPECIFIC NEEDS
problems	wants
difficulties	desires
dissatisfaction	intent to act

THE SOLE PURPOSE OF EFFECTIVE QUESTIONING IN THE SALES CALL SHOULD BE TO UNCOVER BASIC NEEDS AND TO THEN DEVELOP THEM INTO SPECIFIC NEEDS.

To make sure that you understand the difference between Basic Needs and Specific Needs, test yourself below. In each case, determine whether or not the statement from the client is a statement of a Basic or Specific Need. Answers are provided in the boxes at the end of the chapter.

BASIC vs SPECIFIC NEEDS

Simply circle B for Basic Need or S for Specific Need

1. It would be nice to have a method to retrieve information from suppliers about previous dealings with a prospect.   B   S

2. I take the principle of on-the-job safety very seriously.   B   S

3. Turnaround time is a challenge for us with order processing.   B   S

4. It would be great to minimize paperwork   B   S

5. It is time consuming to maintain call objective reports, but that is going to change over the next six months.   B   S

6. Order processing has to be quicker since head office handles over 250 orders per day.   B   S

7. Writing, filing and discussing these reports takes much too long.   B   S

The C.O.L.O.R. Selling™ model

Let's take a look at how this innovative model addresses this needs development process. If we were to examine this graphically, the model would not take on a clear, linear image because each of the types of questions can be intertwined at any given point, depending on the progression of the sales call. A priority is to concentrate on the Digging phase of the sales call. We are concerned with asking probing questions to get to one of the sequential stages in the model.

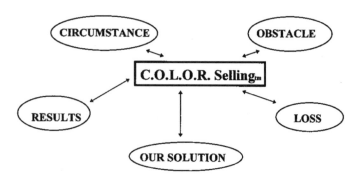

Circumstance questions

As I stated before, most of our sales calls have a very predictable pattern especially with new accounts. We spend a lot of time asking questions about the company, about the buyer, the decision-maker, sales volume, number of employees and so on. All of these questions have one thing in common—they seek factual information or background data about the customer's CIRCUMSTANCES. Let's rethink this strategy.

I used to think that I was complimenting a prospect when I demanded, 'So, tell me a little about what it is that you do here.' I thought it showed interest when I tried to find a personal interest that we may have in common. And, I used to think it would earn me brownie points if I could find a way to ask about their family. It's easy to understand the myth of the Circumstance questions. The myth was that we showed how genuinely interested we were in the account by asking all this fact-finding information. Just ask yourself who benefits from Circumstance questions. The seller! A busy customer can't possibly delight in giving every salesperson detail after detail about his or her circumstances. Don't forget that many of our buyers are purchasing various products and services besides the ones that you and I have to offer them. Unfortunately, they have to answer the same questions no matter what they are being sold.

We talked about the Initializing stage of the sales call and cutting down time in this phase. Well, here is your chance. DO YOUR HOMEWORK! When I first got into business in the early 1980's, I remember attending a national trade show in my industry. While waiting in a booth for one of my vendors who was busy with another client, I literally backed into a woman who was also checking out the 'wares' of this supplier. In a matter of seconds I had succumb to this woman's vitality, knowledge of the industry and charm. I wanted to be her when I grew up! A few minutes later, it was my turn to speak to my vendor and I excused myself. As I approached my supplier, he greeted me with, 'Hey, Jeff, I see you met Cathy.' I explained to him how impressed I was with this lady and he filled me in on some of the details. He told me that Cathy had been in the industry for two years; about the same as me. He also told me that she had been recognized for being the number one salesperson in the industry. Her sales figures were ten times mine and I wanted to know why. I tracked Cathy down at another booth and cornered her looking for answers.

'What's your secret?' I asked. She rolled her eyes and laughed as she said what has become my credence for success in sales. 'When I got into this industry I decided to DO THE THINGS THAT NOBODY ELSE WANTED TO DO!' While this sounded great, I didn't understand. She explained, 'I do my homework!' She went on to tell me that she had found that the common flaw in this particular industry was that salespeople were not willing to do research on a prospect or a client. She said that she did her research on prospective clients. When she decided she wanted to do business with them (did you read that right? WHEN SHE DECIDED SHE WANTED TO DO BUSINESS WITH THEM, not the other way around), she called to try to get the initial meeting. In that meeting she would make it clear to the buyer that she was different than most other salespeople in her industry. She would say, 'IF WE DECIDE TO WORK TOGETHER' (again, notice the language: she didn't say 'If you choose me' or 'If you decide to work with me'), I would ask you to allow me to come work here, free of charge, for one week. Put me in as many departments as you can to analyze your challenges as they relate to my business.' She told me that not all prospects agreed to this, but the ones who did were her clients for life. Why? She became an indispensable part of their team and discovered needs for her products and services that the client did not even know they had.

Now, I am not suggesting that you should spend a week with one of your prospects, but I am suggesting that you find a way to become an indispensable part of their team. Doing your research in advance will set you apart from many other salespeople. How do you do this? Try your local library. Call the customer's assistant prior to the meeting and ask for information. Get hold of a company's annual report. Surf the net to pull down information on the company. Find other local vendors of non-competing products who are doing business with the company or even with the specific buyer on which you are going to call. Don't you think it would be more impressive if you walked into a customer prepared to discuss their recent layoff of 200 employees or their expansion into the South American market, rather than asking all types of Circumstance questions? Be prepared and try to cut down the amount of time spent in asking Circumstance questions.

I am confident from my observations that Circumstance questions are not related to success in sales. Inexperienced salespeople ask numerous Circumstance questions. Experienced salespeople do not.

Obstacle questions

More experienced salespeople are able to ask 'Basic need' discovery questions like:

"Are you satisfied with your current vendor?"

"What is it about order processing that makes your job ` difficult?"

"Do you face any challenges in hiring 250 new employees this year?'

What is the common factor in these questions? If you said that they probe for challenges, difficulties or dissatisfactions, you are correct. Even better, maybe you realized that these questions uncover a Basic Need. I have found that the ratio of Circumstance questions to these Obstacle questions asked by salespeople is directly related to their time in their specific industry. Experienced salespeople ask a higher proportion of Obstacle questions.

It shouldn't surprise you that Obstacle questions have a far more positive effect on buyers than Circumstance questions. If you can't solve a customer's challenge then you have no basis for a sale in the first place. If, on the other hand, you can begin to uncover challenges that you can solve, then you're potentially providing the buyer with something useful. Obstacle questions are like the foundation of a sturdy home. If you don't have a strong foundation, you have no basis to hold up the rest of the house. Likewise, without Obstacle questions to uncover basic dissatisfactions and challenges, the rest of the sales process is a moot point.

Again using our house-building analogy, you couldn't live in a home that only has a foundation. Many salespeople seem eager to offer one of their solutions during the Obstacle questioning process. They hear a basic dissatisfaction and they are quick to 'sell' one of their solutions. One of the major things that differentiates C.O.L.O.R. Selling™ from most other models is that it emphasizes that **you must not offer solutions too quickly in the sales process.** You have to understand that we are only uncovering Basic needs and a customer is usually not prepared to 'buy' based solely on a dissatisfaction or challenge. If you have been doing what you do for any length of time, you tend to want to solve a client's challenge as soon as you hear it. This is the 'B.Y.T.' part of the model; Bite Your Tongue! Train yourself to keep your mouth shut until you can probe a little deeper and develop this Basic Need into a more Specific Need.

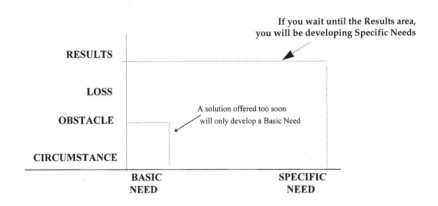

I bet if I hypnotized you and took you back to your early days in selling, you would be amazed at the amount of Circumstance questions you asked. Then you left an account feeling great because you 'hit it off' and you knew 'there was going to be a lot of business coming my way' in the near future. Yet, you didn't really discover any challenges that needed to be solved immediately. Then came the day where you started asking these Obstacle questions and customers started to take notice because you began to show an interest in their problems. This was a turning point in many of our careers, but unfortunately, many of us never took it any further.

KEY WORDS TO BEGIN YOUR OBSTACLE QUESTIONS:
"What challenges do you face....?"
"Are you happy with.....?"
"Can you think of any problems you face...?"

So your challenge is not to be satisfied with what you uncover from asking Obstacle Questions. Remember, these uncover Basic Needs and we need to take these to the next level. Before we go on, let's take a short inventory of the difference between Circumstance (fact-finding) and Obstacle (uncovering dissatisfactions and challenges) Questions. The answers are at the end of the chapter.

CIRCUMSTANCE vs. OBSTACLE QUESTIONS

Simply circle C for Circumstance or O for Obstacle.

1. Who will be involved in this decision?   C   O

2. Do you find it difficult to find time to check the administrative reports from your salespeople?   C   O

3. How much time do you spend every week checking the administrative reports from your salespeople? C   O

4. Does Mary find it difficult to order equipment from the current catalog?   C   O

5. Have you experienced errors in shipping?   C   O

6. How satisfied are you with your existing vendor? C   O

7. How much money is budgeted for imaging equipment?   C   O

Loss questions

Most sales people are able to do an adequate job of asking Circumstance and Obstacle Questions. Your challenge? Don't stop there. Now, don't misunderstand me. In some cases, Circumstance and Obstacle questions may be enough to secure the order, but I would venture to guess that most of the time, you will need to develop a more substantial working relationship. As a matter of fact, these questions illustrate the difference between what I refer to as 'commodity selling' and 'program selling'. The first is always a one-time sale even if it is a repeat customer. You find yourself having to sell and re-sell every time you approach the buyer and, in most cases, their decision will be based on price. Program selling involves developing the relationship with the client, being the source to solve specific business challenges and getting involved with the client's business.

Loss questions are directly related to this concept of program selling. By taking a Basic Need and probing deeper, we begin to demonstrate to the client our desire to solve their specific challenges. The central purpose of the Loss question is to take a challenge that the buyer perceives to be small and build it up into a challenge big enough to justify action. You must find out *what effect* this challenge has on their business or their department or their position in the company.

You can see immediately that Loss Questions are especially powerful in selling to decision makers. It's often possible to achieve a positive outcome from calls on users or influencers simply by asking effective Loss Questions. Decision makers seem to respond most favorably to sales people who uncover possible losses. Maybe this isn't surprising since a decision maker is a person whose success depends on seeing beyond the immediate problem to consequences or possible losses. You could say that a decision maker deals in possible losses. The intent of this line of questioning is to get the buyer thinking of the possible consequences of failing to address the challenges that you have uncovered.

Asking Loss Questions is not a new discovery. World class sales people have been asking them for a long time. The ability to walk the client through a sequential line of questioning is the skill that many lack. The following is an example of what a conversation might sound like using our three types of questions so far:

> *Salesperson:* How many travel agencies does your company work with at this time? (CIRCUMSTANCE)
> *Client:* Since everyone can choose their own, I can't answer that.

Salesperson: Does this pose any *challenge*s to the company? (OBSTACLE)
Client: Now that you mention it, there certainly is a lack of consistency in our travel programs.
(NOTE: If you had a solution to these travel challenges, you would be tempted to offer a solution at this point of the conversation. A world class sales person probes deeper)
Salesperson: What effect does lack of consistency have on the company? (LOSS)

There is one major weakness to asking these questions. Just by definition, they make the customer more uncomfortable with their challenges and we do not want to associate this uneasiness with our solution or product or service. Skilled sales people develop the seriousness of the challenge and then soften the blow through our last line of questioning.

KEY WORDS TO BEGIN LOSS QUESTIONS
"What effect does this have...?"
"How does this affect...?"
"What would happen if...?"

LOSS QUESTION EXERCISE

Below are four statements you could conceivably encounter from a client/prospect. On a separate piece of paper or in the space provided, write down as many questions (beginning with 'What effect: ') as you can think of.

CHALLENGE	LOSSES
CHALLENGE 1 'Occasionally, we do find an inventory level which does not match our vendorís actual merchandise count'	
CHALLENGE 2 'We have experienced errors in accounting, but this is not a very serious problem'	

CHALLENGE 3
'We love the idea of using a
catalog to order. We just wish
Bob from "Get Rich Industries"
could better explain how to use
his catalog.'

CHALLENGE 4
'The last sweater order we
received was packed so tightly
that every garment was creased'

Results questions

Loss Questions must be followed up with Results Questions. Now, you may think I have skipped the second "O" in our model, but this involves Our Solutions (Features and Benefits) and I think we should cover the four types of questions first. Besides, a model based on C-O-L-R-O just didn't work for me. So allow me to get outside the lines a little bit and look at the final type of question—Results—before we return to the "O".

After we have made the customer feel a little uncomfortable with possible losses associated with their Basic Needs, we must now focus his or her attention on the results rather than the problem. Results questions create a positive problem-solving atmosphere where attention is given to solutions and actions, not just losses and difficulties. Results Questions also get the customer telling you the benefits of your solution. Finally, Results Questions are specifically linked to success in sales that depend on maintaining a good relationship. They are questions which garner 'feel good' replies which center on solving the challenge you have uncovered. Remember, we are dealing with a more sophisticated buyer; one who feels comfortable that you can solve their specific challenge.

As you can see, there is a connection between Loss and Results Questions. Another major benefit of these questions is that the Loss Questions build up the challenge so it's perceived to be more serious and then Results Questions build up the usefulness of your solution. It's the use of these last questions that prevents customers from unfavorable perceptions brought on by the Loss Questions. Results Questions ask about the value or usefulness of solving the problem.

Examples of Loss Questions:
"Is it important to you to solve this challenge right away?"
"Would it be of benefit to you to have a suggestion program in the plant?"
"What if we could develop a program whereby your shoppers were rewarded for frequent purchases of our product?"

When you get the customer discussing how your solution will help, then you reduce objections. They can't possibly object to solutions that they have agreed would help them in the first place. Results Questions get them to "buy" into your ideas and solutions. By using these questions, you can get the customer to explain which elements of the challenge your solution can solve.

KEY WORDS TO BEGIN YOUR RESULTS QUESTIONS
"Would it be of benefit....?"
"What if....?"
"If we could help you with....?"

Simply put, Loss Questions are problem-centered while Results Questions are solution-centered. You can see that Results Questions offer solutions in the form of a question. The old way of selling found the salesperson presenting idea after idea in hopes of closing the sale. By using this type of question, we now have the buyer closing the sale for us.
Continuing our example:
Salesperson: How many travel agencies does your company work with at this time? (CIRCUMSTANCE)
Client: Since everyone can choose their own, I can't even answer that.
Salesperson: Does this pose any challenges to the company? (OBSTACLE)
Client: Now that you mention it, there certainly is a lack of consistency in our travel programs.
(NOTE: If you had a solution to these travel challenges, you would be tempted to offer a solution at this point of the conversation. A world class sales person probes deeper)
Salesperson: What effect does this lack of consistency have on the company? (LOSS)
Client: Actually, I know that the accounting department has a tough time reconciling the travel budget with so many unknown entities.
Salesperson: What benefit would there be to having an in-house travel agency? (RESULTS)

Now, let's see if you can determine the difference between the Loss Questions and Results Questions. Answers are found at the end of the chapter.

LOSS vs.RESULTS QUESTION EXERCISE

Simply circle L for Loss or R for Result

1. So, ideally you'd like a way of speeding up the redemption claim process?   L   R

2. Do these difficulties with the quality of your catalog lead to any problems with your employees?   L   R

3. In what way might a suggestion program help you to create your new mission statement?   L   R

4. So, doubling the amount of items offered, would get Mr. Dobbs off your back? Can you see anyother ways you might benefit?   L   R

5. Am I right that the motivation problem in turn leads to a fall-off in productivity?   L   R

6. Do you think that having one photocopier slows down your administrative people?   L   R

7. What would happen if we installed the new LX2000 on a trial basis for a month?   L   R

Our solution

Tied in closely with Results Questions is the final "O" in our model. 'Our Solution' involves offering the features and benefits of what it is that we have to offer. Again, I cannot emphasize enough that you must wait until you have built the client's Basic Need into a Specific Need, in the Results Questioning portion of the sales call to begin to offer the features and benefits of your solution. Your goal should be to concentrate on the benefits you offer vs. the features of your service and/or product. The premise is that we must always put ourselves in the shoes of the buyer who is asking himself or herself, "Who cares?" or "what's in it for me?" after every feature that they hear.

Recently, I had the opportunity to travel with an experienced sales person in the Seattle,Washington area. On the first call with this particular salesperson, I was impressed and mesmerized by her beautifully prepared presentation. This woman had prepared her entire presentation on her laptop computer in full color and in sequential order. Her presentation was flawless, yet the buyer seemed unimpressed. On the second call, I became particularly aware of the buyer's position in the sales call and it hit me! The sales person was giving all the features of her company, her experience and her product line without paying any attention to the benefit to the client. After her presentation, she outlined some of the benefits she offered, but by then it was too late.

I suggested to her that, on our third and final presentation of the day, she try to offer two benefits to every single feature that she put forth to the customer. It worked exceptionally well and I saw a huge change in the demeanor of the client. Afterward, the sales person confessed that it had been hard work to think of benefits for every feature, but that she had felt a difference in the room.

As you begin your quest of 2-1 ratio of benefits over features, I would like to offer an easy system that will ensure you take every feature to at least 2 benefits. Using the following words, you can't fail. Immediately after giving a feature, follow up with the words, "WHAT THIS MEANS TO YOU IS..." and give a benefit. After this, follow up with "WHAT THIS ALSO MEANS TO YOU IS..." For example, the woman in the above sales call began her presentation with information about the company. In our new scenario, it might sound something like this.

Feature: ABC company has been in business since 1939.
Benefit: What this means to you is that we have the experience in the industry to ensure the best sourcing capabilities available in

the Seattle area.

Benefit: What this also means to you is that you can rest assured you are not dealing with a "fly-by-night"operation that is here today and gone tomorrow.

There is another important benefit to you of being more aware of stressing the benefits of what you offer to your client. One of the biggest complaints I hear in all industries is that the sales people are dealing less and less with the actual decision maker. In many cases, because of time constraints, someone has been appointed to screen out possible vendors. It is not possible to get by this "screen" without first selling them on your solution. I liken it to being the director of a play. You can rehearse the players over and over again, but the minute the curtain goes up on opening night, you really have no control on what will be presented. Likewise, you can rehearse this "screen", but you have no control on what happens when it is presented to the actual decision maker. Or do you?

Through the use of our C.O.L.O.R. Selling™ model, we effectively uncover specific needs. Once we have discovered these needs, we must now stress the benefits to our solution or solutions. When the "screen" *does* present your solution to the decision maker, you want them to talk about the benefits you have to offer; not the features. In other words, they may say something like, "ABC company has a lot of credibility in the industry. I don't remember their product line, but I do know that they can solve our bottleneck in production and help in decreasing lost time hours due to accidents in the plant". Your goal should be to simply get the decision maker to want to get more information from you or even better, meet with you directly.

C.O.L.O.R. Selling™ in a nutshell

Asking questions that are important to the customer is what makes this model so powerful. The C.O.L.O.R. questioning sequence taps directly into the psychology of the buying process. Although it is meant to be used in sequence, we all know that the sales process does not always follow a progression. In an ideal environment the application of C.O.L.O.R. Selling™ might sound something like this...

Salesperson: (after the niceties are out of the way...Circumstance) So, in doing a little homework I discovered that you have hired over 280 new employees in just the last 6 months.

Buyer: Yes, it's been an interesting time here at ZBD Industries.

Salesperson (Obstacle): Does having that many new-hires pose any challenges for the company?

Buyer: As a matter of fact, we were just talking about that this morning. One of our biggest problems is that we are running out of parking spaces for our employees.

(Salesperson has uncovered a BASIC NEED—a dissatisfaction— but rather than offer a solution, they dig deeper.)

Salesperson (LOSS): What effect has that had on your department?

Buyer: I have noticed a lot of lost man-hours due to lateness over the past few months. I never really thought about it being tied to the lack of parking spaces

Salesperson: (RESULTS): Would it be of benefit to you to have some type of program that would encourage car pooling among your employees in the plant?

Buyer: It might just cut down on that lost time!

Salesperson (RESULTS): How else might it help?

Buyer: Well, it might encourage a sense of teamwork. I have been looking for a way to increase teamwork in the plant to help in productivity as well.

Is it always going to go this smoothly? Probably not. The nice thing about C.O.L.O.R. Selling™ is that it isn't a static model. You will find times where it is necessary to ask five or six Loss Questions in a row. There will be times when you ask *What effect...?* and the customer says "None!" which forces you to go back to Circumstance or Obstacle Questions. As we have seen, buyer's needs move through a clear progression from Basic to Specific. The C.O.L.O.R. Selling™ model simply provides a road map for you; guiding your sales calls through the steps or needs development until you discover the specific needs of your buyer. The more specific needs you uncover, the more likely the call is to succeed.

Four things to remember when it comes to C.O.L.O.R. Selling™ :

1) PRACTICE ONE NEW BEHAVIOR AT A TIME
If one of these questioning techniques seems a little foreign to you, then practice that one for as long as it takes you to feel comfortable. Don't move on to the next type until you're confident you've got the first one conquered.

2) TRY THIS NEW BEHAVIOR AT LEAST 3 TIMES PER WEEK
Different theories proclaim different amounts of time, but I

suggest trying one of these techniques three times per week until you are proficient.

3) IT'S QUANTITY BEFORE QUALITY
Believe it or not, asking a lot of questions is more important than necessarily asking the right kinds of questions in the beginning. I just want to make you more aware of the questions you ask.

4) PRACTICE IN SAFE SITUATIONS
Until you feel more comfortable, I wouldn't suggest you practice these techniques on huge new prospects or your largest clients

I would suggest you focus on the Digging Phase of your next sales call. Use the words provided for you throughout this chapter and remember, C.O.L.O.R. Selling™ is not a rigid model. Selling by any fixed formula is a recipe for disaster in the large sale. Use C.O.L.O.R. Selling™ as a guideline to probe, develop needs and position a buyer to take action by choosing your solution.

Answers to exercises

BASIC vs. SPECIFIC NEEDS

1. BASIC ('It would be nice'---a statement of dissatisfaction)
2. BASIC (expressing basic unhappiness with situation as it is
3. BASIC ('is a challenge for us' a statement of dissatisfaction)
4. BASIC ('It would be great')
5. SPECIFIC ('that is going to change:'—a specific want or desire)
6. SPECIFIC ('has to be quicker'—a specific want or desire)
7. BASIC (expressing dissatisfaction)

CIRCUMSTANCE vs. OBSTACLE QUESTIONS

1. CIRCUMSTANCE
2. OBSTACLE ('Do you find it difficult: 'probing for challenges)
3. CIRCUMSTANCE
4. OBSTACLE ('Does Mary find it difficult: ')
5. OBSTACLE (This one has been argued both ways—I could be wrong, but I think it's probing for a difficulty or dissatisfaction)
6. OBSTACLE ('How satisfied are you: '—great way to ask an Obstacle Question)
7. CIRCUMSTANCE

LOSS vs. RESULTS QUESTIONS

1. RESULTS ('So, ideally you'd like:' solution-centered)
2. LOSS (could be re-stated, 'What effect do these difficulties?')
3. RESULTS
4. RESULTS (gets client to suggest other solutions as well)5.
6. LOSS
7. RESULTS
8. LOSS

"The new wave of world-class salespeople recognize that their roles have reversed. Instead of being the <u>giver</u> of infomation as they have been in the past, now they must be the <u>seeker</u> of information."
-Jeffrey Tobe

About Jeffrey Tobe

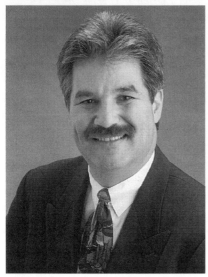

Insider Magazine recently dubbed Jeffrey Tobe, "the guru of creativity." Prior to his professional speaking career, Jeff had been involved in the advertising industry for over ten years. During his last three years in that business, he won five international Golden Pyramid Awards for creativity. Jeff was also recognized as a leader in the sales management arena by Sales & Marketing Executives International.

Jeff was born in Fergus Ontario, Canada and now resides in Monroeville, PA with his wife Judy and their two daughters. He is a member of the National Speaker's Association and the Pennsylvania Speakers Association.

For more information and a free marketing video, contact:
1144 Colgate Drive
Monroeville, PA 15146
Toll free: 1-800-875-7106
(412) 373-6592
Fax: (412) 373-8773
E-mail: CRE8IVA@aol.com

Company Profile

Coloring Outside the Lines offers customized, creativity-in-sales-and-marketing keynotes, seminars and training. From your meeting's opening, motivational address to a long-term training program for your sales force, Jeffrey Tobe and his associates bring you fast-paced, up-to-the-minute, participatory programs. Before any new sales or customer service approach can be broached, you need to be willing to get outside of your comfort zone and 'stop looking in your rear view mirror' at what you have always done in the past. Instead, start looking through your windshield to see what's coming down the road ahead.

We have no static program. What this means to you is that we can design a program to fit your specific time parameters, budget and needs.

Most Requested Programs (in addition to C.O.L.O.R. Selling™)
Coloring Outside the Lines™
Creativity in Sales and Marketing for the 21st Century
This is the company's 'signature' presentation encouraging participants to look at their challenges from a whole new perspective in managing the change that is inevitable with innovation.
Keynote, 1/2 day to 2 day workshop available
Listening Between the Lines...
Effective Listening Techniques to Better Sales Relationships
Information is power! And yet, this communications tool is the least studied, the least practiced and the least understood of all. Learn the 9 steps to more effective listening and how you gain the competitive edge by keeping your mouth closed and your ears open.
Keynote, 3-6 hour module available
Who are You Selling to Anyway?...
Understanding Your Clients' "Buying Style"
By discovering your unique behavior in the sales process, you can better understand how to sell to a buyer whose 'buying style' is incongruent with your 'selling style'. This is vital if we are to be able to build long-term, professional relationships.
Keynote, 3-6 hour module available
Outside the Lines Customer Service...
Professional Service that Works!
This program provides employees with a refreshing and powerful system for better, more creative, customer service. Individual skill-building exercises combined with group activities focus on identifying strategies for customer-friendly service.
Keynote, 5-15 hour module available

Chapter 8

Selling Through Negotiating

by
Dave Jakielo

Keep in mind that the only goal of any negotiation should be a win/win solution or no deal.

—Dave Jakielo

To be a successful salesperson you must possess many skills. One of the most important skill sets is the ability to negotiate. Mastering negotiating skills will help you increase your sales and maximize your income. Negotiations do not occur only in a business situation. You need to negotiate throughout the day. You negotiate with your boss for a raise or promotion. You negotiate with your co-workers to help handle the work load. You negotiate in a romantic relationship. You really need to negotiate when it comes to four teenage daughters and two bathrooms. Given that negotiating is such a major part of our life, why not invest the time and learn how to do it well?

Keep in mind that the only goal of any negotiation should be a win/win solution or no deal. A win/win outcome occurs when both parties achieve a mutually satisfying and beneficial agreement. Anything less and it is probably the last time you will deal with each other. When you enter a negotiation with the goal of reaching a win/win solution you usually will achieve your goal. Remember almost everything is negotiable. The first area we need to be aware of is that there are certain common facts about negotiating.

The facts about negotiating

- You are constantly negotiating with the various parties throughout the day.
- Anything you will ever want is owned or controlled by someone else.
- There are predictable responses to the maneuvers that take place.
- There are three critical factors of every session—Power, Information and the Time element.
- Remember you are dealing with people not just issues.
- People are different, you must adjust your personality style to their style.
- It's important where negotiations take place, preferably on your turf.
- You are in a bad position if negotiations are narrowed down to

one issue.
- Never, never give a concession without getting something in return.

The art of being a successful negotiator is working with people. The goal or object of any negotiation is not to get the best of them, but you need to work together to reach an acceptable solution.

I have been involved in hundreds of negotiating sessions, and I have found that there are three reactions that are predictable:
- If someone takes your first offer you wish you went lower.
- If they jump at your offer you think there is something wrong.
- If you get everything you want you're not asking for enough.

To keep the above situation from happening, you must do your homework. (I will discuss this in section four of this chapter.) Don't fall into the trap that you think people must want the same things you want. What is important to us may not be important to them.

Six styles of negotiating

Even though we should always be focused on a win/win solution it is important for you to recognize the different styles you may encounter at various points in your career. Many people feel that everything is negotiable and most times that is true because prices are usually set arbitrarily. We're typically not good negotiators because of fear of rejection. The only way to get over this fear is to practice, practice, practice the basic skills of negotiating. The goal is to satisfy both of the parties' needs.

Win/Lose—This situation is a common occurrence. This is when you are satisfied with the results but the other party is not satisfied. The big question you need to ask yourself when this situation occurs is, will they ever want to do business with you again? When people feel that they have been taken advantage of they will either avoid you in the future or try to get even. Remember your win is only temporary and short-term. You've blown a chance for future business. This one sale may seem great but you probably have thrown away any chance for future commissions. This happens quite often because this is the style with which we are most familiar. While we were growing up, we learned this type of behavior from our parents, teachers or any one in authority. Usually they won and we lost, many times the only explanation was BECAUSE. I wouldn't recommend when a prospect asks you why your price is so high you say, "BECAUSE." To avoid win/lose situations we need to deprogram ourselves of this type of thought process that may have been drummed into us at an early age.

Lose/Win—This is when you are not satisfied with the results but the other party is satisfied. Some people allow themselves to be railroaded into a decision. They do not like confrontation and they do not want to offend the other party. When a person gives into this type of negotiation once, you can rest assured that it will happen again. Be careful, you can become used to giving in. It can become second nature.

A few years ago I had to negotiate with a client that was a "lose/win" negotiator. He always won because at that time I had not learned the skills of negotiating successfully. He always wanted me to lose and he had to win. He was successful since I wasn't prepared to deal with him on his level. He used many of the tactics we will be discussing. My goal in this chapter is to explain the skills you will need to prevent this from happening in your future negotiating sessions.

It's funny now that I think about it. Before I learned how to conduct a successful negotiation I was giving out concessions like life jackets on the Titanic. It's the old, if I knew then, what I know now, the results would have been different. Well, you're in luck, read on and protect yourself from this type of person.

Lose/Lose—The signs of this situation are that both parties usually possess a high level of emotional involvement. Both parties would rather come to a ridiculous agreement than have the feeling that the other person won. Rather than let the other party feel that they won, they settle and neither party is happy. This often happens in a nasty divorce. The parties' actions are directed to try to hurt the other individual. A friend of mine was going through a divorce. He knew he would be instructed by the courts to sell their house and split the proceeds or pay his soon-to-be ex-wife half of the equity. Well, this was such a bitter divorce that rather than do either, while the divorce battle was going on, he defaulted on the mortgage and let the bank repossess the property. Neither of them ended up with much of anything from the house.

Compromise—A compromise occurs when two parties cannot agree on an issue and they come up with an entirely different third solution. Some wants are fulfilled but some are still unfulfilled. Both parties are partially satisfied yet, partially unsatisfied. Since neither party has a strong positive feeling they may not negotiate together again in the future.

No deal—You agree to disagree. You walk away without entering into an agreement. We cannot find a solution that would benefit both of us so lets go our separate ways. It's better not to enter into an agreement that you will be unhappy with, rather than get into a relationship that will undoubtedly lead to future disagreements or conflicts. This often happens if you have issues that can't be resolved or have strong opposing opinions.

Win/Win—I'll reiterate that this should be the only goal of every negotiation. This concept is based on the principle that there is plenty for everybody, that one persons success is never achieved at the others' expense. Completing a win/win negotiation leaves both sides with a feeling of contentment. A strong bond may be formed which will lead to future successful negotiations.

Three stages of negotiating

There are three stages of negotiating, just like a larva—becoming a caterpillar then a butterfly. You need all three steps to end up with something beautiful. The three stages are:

Establish criteria. Why are they making their request?

Get all the information. Find out all you can, don't jump to conclusions. We, being of an impatient nature, sometimes want to go to the bottom line too quickly.

Strive for compromise. To better explain this three step process consider the following: Your son comes to you and wants to borrow the car. You respond by jumping all over him and saying, "You always want to borrow the car" and a shouting match follows. This entire situation could have been avoided if you would have just followed the three stages of negotiating:

- Establish criteria. Find out why he wants the car. One of the reasons he asked was because mom wants him to pick up a prescription for her and then he wants to go to the movies.
- Get information. Who is he going with to the movies. When are they going and when will they return.
- Compromise. Have you cut the grass? If the answer is no you can make that a stipulation that you can go after you completed your chore.

Many arguments can be avoided if you follow the above formula.

How to prepare for a successful negotiation

Attempting to negotiate with someone before you are properly prepared is like baking a cake without a recipe or without all the basic ingredients. You need to know the answers to the questions below before you even enter the room to negotiate:

- What will be the subject matter and issues for discussion?

- Make a list of both resolved and unresolved issues.
- What do I have in common with the person across the table?
- Do we come from the same backgrounds? Are we both in marketing? Will I need to be prepared to give a presentation from a perspective other than mine.
- What are their needs and objectives that I should be thinking about?
- Do they want to drive a car for prestige regardless of price or are they just interested in basic transportation?
- What's the style of the person with whom you are going to negotiate?
- Is it always their way or the highway or are they interested in finding an equitable solution? If you don't know the party you're dealing with sometimes a business acquaintance can give you an insight into the negotiating style of this person.
- What is my opening package or starting position?
- What are you going to offer at the first meeting? Never play it by ear, always have a detailed plan.
- What am I trying to accomplish?
- What is the minimum that will be acceptable to you? Determine your bottom line ahead of time.
- At what point do I walk away?
- When do you have to admit that their demands will lead to a losing situation? When should you recommend that you cease to do business with each other?
- What are the current positions?
- Where are the differences?

Tactics of negotiating

The purpose of tactics or techniques, which some consider to carry a negative connotation, is not to take advantage of your negotiating partner. You need to use them as tools for a successful win/win negotiating session.

You will need to know and be able to recognize these techniques even if you do not use them. If the party you are negotiating with knows and uses these techniques you must be aware of what is happening and ready to react. If you allow the other party to achieve success with any of these tactics you will not be able to go back in time and change the outcome.

Don't use hard core techniques on someone who doesn't have any negotiating skills. After the negotiation is over and they have had time to think about what occurred they will be very angry with the way you handled the situation.

Again, even if you don't use any of these tactics you need to know when they are being used against you in order to protect your position.

Asking for more—This occurs after an agreement has been reached and one party, at the last minute, tries to get more. With this technique they never ask for everything up front. Then after you think a final agreement has been reached they ask for more on the way out the door. An example of this technique occurs when you have just made a sale at a good margin. You have agreed on a price and quantity, and are about to leave when they say, "That does include shipping cost, doesn't it?" They realize that it's a good time to ask for more when the negotiations have been completed. The reason this is true is because people feel good and are willing to give in on an issue they may not have agreed to if it was part of the original negotiation. They wait for the decision to be made then ask you for more because you are vulnerable.

A successful counter tactic is to make them feel cheap. I once heard a story of a man who was selling his car, and both parties had agreed on a price. As the buyer was sitting at the seller's kitchen table writing the check he said, "And that will include a full tank of gas?" The seller turned the tables and said, "Wait, you just negotiated a very good price. You're not going to try to get a tank of gas from me too, are you?" Be careful if you find yourself in this type of situation you're very vulnerable to giving concessions that you would not have agreed to in the beginning.

Problem transference—This is when someone tries to give you their problem. The customer says, "I only have $3000 dollars for a computer so don't waste my time with anything out of that price range." A counter tactic is to test for validity. Ask the customer if you can show them a computer for a $1,000 more than their spending limit, that will do twice as much as a $3,000 model, will they take a look at it?

Use of higher or limited authority—Many times, just when you think you have made a sale, your prospect says, "I'd like to buy it but I have to check with a higher authority." In this example let's say it's the vice president of purchasing. Here is a series of counter tactics that can be utilized.

- Appeal to their ego—"Well, the vice president of purchasing always takes your recommendation, doesn't he?"
- Get their commitment—"And you will recommend it to him, won't you?" They usually will not make up a story when you ask them this question. In most instances I have found that they

will tell you why they cannot make a recommendation. This is a good way to find out additional objections or the real issue keeping them from a decision. When you find out what is blocking their decision then you can start to resell.

- Use the qualified "subject to" close—OK, I'll write this order up and it is "subject to" the vice president of purchasing review. He will have the right to decline, after his review, for a specific reason. You must remove the "higher authority" excuse before they use it. Sometimes there isn't a higher authority, it's just a stall tactic. Get it out of the way quickly. Example: Let me understand, if we can agree on this are you willing to buy today? This eliminates their ability to refer it to a higher authority. If they use the higher authority stall, you need to ask yourself, "Am I talking to the right person?" Then say, I understand you don't have the authority. Whom do I need to talk to get a decision today?" This response lets the person know you are not going to just accept their stall. Another tactic is to ask for the name and phone number of their boss. Then pull out your pen and paper and wait for their response. This may seem harsh but remember the "higher authority" stall is a strong tactic that they are using against you. If they do not have the authority then you should be talking to someone else. This tactic is most often used to take the pressure off them of having to make a decision or coming right out and rejecting your offer. You always need to test the limited authority stall to see if it's valid.

Red Herring—This technique is sometimes considered to be a dirty trick. This occurs when one party focuses on a minor point to get their way on a big issue. Usually this occurs with highly emotional issues, like in a divorce. For example, the wife wants the couple's art collection but the husband knows it will hurt the wife if he doesn't give it to her. So the husband acts as if he wants the art. The wife then changes her request to, "Well, I only want these three paintings." She really doesn't want those three. She wants all the others. The husband, thinking that he will be hurting her if he keeps the three she requested says, "No way, I get those three paintings and you can have the rest." Little did he know that because of his emotional blindness, he gave up what the wife really wanted.

Squeeze tactic—A customer enters a store to purchase bedroom furniture. The salesperson says it's only $2,500. You respond, "You'll have to better than that." Your response puts pressure on the salesperson to start shaving the price without you, the buyer, giving any concessions. A person using this technique tries to keep pushing to get the other party to name their bottom-line price. A counter tactic to the customers' response is, "OK, how much better will I have to do?" They may ask, "Are you really serious about buying this today?" If the customer is really serious about buying, it will get things moving. If they won't give you an answer or any additional information about the possible purchase, you are probably wasting your time.

Trade off—You trade one issue for another, or each party makes their offer and you both decide to split the difference. You compromise: "I'll pay your asking price if you will deliver it at no extra charge."

Set-aside technique—This tactic is very effective when there is an impasse or you have an issue that causes a deadlock situation. If someone says, "No way can I pay more than $1,000" but your cost is more than that amount, don't argue the point; it will only cause both parties to become angry with each other. Set that issue aside and clear up smaller issues like, how do you want it packaged, when would you like it shipped. The reason to set the price issue aside is because it will be easier to solve after you have gained some momentum by obtaining "yes" answers on other issues.

It's incorrect to think that you must settle the big issues first. Tackling the big issues first usually stalls the process and you may never be able to move ahead. If you do find yourself in a deadlocked situation, the only way to solve it is to bring in a third party, an arbitrator, who is perceived as reasonably neutral. Bring in a neutral party, then have each side restate their positions. This will help you identify all the critical issues that are causing the deadlock.

Good guy bad guy—This is one technique we are probably all familiar with. We see it on TV when two police officers are interrogating a suspect. Car salespersons are also famous for using this technique. As I stated before, little decisions often lead to big decisions. This is almost always the case when you're dealing with two people in the negotiation process. With this technique one person usually states, "I'd like to sell it to you for that price, but I don't know if I can get my sales manager to agree." Don't play this game; you cannot win, but you can use counter tactics. One is to go over their head to their boss. Tell the boss that they were doing "good guy/bad guy" to you and say "I know you do not approve of that, do you?" Explain to them, "I know what you're doing, so anything you say I am also going to attribute to your sales manager." If you take this stance it very rarely backfires, but if it does, that is an indication that they weren't playing fair and you're better off not dealing with them. Remember, it's always harder to negotiate with more than one party.

Feel, felt, found formula—Don't ever try to argue a position, reach a stalemate, then try to go back later and try to bring them around to your point of view. You must strive to change their mind without an argument. Here is an example of this technique: A car salesperson is trying to sell a four cylinder car. The buyer says, "I don't want a four cylinder car, we have too many hills in our area." So the salesperson follows the three steps. FEEL = He says I understand exactly how you feel about four cylinders. FELT = Yes, most people I talked to felt the same way about four cylinders. FOUND = However, we have taken a closer look, and examined how the car performs on our hills. Taking into consideration the extra fuel economy you will realize, we have always found that it is the best way to go.

Flinch or winch—When price is mentioned flinch as if you just suffered personal pain. Let your face show how shocked you are that the price is that high. This should be your reaction no matter what the price. This reaction alone will usually have the seller drop the price, especially when it has been set arbitrarily. This also stops them from trying to add extra charges after you have reached an agreement.

Question method—Use any of the following questions. Ask "Can't you do better than that?" Ask this question even if you think it's a great price. Ask "Is it ever on sale?" When you are told the sale price immediately, offer to buy it at that amount. If they respond, "but it isn't on sale today," tell them to ask the manager if they will accept your offer. One last question could be "What's the best you can do if I were to buy it today." Remember no one will ever sell you anything at a loss. Negotiating for the lowest price may affect someone's commission but you're not hurting them.

Silence—Never underestimate the power of silence. If they make a request or a demand you can't meet, remain silent. Almost every time, whoever speaks first loses. Most people cannot stand silence. When you wait, many times they will start talking and change their position. When someone gives you the silent treatment, you can use one of two counter tactics. The first is to remain silent and wait them out. The second is to just restate your last offer. Never give any concessions during the silence.

Low-ball offer—This is where a salesperson will give you a low price to get you to say yes. Once you agree, then they start with, "By the way." A good example is when they quote you a low price on a computer and you say, "OK, that sounds good." Then they start "by the way, you'll want to upgrade the memory so it will run more applications." "By the way, you'll need a color printer and a high resolution monitor." These are all add-ons and are sold at high margins.

Written word—They put terms in writing so they seem not to be negotiable. Like an apartment lease. Most people believe that if it's in writing it cannot be changed. When someone gives you a written document they want you to believe that they are powerless to negotiate or change the written word. A counter tactic is to indicate to them that the terms are not acceptable and you will not be able to reach a deal. You'll be surprised how eager they will be to negotiate.

Outrageous behavior tactics—Someone acts outrageous and forces the other party to make a move without them having to make any concessions. An example is someone who turns over a table or rips up a contract. The goal is to rattle the other side. No one likes volatile confrontations. Once I was in a meeting and the client slammed his fist down on the desk. A counter tactic to this behavior is to remain silent. Let them settle down. Caution, avoid the temptation to respond emotionally. Do not try to fight back just; defuse the emotion.

Trial Balloon—Use a commitment question to see where they stand. Say something like, "Would you like this blouse in red or blue?" If they answer this question they are sold. Best counter tactic is to answer their question with a question. Well, if I did want a red one what is the price? Always try to get the other party to make the first move.

Hidden meanings in conversation

You need to be able to read the other party's hidden agenda in negotiations. The other party can learn a lot about your hidden agenda by observing the way you talk or by carefully listening to your tone. While you are trying to figure them out be careful in what you give away. Listen carefully to the words and tone of voice other people use. Many times people mean just the opposite of what they say.

Here are some examples of how people use words to their advantage:

When they say	They really mean
as you are aware	usually you are not
by the way	it means by their way
before I forget	they won't forget, here comes an important request

There are words people use that mean the opposite:

When they say	They really mean
We can work out the details later	there is a great deal of negotiating to go.
Don't worry	start worrying
In my humble opinion	they don't consider their opinion humble

Watch out for the following expressions:

When they say	They really mean:
Frankly, Charlotte I don't give a damn	yes, he did give a damn
To tell the truth	probably not telling the truth
Honestly	does that mean they have been dishonest up to now?

Some great put off lines are:

When they say	They really mean
I'll try my best	you know it probably won't be good enough
I'll see what I can do I'll give every effort	when hell freezes over the answer's no but give me credit for trying
I'll think it over	don't call me I'll call you

Sometimes they may try to throw you off track.

When they say	They really mean
I'm not an expert but	yes, they are an expert.
I don't mean to be personal	but they are going to be very personal.
I don't mean to intrude	look out they are getting ready to intrude
I need a big, big favor	They set you up. You think they are going to ask for the moon. However, it's a minor request and you easily agree.

Sometimes people send up trial balloons. "I haven't given it a lot of thought." Yes they have, and you're getting close to a deal. Or, "off the top of my head," they are not sure if you'll accept what they are proposing, but they will try presenting it anyway.

Remember there is a danger of trying to read too much into a situation; you can be carried away. Listen and try to understand what the other person is saying, but don't go overboard. For example, some people will not leave the house if their horoscope says to stay in today.

Body language: what are they really saying

Experts say that 20 percent of what we communicate is done with words. The remaining is through body language. A marvelous benefit we have over the animal world is that we can use our voices and our language to probe the messages we are receiving non verbally, in order to see if our assumptions are valid.

One important thing to keep in mind, the explanation of body language I am relating applies to Americans. In other cultures, body language may mean different things.

Listed below are some of the more common body language cues:

Discontinuing eye contact—If you are talking with someone and they look away for an extended period after having maintained good eye contact, it's almost a sure sign that they disagree with something you said or have lost interest in the conversation.

Beginning eye contact—Also, the opposite is usually true. If someone has not been facing you and suddenly turns towards you and begins making eye contact, you have finally caught their attention and are getting your ideas or points across.

Slouching—When a person is not sitting in an attentive position and they are slouching in their chair, you would be wise to take it as a sign of disinterest or a heart attack.

Grasping a chair arm and locking ankles—This occurs when a person is in an anxious state. You see it when someone is late getting to their next meeting. This posture may signal that the person is holding back information or trying to hide their true feelings.

Clenching a fist or banging a hand against a table—These are warning signs that they are about to blow their top. (You probably wouldn't be where you are today if you didn't already know that.)

Wringing Hands—The person is nervous. Your first task is to try to make them relax. You can achieve this by smiling, looking them in the eye, and leaning slightly forward.

When interpreting what people are saying keep the following points in mind:

Visual cues are more important than words.

Then listen for voice tone (pick up commitment, enthusiasm, disinterest, skepticism and other messages).

Least important are the words themselves.

It's your responsibility to ensure that your body is sending the right message. In most cases while you're trying to read them, they are trying to read you. When you are dealing with others you should;

Sit or stand erect. Never lean against a wall, desk or table.

Maintain eye contact. If you feel uncomfortable doing this, it's OK. Many people do. One way around this problem is to pick a spot in the middle of the person's forehead right above the eyebrows and concentrate there. They will never know you're not looking directly into their eyes.

Do not cross your arms and legs.

To emphasize that you are paying attention, nod your head occasionally and respond affirmatively. Say "I understand"—"I see"—"Yes". Another technique is when they have finished making a point, repeat the point. This will indicate to them that you really were paying attention.

To show authority, sit at the head of a table or stand while others are seated. Pay attention to your posture and gestures. Remember not to give too much away non verbally.

Let me share with you a personal story that happened to me. A few years ago my wife and I decided we were going to buy a second home. A place to use as a "get away" where the whole family could relax. We decided the type of place we wanted. We knew it had to be on the water and we wanted it to be no more than an hour away. We also determined how much we could afford. I was proud that we were so well prepared. As fate would have it, we found the perfect place. I was so excited that we found exactly what we were looking for that I couldn't control my facial expressions or hide my enthusiasm. The seller didn't have to ask if I was interested. I'm sure my lack of control cost me a few thousand dollars in the negotiations. So be careful what you show with body and facial expressions. I learned my lesson.

Qualities and skills of successful negotiators

The process of negotiating is a life-long process, ongoing, never ending. Unless you are planning to be a hermit and living in a cave, you will always have interaction and exchange with other people. To become a successful negotiator you need to possess the following qualities and learn the following skills:

- You must be able to bargain, trade and compromise.
- You must be open-minded, adaptive and creative.
- You will need to consider all types of options and possibilities.
- You must avoid situations of fixed positions where people dig in their heels. Instead, be flexible, and look for areas of compromise.

- Successful negotiators are cooperative versus competitive. You need to reach collaborative solutions that are beneficial to each party.
- You will need to be innovative or try unusual ways to get both parties what they want.
- You must be honest, direct and non manipulative. Placing great value on the relationship and looking forward to both parties getting along after the negotiation.
- You must have the desire and exert the effort to acquire the skills of negotiating.
- You will need to understand how the different tactics and techniques work.
- You must have a willingness to practice. Once after working an entire day at a trade show in Chicago, I went to check into my hotel. To my amazement even though I had a confirmed reservation the desk clerk told me that there were no vacancies. She offered to call around and find me another hotel. It was around midnight, I was dead tired and I didn't want to have to travel to another hotel. So I asked to see the manager. When I explained my situation, she said she was sorry and if I didn't mind sleeping in one of their unoccupied hospitality suites she would have a bed brought in immediately and only charge me $25.00. This solution was acceptable to me, but I wouldn't have had this offer extended if I hadn't asked.
- Strive for win/win solutions; use your skills properly. Never take advantage of anyone. Always protect your integrity. You can always find another deal, but you cannot go shopping for a new reputation.

Understanding the powers of negotiating

The power or ability to influence other people, whether you have it or you create the perception you have it, doesn't matter. Some of the various types of negotiating power are:

- Legitimate power—This is anyone who has a title.
- Reward power—If they can hand out the rewards.
- Intimidation power—A state trooper who pulls you over on the highway.
- Consistency power -If you always display a consistent set of values and always play it straight in dealings with people.
- Charismatic power—Having an overwhelming personality like an entertainer.

- Expertise power—A doctor or a lawyer who use their own language to make you feel they have power.
- Situation power— A driving examiner who can pass or fail you. Outside that job they have no power.
- Informational power—The sharing of information bonds. Secrecy or withholding information tends to intimidate and give you control.
- Knowledge of the needs of others—He who knows the most wins.
- Appearing to be indifferent.—Acting as if you do not care how things turn out.
- Real or implied scarcity—Saying you only have one or a few left. Be careful if you're bluffing it may be interpreted that you're dishonest.

You can convey authority by your dress, the way you walk and carry yourself. When I was in sales full time, almost every time I walked through a hospital to an appointment, people assumed I was a doctor. I conveyed this perception by dressing in a suit, walking like I owned the place (this is accomplished by a quick pace and a smile) and not carrying a briefcase so I didn't look like a salesperson.

Common negotiating mistakes

Do not enter into a negotiation with artificially high demands hoping to reach a quick compromise.

Take time to discover what it is the other person wants. Two children were on the patio fighting over a cup of Kool aid. Since it was the last cup of Kool aid the mother rushes out with another cup and divides the drink by pouring half into the empty cup. The one youngster drinks his down, the other pours the Kool aid in the grass and starts playing in the sand box with the empty cup. If the mother would have taken the time to "discover" what each child wanted there could have been a better solution.

Don't close your mind to an unfavorable option too fast. As you progress in the negotiations, something that seemed outrageous at one time may make sense now or can be used to gain another concession.

Don't try to handle the toughest issues first. You may have a tendency to think you must solve the biggest issue first. You say to yourself: "If we can reach an agreement on this big issue the rest will be a cake walk." That's not the case; try to build momentum by getting the other party to say yes a few times on small issues.

Don't assume. Many times we make the mistake of looking at a solution only through our eyes. We think everybody must want what we want. Take the case where you need a business loan and you are nervous because you think the loan officer will say no. Surprisingly, the loan officer was just chewed out by his boss for not making enough loans. He needs you, too.

Don't get defensive and hoard information. Let the other party know pertinent information, it may help them understand your perspective. Once I had contracted with a painting firm to paint the exterior of my home. The price included two coats. The crew arrived bright and early one morning and painted the first coat. About noon they stopped and started packing up. Well, having had problems in the past with contractors not completing their jobs, I rushed out of the house and said "Oh no you don't, I paid for two coats, if you leave now I'll never see you again!" The contractor calmly picked up one of the paint cans and showed me the label where the manufacture recommended that the paint be allowed to dry for at least eight hours between coats. He assured me that this was standard procedure and they were headed off to apply a second coat to a house in the next subdivision and would be back first thing in the morning.

Don't leave details up in the air. Negotiate your price before you deliver services or goods. I've seen case after case where the services to be rendered weren't clearly spelled out and one or the other parties ended up in a losing situation.

Don't be afraid to develop one of the most important powers: walk-away power. There is no contract or sale you can't live without. Most bad deals occur because one side gives up their walk-away power. When you say I'm going to make the deal at any cost, you're in trouble. I remember one occasion where a client and I were negotiating a contract extension. All the issues had been resolved except the price. We had set this issue aside earlier in the negotiations and agreed on the other twenty or so points. No matter how much I tried to resolve the price issue the client insisted I go lower and if I agreed to his price it would have meant zero margin. Well, no one ever likes to lose a sale but I knew if I agreed to the price he was willing to pay, in the long run it would be a lose/ lose situation. I would have lost because there wasn't any profit for the company and if we cut back on service, it would hurt our reputation. He would have lost because our employees wouldn't give him the level of service he needed to be successful. It would have been in the back of their minds that this was not a profitable deal and they might not have devoted the proper effort.

So I took a chance and explained that since he couldn't pay my price and I couldn't enter into an unprofitable contract, we needed to break off negotiations. Without saying another word, I picked up my papers and took the contract off his desk and started to walk out. Before I got to the door he broke the silence—remember, he who speaks first loses—and stated that maybe the price was OK. To this day I wonder what the outcome would have been if he had remained silent.

Sign of a successful negotiation

- A good negotiation is when both parties' major interests have been met. They can walk away feeling they both have accomplished something important. No one should feel that they have been taken advantage of or got the short end of the stick.
- Each party cared about the objectives of the other.
- Each side needs to feel that both sides were fair. For example, you don't feel bad losing a game if each side played fair. But if one side cheated, the other side is very angry. No one wants to experience the feeling of betrayal. Both parties' feelings should be that negotiations were tough and they fought hard but they listened to each point of view.
- Need to feel that you have enjoyed dealing with each other. And would work together again. Not to outdo each other or get revenge but to have another win/win situation.
- Each party is willing to keep the commitments and will uphold the agreement. You should never feel that either party will back down or change their mind later.
- The outcome is better than any alternative you can imagine.
- People will not give you what you want if you dominate them. They will agree only after you give them what they want.
  If you later think you made a bad deal, don't be afraid to go back and say you made a mistake or you changed your mind. It's OK to say you're not happy with this deal; let's re-open and re-negotiate.

Tips for negotiating success

Have negotiations in your office, house, car. If they invite you to their office and you can't counter by having them come to you, try for a neutral site like a hotel or restaurant.

Positioning—Opposite sides of the table are bad. Don't sit face to face, try for side by side. Whenever there were more than one of us on the negotiating team we always tried to split up and sit on different sides of the table. Try to alternate your seating pattern if possible. Always try to sit next to your major negotiating opponent not across from them.

Timing—A relaxed time schedule is recommended. You don't want to be rushed. If there is not enough time to arrive at a win/win solution, you're better off postponing the negotiation until a later time. Be careful; some people use this as a tactic against you. They will meet you and say, "I only have a few minutes." It's best to not start the session and reschedule.

Control your emotions. Once you let yourself get emotional about an issue it fogs your thinking patterns. You will find that you can't agree on anything even the little issues. If a person usually makes you angry or intimidates you, it will hurt the outcome. Take time to analyze how the other party is making you feel and adjust for that. Don't be afraid to take a time out or give someone else the floor.

When dealing with difficult people, *use tactics that will keep the negotiations on course without offending anyone.* This is often hard to do but you need to stand your ground; giving in will only lead to more demands. Use a statement like, "What you're suggesting is not an option." Being assertive without having a smart aleck tone or attitude will help you move on to the next issue.

Be aware of the other parties' perceptions. You want a raise because you think you deserve one. But your salary is already close to your bosses, and they don't want it to get any closer.

Ask open ended questions. If after some discussion your boss still isn't offering a raise, don't force the issue by asking "Are you going to give me a raise yes or no?" Instead ask an open ended question like, "If you can't give me a raise are there other duties I need to take on to advance my career?"

If someone is pressuring you to make a quick decision say "If I have to answer now the answer is no, but if I can have some time to think about it my answer may be different." Use this tactic when you need to buy time.

Prepare for negotiations. The process must start before you meet face to face. Do your homework and prepare in advance. The more information you have the better you will do in negotiations.

Never, never say yes to the first offer.

Seek win/win solutions all the time. Remember you're trying to build a strong relationship for the future.

Take every opportunity to practice. Try negotiating with friends, family etc.

Know what you want. This may seem like common sense but you need to know exactly what you want. Many times we go into a negotiation with a vague or general idea of what we want, we think in generalities of a contract or a sale. However, we fail to plan for details like shipping cost, delivery dates or start up time. When we are not prepared, we end up giving concessions we wouldn't have offered if we were better prepared.

Know ahead of time what concessions and compromises you are willing to make. You must have a plan, you need to know what you must have, what you would like to have and what would be great to have.

Rehearse the session with your peers for practice. Let them play the devils advocate. Have them bring up what if scenarios. Anticipate compromises. This way you won't panic when they come up. Never want anything so badly that desperation causes you to make a bad deal. Have alternative ways to reach your ultimate goal.

Don't accept an unattractive offer. Just because you have invested time and money it doesn't make you obligated to accept a bad deal. Remember, you'll survive if you walk away. As Kenny Rogers said, "Know when to hold them, know when to fold them."

Knowledge is power. The more information you know about the people, their organization, and the issues, the sharper the edge you'll have.

Comfort—Have comfortable chairs, something to drink.

Keep your attitude positive, calm, patient, low keyed.

Don't plan a session close to lunch or dinner times. Things always go better after eating.

Remember everything someone asks for is an issue. Never give a concession without getting a concession in return.

You must approach each negotiating session as a unique experience with thought and planning. Don't rush into a session like a battle, firing off techniques indiscriminately. Weigh each offer on its merits and respond accordingly. Be alert and give every move plenty of thought.

Remember value is in the eyes of the beholder and everything is negotiable. Most importantly, you'll never go wrong if you always strive for win/win solutions.

About Dave Jakielo

Dave Jakielo, has over 25 years of hands on management experience with two multi million dollar corporations. Dave has been speaking, consulting and teaching business methods to managers, clerical staffs, business owners and other professionals throughout the country for over a decade. Programs are designed to be educational, informative and entertaining.

Dave has extensive experience in sales, marketing, business start-ups and turnarounds, acquisition assimilation, customer service, negotiations and managed care contracting.

For the past fifteen years, he has been speaking nationally on business issues, general management, motivational and personal development issues. Being a magician, Dave can include a magical theme in his presentations to enhance participant's retention of the material.

Dave is a Board member of the International Billing Association (IBA), a member of Medical Group Management Association (MGMA), a member of the Pennsylvania Speakers Association and a member of the International Brotherhood of Magicians.

Dave is a graduate of the University of Pittsburgh with a Bachelor of Science in Business Administration. Dave has trained at the Buckley School of Public Speaking. He is President of his own seminar, training and consulting company.

For more information, contact:

Dave Jakielo
Dave Jakielo Seminars & Consulting
86 Hall Avenue
Pittsburgh, PA 15205
Phone/fax: 412-921-0976

Company profile

David F. Jakielo Seminars & Consulting , is a firm that helps companies increase profitability, assists non-profit organizations to achieve their goals and works with individuals to enhance their careers. This is accomplished through seminars, in house training and consulting.

Program lengths are modified based on clients' requirements. Seminars are available for groups or can be held in-house for your company.

Sample of Seminars and Training Topics

General business

The Art of Negotiating—Conducting successful win/win negotiations.
High Impact Selling—Maximize your efforts to ensure your highest earning potential.
Life After a Merger—Presentation revolves around the most important aspect of mergers—the human element.
First Class Customer Service—How to keep them coming back.
So You Want To Stay In Business—Covers leadership skills, style, development and responsibilities.

Health care

Getting Paid for What You Do—Collecting from patients, insurance companies, the importance of coding and negotiating with third parties.
Managing Your Practice as a Business—How to compete in today's marketplace. Examine cost, marketing, staffing, accounts receivable etc.
Managed Care "Surviving the Future"—Examine what's occurring throughout the U.S. with HMO's, capitation, Global payments.

Chapter 9

Dick & Jane Communication

by
Anne Louise Conlon Feeny

*Why can't a woman be more
like a man?*
—Henry Higgins
My Fair Lady

Grousing about his protege, Henry loudly moans that she—and all women are "silly, demanding, and indecisive." For her part, Ms. Doolittle voices her frustration with Henry's petty arrogance in a later soliloquy; thus, their battle of the sexes raged. Little wonder, since they never talked to each other about what was bothering them. Nor do they attempt to view the situation from the other's seat. The play's pre-determined happy ending triumphs over their angst, however, as they discover they're not really angry, they're just in love!

Is it any wonder, then, that communication with the opposite sex resembles a mine field? We've been sold an ordnance lode that regularly bombs in a social setting, and can prove even more explosive in business. Missing Lerner and Lowe's loverly score to steer the way to that happy ending, you're left with communication skills that not only interfere with your ability to sell effectively but can also put you at risk with the law.

Alas, even Henry's bromide offers no solution. Even if Eliza became just like him, that would result in one particular woman behaving like one particular man. It doesn't allow for men and women being different from one another, within their genders. Stereotypes to the contrary, all Dicks are not alike and all Janes are not alike. There are basic personality and style traits (based on both nature and nurture) that create differences you should know about, before even attempting to enter the world of gender differences. Learning about them can begin to ease the challenges of selling to people who are different from you.

Ancient discoveries

The ancient Greeks categorized styles by four basic sets of characteristics; throughout history, social psychologists like Carl Jung have continued to research the topic and translate their findings. If you've never assessed your personality or style, you'd benefit from the discovery. Understanding about styles and how they influence the ways people communicate can build your confidence and increase your comfort level when meeting with customers, especially those who are not like you.

There are many assessment instruments available; in my career planning practice, I use the DISC Personal Concept. Like many such instruments, the DISC behavior profile offers a choice of four basic styles: D = Dominance, I = Influence, S = Steadiness, and C = Compliance. In each of you, one or two of these tends to be more dominant than the others. The DISC Personal Concept is highly accurate (95%), self-scoring—I help clients interpret the results, and reasonably priced.

NOTE: A variety of other tools is available; scoring and interpretation frequently require a trained or certified consultant. Whatever you or your organization seeks to accomplish, be sure to hire a qualified professional to administer the instrument and interpret the results.

A matter of style*

Every day you assess others based on the way they communicate with and react to you. And, they, in turn, assess you. Sometimes you meet people with whom you get along well immediately, who understand and respond positively to most of what you say. As a result, you're comfortable in their company, and look forward to seeing and even working with them again. You describe that comfort with comments like, "We are really in synch," or "We are on the same wave length," or even, "We speak the same language."

On the other hand, when you meet people who either greet your clever repartee with blank stares, or question everything you say, you start looking for the exit. And, you opt not to be saddled with their company again. Ironically, they probably feel the same way about you. "How could they?" you ask when you're so witty and garrulous, or so studied and precise. The truth is that witty and garrulous people can drive studied and precise people right up a wall, and vice versa.

Those diverse behaviors result, in part, from your different personal styles, some of which can reflect others' expectations of you. The most important thing to remember is that those differences don't make you evil, just different. The goal in helping you to identify your dominant style(s), is not to suggest that you change who you are. But, to enable you to identify different styles, respect those differences, and communicate more clearly with others—to speak their language.

* The information about the DISC Personal Concept is taken from my career planning workbook, *Exploring—finding a path to feed your soul.* Much of it is copyrighted by and used with the gracious permission of Jack Mohler, president of Jack Mohler Associates. For additional information, call Jack at 770/819-7362/7392 FAX, or write to him at Jack Mohler Associates, 1922 North Creek Drive, Austell, GA 30001.

Understanding your personal concept

One of the features I like most about the DISC Personal Concept is that it provides a three-faceted behavioral profile:

- The Private Concept, which is your self-concept, or the "real you."
- The Projected Concept, which is the mask you wear, or the behavior you want people to see.
- The Public Concept, which is the average of the other two. On a given day, it is the presumption made by others as to the "real you" based on their brief exposure to you.

The Private Concept—the real you reflects the way you behave and communicate when you are with people you know well, or when you are in the confines of your home. Or, perhaps, the way that slips out when you are under severe stress, and your Projected Concept "mask" slips. (Whenever you are under stress, you tend to default to the behavior(s) most comfortable for you.)

The Projected Concept reflects the way you believe it is appropriate for you to behave and communicate, given your family background, gender, social or economic status—whatever your influencers. It can also indicate the stress you are placing on yourself to achieve.

The Public Concept represents the interaction between your Projected Concept and your Private Concept. Your Public Concept reflects your behavior as observed by a casual acquaintance on a given day.

You play many roles in life—employee, spouse, parent, partner, offspring, sibling, sales rep, customer, etc. No doubt, you travel in and among some of these roles every day, and will many times create a different impression in each one.

That doesn't mean that you—or anyone else—go through life consciously and deliberately "faking it." Psychologists who studied people as they went from role to role found that most subjects felt they were presenting true and accurate pictures of themselves from moment to moment.

Apparently, individuals are capable of wide ranges of behavior depending on the context. They may appear dominant and powerful in one setting and weak and submissive in another. Yet, in all settings, people usually feel they are honest and authentic. In effect, we believe our own performances.

The idea that people are acting a good deal of the time may not be hard to accept. That they are acting all of the time is. Surely, there is a person behind the act, a person who is being more or less truthful about herself.

But, what is this true self? Psychologists have found this question difficult to answer. They have learned, however, that the way a person views himself—the Private Concept—is affected by the performances he puts on, and others' reactions to those performances.

It appears that these performances are prompted by a tendency for people to see themselves only through the eyes of others. That explains their strong need for social approval. If they frequently find themselves the object of disapproval, they inevitably think ill of themselves (Private Concept). To avoid this disapproval, they may behave the way they think others expect them to behave (Public Concept). When people put on performances, they often deceive themselves as well as their audiences.

If someone tries to impress others with how intelligent and cultured she is and they react favorably, she will start thinking that she is smart—even though she may previously have felt that she was not very bright. Consider our afore-mentioned Eliza Doolittle. She dressed in rags, sold flowers in the street, and "howled like an alley cat," until Professor Higgins took her under his tutelage. If we could have measured her opinion of herself the day before he began tutoring her, versus the day she appeared at the exclusive Ascot races, we'd probably see rankings at opposite ends of the scale. Dressed like royalty and speaking the king's English with grace and poise, she no doubt viewed herself as the intelligent, cultured creature she saw in others' eyes. This behavior, observed by a casual acquaintance on a given day, is called the Public Concept.

In addition, people usually try to fit their private concept and their roles together. For example, a person who sees himself as a quiet, studious type will try to find an occupation—being a librarian or a researcher—that fits that image. Then, he will act even more like a quiet, studious person because the belief is that such behavior is expected of a librarian or a researcher.

Impressions of ourselves

Why are people so interested in controlling and managing their impressions anyway? The primary motive for this kind of behavior is the need for approval. Acting in ways designed to get approval fulfills an individual's need for security and acceptance. If a person abandons her "mask," she may face exclusion from certain areas of society.

Sometimes, people feel that to fit in, it becomes necessary to maintain a "front." For instance, an employee may behave "properly" on the job, especially in front of his boss. He may smile and never complain about the workload and unrealistic deadlines in hopes of being seen as worthy of promotion.

But, the minute he leaves the office, his behavior changes. His work audience will probably never see how he behaves with close friends and associates. There is an inconsistency in his performance, and he is careful to keep the two audiences separated. In each situation, he is giving the performance he feels will gain approval from the people around him.

Impressions of others

It takes people very little time to make judgements about each other, even on the basis of limited contact. The impressions two people form of each other nevertheless influence the future of their relationship.

People tend to be sympathetic to someone who seems shy, to expect a lot from someone who impresses them as intelligent, to be curious about someone who appears deep and interesting, and to be wary of someone who strikes them as aggressive.

Forming an impression of a person is not a passive process in which certain characteristics of the individual are the input, and a certain impression is the automatic outcome. If impressions varied only when input varied, everyone meeting a particular stranger would form the same impression—which is, of course, not what happens.

One person may judge a newcomer to be "quiet," another may judge the same person as "dull," and still another may think the person "mysterious." These various impressions lead to different expectations of the newcomer, and to different patterns of interaction as well.

One reason that people develop different impressions of the same stranger is that they form their impressions on the basis of their own set of prejudiced assumptions about how people behave. Everyone has definite ideas about the behavior of others.

For example, some people tend to distrust those who talk a lot. Their bias may be that, "People who talk a lot are superficial." Others may assume that attractively dressed people are good workers. Their bias may be, "People who take care of their appearance are likely to be thorough about other things, too."

People are always making guesses, judgements, or predictions about one another on the basis of limited information. As a result, they are sometimes highly accurate, and at other times, inaccurate or completely in error. The methods used to make these judgements are generalization, stereotyping, and emphasis of certain traits.

Generalization

Judgements of others are often inaccurate because they are broad generalizations based on only a few facts. The more general the judgement, the more necessary are specific facts for the judgement to be accurate.

Judgements of an emotional state are the easiest to make. If someone approaches you shaking a fist and shouting, you can be fairly confident in judging that she is angry. If she makes a frequent habit of carrying on this way, you may judge her to be hostile or aggressive.

Aggressiveness is a trait, an enduring aspect of a person's behavior. Having judged a person as aggressive, you may predict that she is not likely to take things lying down and that she frequently gets into squabbles.

A person's behavior is a composite of all of her traits. By knowing someone's personal style—Dominance, Influence, Steadiness, or Compliance—you may feel confident in making even general judgements about her behavior. But, a little learning does not an expert make.

Stereotyping

Quite often, people categorize others on the basis of their clothes, style of speech, occupation, or other such small bits of information. Once a person has been "labeled," he is considered to have the characteristics associated with the category. This process is called stereotyping. Predictions made about this person can be seriously in error.

The errors that result from stereotypes have had widespread effects in our society. Most people have had to face being pre-judged by someone else on the basis of race, religion, or gender.

Stereotypes exist on a personal level, too. A person may, for some reason, feel that all people with black hair are romantic. Another may categorize all people who laugh easily as flighty.

Stereotyping is a way of simplifying the task of making judgements about people. This tendency to simplify causes what psychologists call the "Halo Effect." Once you've decided that a person is good, for example, it is then difficult to see anything bad about that person.

On the other hand, if you feel negatively toward someone, you may find it difficult to see any good points. This is sometimes called the "Horn Effect."

Emphasis of certain traits

Certain traits seem to weigh heavily in people's judgements of one another. For example, judging a person as warm or cold may have a significant effect on what other traits she will appear to have. One thinks quite differently about the generosity of someone who is friendly and outgoing than one does about someone who is blunt and rude.

People often make mistakes in forming impressions of others. Impressions are only educated guesses about how people are likely to behave, and they sometimes have to change as one gets to know a person better.

The biases that one uses to make judgements about people change, too, as one learns more through observing and listening. Psychologists have found that people tend to judge others with the same assumptions and categories they use to judge themselves. Therefore, the implication is that by learning more about ourselves, we can learn to judge other people more accurately.

One psychologist particularly interested in people and their behaviors was Dr. William Marsten. While at Columbia University, he developed a system of identifying and categorizing these behaviors, labeling it his four-factor theory.

He concluded that there were two sets of factors which interact to determine behavior: the environment itself and the way people respond to the environment.

Marsten believed that people exist in either a favorable or an unfavorable environment. (Since a neutral environment does not work actively against you, he classified it as favorable.)

Within their environments, people can react in one of two ways: they can be active or passive. To allow for degrees of behavior, Marsten represented the environment as a continuum, from extremely unfavorable to highly favorable. People's responses to those environments are also represented as a continuum, from highly active to extremely passive.

Combining the ranges of these two factors resulted in his developing a diagram of four basic kinds of styles. You can behave actively in either a favorable or an unfavorable environment. Or, you can behave passively in a favorable or an unfavorable environment. The four environments are illustrated in Figure 1 on the next page.

FIGURE 1, Marsten's Four-Factor Behavioral Model

(ACTIVE)

INTENT: TO CONQUER DOMINANCE	INTENT: TO PERSUADE INFLUENCE
INTENT: TO AVOID TROUBLE COMPLIANCE	INTENT: TO BE SUPPORTIVE STEADINESS

(PASSIVE)

Understanding the behaviors

In the upper left-hand quadrant, the environment is unfavorable, or antagonistic, and the behavior of the person in that environment is active. Her goal is to overcome, or provide "Dominance" in this environment, and this behavior refers to the D in DISC.

In the upper right-hand quadrant, the environment is favorable, and the behavior of the person in that environment is active. His goal is to persuade or provide "Influence" in this environment, and this behavior refers to the I in DISC.

In the lower right-hand quadrant, the environment is favorable, and the behavior of the person in that environment is passive. Her goal is to be supportive or provide "Steadiness" in this environment, and this behavior refers to the S in DISC.

In the lower left-hand quadrant, the environment is unfavorable, and the behavior of the person in that environment is passive. His goal is to conform, or provide "Compliance" in this environment, and this behavior refers to the C in DISC.

Most people have strengths in two of the quadrants. By now, you can probably tell that people exhibiting high S or high C behaviors could have a terrible time communicating with people who exhibit high D or high I behaviors (and, vice versa). Unless both learn to understand and value their differences, and make adjustment in the ways they communicate, they might as well be speaking different languages to each other.

By now, you may be saying, "But, I can behave any number of ways, based on the situation, the people, etc." That is true. You are all interesting and different mixes of behaviors from all four quadrants. But, you all also have preferred styles and it's helpful to:

- recognize what they are (quirks and all),
- understand how others may view them and you, and
- determine how to deal most effectively with those whose styles differ from yours.

Please be assured that no one is telling you that you're not okay or that you need to change. That is your decision. Part of the learning, however, is being honest with how others perceive you.

If you prefer not to be perceived that way, you can look at your behaviors, and make a conscious effort to mollify or change them. But, don't expect to change overnight. Your behavior was pretty well set before you entered first grade, so only deliberate, conscious effort is going to alter your style.

One colleague of mine, who is a wonderful person and a fine manager, was horrified that his behavior ranked so high in the D quadrant. He actually cared quite a bit about the people he managed, and wanted to come across to them in a more supportive, caring way.

Because he tried so hard, he narrowly lowered his D score. Not enough to satisfy him, however, which wasn't surprising. People in the high D quadrant are not known for their great patience and low satisfaction levels. Jeff was a quick decision maker with excellent leadership qualities. He had been a Green Beret in Vietnam, and High D decision making was called for in the kinds of stress and trauma he experienced on a daily basis.

Despite his efforts, he wasn't going to convert himself to another quadrant. What I think he finally realized was that that was okay. What's important is being conscious of our behaviors, and becoming flexible enough to adjust our styles to those of our audiences.

Let's talk in more detail about each quadrant. As was mentioned, there are ranges of behavior within each. The High-D person is a self-starter who thrives on both challenge and competition. She is usually direct, positive, and straight-forward. She tells it like it is, sometimes bluntly. She likes to be center stage and in charge. She fights hard for what she thinks is the way to go, but can accept momentary defeat and is not a grudge-holder.

High-D people prefer variety, the unusual, the adventurous. They are apt to lose interest if they feel a job becoming routine, so they must be kept constantly involved. A High-D person is prone to making job changes, especially early in her career, until the right challenge is found. She is self-sufficient and an individualist. Demanding of self and others, she is discontented and dissatisfied with the status quo.

The High-I person is outgoing, persuasive, and gregarious. He strives to make his opinions and beliefs prevail. He is very comfortable in one-on-one situations, with an outgoing nature that typifies the image of the "natural salesperson."

His basic interest is in people. The High-I person is poised and meets strangers easily. People tend to respond to him naturally.

Because of an inherent trust and willing acceptance of people, he may sometimes misjudge their intentions and abilities. High-I people are easily met, name-dropping conversationalists, who sell themselves well. They are friendly competitors and optimistic managers. They are fashionable dressers who join organizations for prestige and personal recognition. They usually have a wide range of acquaintances, and get along well with others because of their innate optimism and people skills.

The High-S person is usually amiable, easy-going, and relaxed. She is warm-hearted, home-loving, and neighborly. She tends to be undemonstrative and controlled, concealing feelings from others, and is apt to be a grudge-holder. Most of the time, she is even-tempered, low-key, and unobtrusive. She is complacent, prone to leniency, and emotionally mature.

The High-S person strives to keep things the way they are, and dislikes change. Once underway, she works steadily and patiently. She dislikes urgency and the pressure of deadlines. She is usually very possessive and develops strong attachments for things, family, and departments. While High-S people seldom argue or openly criticize, they can quietly resist and slow things down. They are passive resisters, if they care to resist at all.

The High-C person proceeds in an orderly way. The methods he uses are usually predetermined and he is precise and attentive to detail. High-C people strive for a neat, orderly existence, and tend to follow traditional procedures and established systems. They prefer to adapt to situations to avoid conflict and antagonism. The need for self-preservation causes them to document everything they do. If the "book" calls for it, then it is fine.

The High-C person is naturally cautious, conservative, and tentative in decision-making. He prefers to wait to see which way the wind is blowing. Once his mind is made up, however, he can be very rigid. He tries to be what you want him to be. He tries very hard to avoid conflict and stepping on toes. The High-C person is usually reserved, conservative, adaptable, open-minded (up to a point), and diplomatic.

Probable strengths

Every style has probable strengths and possible weaknesses. Most of us are better served if we capitalize on our strengths, while not allowing ourselves to be consumed by our weaknesses. Areas of probable strengths include:

High-D—Probable Strengths
The High-D person will usually be:

positive	self-reliant	aggressive	pioneering
courageous	competitive	results-oriented	hard-driving

High-I—Probable Strengths
The High-I person will usually be:

a good mixer	optimistic	enthusiastic	outgoing
persuasive	eloquent	perhaps charismatic	

High-S—Probable Strengths
The High-S person will usually be:

predictable	consistent	relaxed	considerate
loyal	accommodating	generally self-controlled	

High-C—Probable Strengths
The High-C person will usually be:

agreeable	cooperative	thorough	adaptable
conscientious	precise	well-disciplined	frequently perfectionistic

Possible weaknesses
There is no perfect person; each of us has possible weaknesses. Unfortunately, what we perceive as strengths in ourselves, others may perceive as weaknesses. By better understanding ourselves, we can capitalize more fully on our strengths and minimize our weaknesses. Areas of possible weaknesses include:

High-D—Possible Weaknesses
The High-D person may at times:

overstep authority	take chances	be egotistical	resent restrictions
be too demanding	take on too much	shoot from the hip	be inattentive to detail
stir up trouble	become dissatisfied with routine work		

High-I—Possible Weaknesses
The High-I person may at times:

over-sell	talk too much	misjudge capabilities	act impulsively
trust people too much	appear superficial	jump to conclusions	
be too concerned with being popular		waste too much time in people dealings	
over-estimate results of projects		over-commit in setting objectives	

High-S—Possible Weaknesses

The High-S person may at times:

resist change	try to keep things the way they are	move too slowly
be too lenient	have trouble meeting deadlines	delay starting new projects
be possessive	put off making decisions	hold a grudge
wait for orders before acting	be too patient with mediocre performance	

High-C—Possible Weaknesses

The High-C person may at times:

pass the buck	get bogged down in details	need too much guidance
be defensive when pressured	be a nit-picker	be a tentative decision-maker
resist full responsibility	cooperate to avoid controversy	not act without precedent
spend too much time checking and re-checking		be too dependent on "rules"

As we build our careers, we usually look for the kinds of work and work environments that support our personal types. Let's consider what aspects of a position might best match the different types.

High-D positions demand:

getting results	accepting challenges	making decisions
expediting action	reducing costs	solving problems

High-I positions demand:

contacting people	motivating others	helping people
exhibiting poise	generating enthusiasm	speaking well

High-S positions demand:

exhibiting patience	developing special skills	performing to standards
using concentration	staying in one place	being loyal

High-C positions demand:

following directions	concentrating on details	being diplomatic
adhering to procedures	avoiding trouble	controlling quality

A Note of Caution: Our society loves to categorize people into boxes with the mistaken notion that it increases understanding. This information was included to expand your thinking. The opposite will occur if you use personalities as just one more way to stereotype people.

Back to Dick & Jane communication

Personal style is just one of the filters we use to gauge our opinion of others. Returning to Dick and Jane, we'll address the issue of gender differences. Men and women are different; they differ not only in their biology, but also in their thinking, their behavior, and their speech.

There's that word again—different, a seemingly neutral characterization that slanders no one, nor declares anyone better or worse than another. But, different from what? To evaluate anything, including a gender or a culture, you have to measure it against a specific standard.

In the United States, that standard has typically been the white Anglo-Saxon male. That became the benchmark for classifying "normal" behavior, effectively labeling every non-white-male behavior as "abnormal," or at least "substandard." Because that practice was imbedded in the culture, it gave rise to another standard, that of the "reasonable man." For centuries, society, which includes the court system, has made judgements on behavior based on what it believes a "reasonable man" would think or do.

Only through the directed efforts of women and men who realized that, at the very least, that benchmark could not be applied to women, did the notion of a "reasonable woman" evolve. Substantial case law, in particular involving assault and sexual harassment, has now been built around that concept.

This is not to say that the "reasonable man" idea is wrong, but that it applies only to the "reasonable men" who created it. It is not valid for other populations. My purpose in providing this information is not to make white males feel further intimidated. (I have two sons who sometimes feel they represent an endangered species.) Rather, it is to lay a foundation for understanding why basic differences, including gender, create different expectations, assessments, and reactions.

When we compare women, or any other dissimilar population to a white male standard, we are judging them against a standard contrary to their very nature. Why should you care? For several reasons, including,

Customers—

You won't always be selling to people who look and think and speak the way you do. But, they will be buying from somebody.

Wouldn't you prefer that they buy from you, rather than your competition? Your company probably does. To sell successfully to any customer, you'll need to communicate effectively with them. When you find that the other person is not speaking your language, and you criticize that person for not thinking and responding the way you would, you're sabotaging your own goals.

On the other hand, if you can tune into and meet a customer's needs, and provide the necessary follow-up (translate: service) regardless of how different that customer may be from you, you'll increase your success in sales. Remember, the register doesn't ring until the deal is done. And, it doesn't keep ringing unless the need for service is continuously satisfied. Studies show that customers value service even more than price, because most of the time, good service saves them money.

Evolution of personal selling—

Push Emphasis—In the beginning, there was the product. Salespeople sold products by convincing as many people as possible to buy their products. Then they disappeared until the next sales call.

Marketing Emphasis—In the mid-50's, the approach started to shift from a product orientation to a customer orientation. Sales energy was directed toward identifying the needs and wants of target markets and focusing on delivering based on those wants and needs.

Consultative Selling Emphasis—In the late 60's to early 70's, the salesperson further supported the customer by analyzing problems and needs and making recommendations. Markets, too, evolved, with the development of target markets.

Strategic Selling Emphasis—In the early 80's, the selling environment became more complex. An increased focus on niche markets created the need for more planning.

Partnering Emphasis—In the early 90's, the core emphasis targets partnering. That means building long-term, high-quality partnerships—with each customer, that result in repeat business and referrals. Proponents like Tom Peters and Ron Zemke popularized the term "lifetime customer," reflecting the value of listening to the customer. But, if we're functioning from an underdeveloped understanding of the customer, how valuable is the information we're hearing? And how do we best the competition?

CASE HISTORY

Lucille Treganowen, owner of Transmissions by Lucille, and author of Lucille's Car Care *practiced partnering with customers long before the term came into popular use. To demonstrate her respect for customers' concerns, she would ride with a customer in his or her car to determine why the "thing-a-magig" was going "whackety-whack." Even if the culprit were not the transmission, she wanted the customer to get an accurate diagnosis of the problem. Lucille knows that that customer has the potential to tell hundreds of people about her company, and she wants it to be positive.*

CASE HISTORY

Harvey Mackay, owner of Mackay Envelope and author of several books including, Swim with the Sharks without Being Eaten Alive, *employs his list of "66 things you ought to know about your customer," to build lifetime customers. As Ken Blanchard puts it in that book's forward, "Harvey knows more about his customers than they know about themselves...and certainly more than the competition does!"*

Legal Issues, Fines & Job Loss—Title VII of the Civil Rights Act of 1964 forbids discrimination on the basis of color, creed, sex, religion, and national origin. (Actually, the word, "sex" was added as a joke by a member of Congress who did not support the bill and believed it would never pass.) In 1972, an amendment was added explicitly prohibiting sexual harassment. In 1988, court decisions extended coverage to include homosexuals and heterosexual men. Also added was harassment by co-workers, non-employees, and third parties.

Prior to that time, most cases targeted supervisors and managers because they held bay over hiring and promotion decisions and are most directly responsible for providing employees with a safe work environment. In recent cases, managers who have been found guilty of sexual harassment have been fined personally; even senior level managers, including CEOs have been fined and fired.

Definitions

Sexism: A set of attitudes and beliefs that one sex is superior to another.

Sex Discrimination: Treating employees differently and making employment decisions based on sex, rather than on qualifications and experience.

Sexual Harassment: Unwelcome behavior of a sexual nature.

This is where the concept of the "reasonable woman" is supported by case law. In 1991, the U.S. Court of Appeals for the Ninth District ruled "that the question of harassment must be viewed from the perspective of a reasonable woman rather than a reasonable person." It further stated that women who experience mild forms of sexual harassment may understandably worry and in fact view harassment as merely a prelude to further, more violent behavior. That ruling substantiates the reality that sexual harassment is a crime of power, not passion.

Two key tenets of the law are *quid pro quo* and "hostile environment."

Quid pro quo is Latin for "this for that," and describes harassment that hinges a hiring, job retention, or promotion decision on the performance of sexual favors.

"Hostile environment" describes sexual conduct that unreasonably interferes with an individual's job performance or creates an intimidating, hostile, or offensive work environment.

CASE HISTORY

As stated above, sexual harassment can involve non-employees harassing employees. The owner of a small business hired a consultant to provide some team building for his employees. In the course of conducting the training, the female consultant made some sexual remarks to one of the male participants and patted him on the behind. He told her that made him uncomfortable and asked her to stop. On the second day of training, however, she persisted in her offensive behavior. His next step was to sue the company. Rather than suffer through a public trial, the owner settled with the employee out of court.

Sexual Harassment—is it or isn't it?

If you're uncertain about whether or not your contemplated action or comment could be viewed as sexual harassment—or another form of discrimination, consider this:

If you wouldn't do it, say it, act on it, hang the poster, tell the joke, show the magazine to your son, daughter, sister, brother, spouse, significant other,

Or

If you wouldn't want someone else to say or do it to the people you care about, would you still say it/do it?

My sons and my daughter and I have had interesting discussions around this topic. I believe it has been a worthwhile exchange; I've learned a lot. And, that is what all reasonable people deserve to have:

sufficient, ongoing, relevant information that fosters learning and expands understanding of themselves and others.

One research study established the common characteristics of top salespeople as being, "nice." That is, they possessed "self-respect, consideration and respect for others, courtesy, and manners..." Collaboration beats conflict every time. That's the goal of every sales effort, isn't it? Solid collaboration between salesperson and customer; establishment of mutual respect; open exchange of information; creation of the win/win.

The power of networking—In today's marketplace, where people change jobs more frequently, where companies constantly buy and sell other companies, you are bound to encounter familiar faces in new places. That's an enormous plus if they know you bring a solid reputation, as well as an interest in their needs and quality products to fill those needs.

That means not letting your testosterone or estrogen do the talking.

CASE HISTORY

Jane is in sales with a major, New York advertising agency. Leaving a restaurant one night, after taking clients out for drinks, she and five other members of her sales team—all male—spotted three tall, very beautiful, "model-looking" women walking down the street. They wore micro-mini dresses with no bras. Jane's fellow sales reps made various remarks like: "I could do her," and "Bend over, baby & let me drive."

"I felt myself getting smaller and smaller, like the woman in that public service announcement on sexual harassment," Jane recalled. "I called them all (including her boss) pigs, told them to tuck it in & zip it up," said I was going home and left. One of the Dicks came after her cajoling that, "Boys will be boys." "Yes," Jane responded, "but not around me—you wouldn't do that in front of your sister."

"The best part," Jane continued, "was in the sales meeting next morning, when the national sales manager who hadn't even been with them the previous evening, came in and said, "Heard you guys got a little action last night." That pretty much erased her manager's earlier apology.

Jane knew she needed to address the situation, but she cooled off first, and planned her words carefully. Meeting with her manager a few days later, she clearly explained how the incident had made her feel degraded and isolated. "When I realized that I was going to be the only woman on the sales team, I realized there would be some concessions I'd have to make," she explained, "and I have. But just because I was the only woman, didn't mean that my breasts had shriveled up and fallen off and that I had grown a penis. I would appreciate that being remembered.

"At first, I thought he was going to fall over & die. He looked shocked and then he laughed. I needed to express the severity of the incident to him, so I purposely & purposefully chose strong language like that," she added.

"It's hormonal, Jane says, "but you have to consider who's around you when you're doing it." On the whole, she has a relatively healthy relationship with everyone on the team. "I'm at the point where I'm comfortable enough in myself that I'm not going to run into the bathroom and cry— or want to rip somebody's face off...but I have no inclination to be tolerant about that stuff. It's been a real lesson for me in a lot of ways."

"Subsequently, I've heard what a female watcher he is," Jane continues, "he almost got hit by a car once," she chuckles, "as he and a male colleague were crossing the street. But never once, in two-plus years, has anything even remotely similar happened."

Fortunately for both of them, they'd had a good relationship since they started working together. Otherwise, Jane may have filed a lawsuit against the four team members, her boss, the national sales manager, and the company. They could all have lost their homes as well as their jobs. Getting your company sued doesn't bode well for job retention.

Does this mean you should be afraid to open your mouth because anything you say could be construed to be offensive at least and illegal at worst? Not at all. It means that you need to understand and respect others' sensitivities and always act professionally. Your best defense against any kind of accused impropriety is your reputation.

If your behavior is beyond question, then bosses, colleagues and customers would be more inclined to doubt any accusation. If, however, you're known for spewing double entendres, ogling the other gender with lewd stares, telling "dirty" or sexist/racist jokes, you are putting your job at risk. Others may tolerate or even seem to enjoy your behavior, but *they won't put their jobs or finances on the line for you. You are setting yourself up for a fall.*

Why Dick & Jane cross communicate

This chapter shares the name of a series of communication programs I created to enable my clients to simplify their communication processes, and to enable men and women to understand and communicate with one another in a more direct, more dignified manner.

I called it "Dick & Jane Communication" because I wanted to challenge the gender mystique as well as simplify the process. After all, there wasn't much margin for error in interpreting, "See Spot run." While many of our conversations cover more complex topics, we can still strive to build a better foundation for understanding one another.

That includes recognizing that there are basic linguistic (verbal) and behavioral (non-verbal) differences between men & women that contribute to the sometimes humorous, but often frustrating ways we miscommunicate, especially in a business setting. As a matter of fact, many of the problems come from forgetting that you're in a business setting.

Example: Dick the sales rep finds it annoying when he asks Jane the supervisor about her department's needs and she acts vague and coy. Dick really wants her company as an account, but how does he accomplish that if he can't get a clear picture of product usage and potential need?

Example: Jane the sales rep feels insulted when Dick the purchasing agent is more interested in her personal life than in her product presentation.

What's frustrating for sales pros like Dick & Jane, is that they were trained to—or figured out how to be professional sales people. Not everyone gets that level of training, including how to deal with customers of the opposite gender. Rather, females grew up being trained to treat men like dates, mates, dads, brothers, and uncles. And, men became accustomed to treating women like wives, lovers, sisters, mothers and aunts. Neither gender was educated to treat the other like competent, professional adults in a business setting.

How Dick can improve his communication skills

Interrupt Less and Listen More—Men interrupt conversations more than women do, and they interrupt women twice as much as they interrupt other men. Throughout their lives they've been encouraged to speak more than females have, so they actively seek to have the floor as much as they can.

Listen to customers more. Ask them questions, be quiet and listen. Show that you think what they are saying is valuable. Digest what is being said, and make notes about how you can help those customers. As the salesperson, you're the interviewer, so you should be doing only 20-30% of the talking.

Avoid Condescension—This includes vocabulary as well as attitude. And, if you don't think words are important, ask yourself why advertisers spend billions of dollars each year, finding just the right ones to describe their products' benefits.

Don't use the Seven Deadly Sexist Words: dear, honey, sweetie, sugar, girl, chick, and broad.

Why? Because none of those words connotes a competent, professional, female adult. And, some women feel as offended by them as an African American would be by a racial slur.

While there are some females who may not find those words offensive, you won't insult any adult female by referring to her as a woman. If you're not sure how she prefers to be addressed (Jane, Ms/Miss/Mrs Jones), ASK!

Treat customers with dignity and courtesy—When Dick treats Jane with courtesy and professionalism, he's creating a positive image for both of them. He'll also be bucking what her stereotype may be about salesmen. Trust me, she's met some winners! He'll single himself out as someone who understands today's marketplace employs a variety of people. He'll have a better shot at earning her respect and trust—not to mention making the sale!

CASE HISTORY

A colleague of mine was getting prices on new windows for her home. When she asked one of the contractors she was considering a question, he called her "dear," and answered her as if she should have already known the answer. The sales call went downhill from there:

> Jane: *Please don't call me "dear."*
> Dick: *I was just trying to be friendly.*

247

Jane: *Using "Jane" would be friendly; using "dear" is familiar. And I asked the question because this kind of purchase is new for me. I need to work with someone who can respect that, and I don't believe you do.*

Dick was not thrilled with the outcome, so I doubt he realized Jane had actually done him a favor. Not everyone will tell you you've been offensive. They just won't buy from you. That won't, however, prevent them from telling everyone they come in contact with why they shouldn't buy from you. How much potential business did that contractor lose, besides the sale of 25 windows (some custom-sized) to Jane? Think of the referrals she could have provided.

Don't presume the female customer knows nothing about her product/service needs. What she does know is what works or doesn't work in her department, and if you ask the right questions, you will soon know, too. She may even start trusting you and asking your advice about different product features or possibilities. After all, what is the goal? For you to let her know how much you know, or for you to find out how you can best help her make the best decisions for herself and her department?

Don't view the beautiful female customer as an air head. Much of the previous statement applies here, too. I promise you that whether she's a nuclear scientist or not, she will appreciate your treating her with respect and dignity, and you'll have a better chance at becoming a regular vendor.

Don't assume the woman who answers the phone—or is sitting at the secretary's desk—is the secretary and/or immaterial to the process.

CASE HISTORY

Dick recounts seeing other sales reps blow a deal before it has a chance to develop by assuming that the woman at the front desk is insignificant to the sales process. At the very least, she is the linch pin who can decide if and when you get to meet with her boss. More often than not, she is someone on whom her manager relies for a reading on whom is worth meeting.

Surprise, surprise, sometimes she even is the boss— who stopped to answer the phone or look for a file in her secretary's absence. (Women managers are more prone to doing that than their male counterparts.)

Capitalize on the Customer's Knowledge and Experience. You are there to ask questions about customer need, not expound on how much you know. Your knowledge about your products will prove beneficial to the customer only after you discover which benefits are most valuable to her. And, if she's resistant to your sales pitch, you can try pulling on her expertise to win her over.

CASE HISTORY

Dick was new to sales and had the added joy of taking on a territory where his predecessor had made few friends. As if converting unhappy people to satisfied customers wasn't enough of a challenge, one of the women he called on thought he was too young and inexperienced to understand her facility's needs.

Did Dick deal with his frustration by writing her off? Not a chance! He preferred to convert his toughest critic into a mentor. By seeking her advice, Dick capitalized on her expertise. Every time he gets a new or re-designed product to sell, he meets with Jane to get her reading on its practicality and usefulness. "Now," Dick beams, "I have a clinician's view, instead of just a product brochure." He knows that he's not the only one in his territory selling to the medical community; Jane's insights frequently give him an edge over the competition.

How Jane can improve her communication skills:

Be more assertive and less tentative. Females historically have been taught to be more quiet and less direct than men in expressing themselves. Such an approach gives Dick the customer the impression that you don't know enough about your product and how it could benefit him and his organization. Or, that you aren't convinced it's as good as you'd like him to believe. Such behavior diminishes your influence and credibility.

Reduce the use of intensifiers. Women tend to use more intensifiers than men when describing features and benefits.

Example: This widget is very, very durable.

Instead, find some statistics that support your claim; get some evidence. Then, consider using something like these samples.

Example: This widget is 15% more durable than our previous model.

or

Example: This widget is 15% more durable than the 10 other models we tested.

You may even have a synopsis sheet that describes the testing. And, you can connect that product feature to a client benefit.

Feature: Our company has increased the durability of this widget by 15%.

Benefit: That means a 20% less chance of downtime on your equipment.

Eliminate qualifiers. Women demean the value of what they're saying by using phrases like:

Example: This may not be the best solution to your problem, but how about trying...

Example: I know I'm not as familiar with the situation as you are, but could you...

Example: This may not do exactly what you want, but...

If you don't think much of your solution or ideas, why should anybody else? Instead, just offer some suggestions and get some feedback.

STOP attacking and start supporting other Janes—anywhere, any time. In every survey that I've done with my audiences, one of the biggest complaints they (both Dick and Jane) voice about working with women is: Women can't get along with other women—they're mean and catty to each other.

I've heard women criticize other women about everything from their hair and their clothes to their homes and their cars. You will never hear a man cut down other men the way women can cut down other women. They may think it, but they won't say it—not in front of women, anyway. They may kid or tease one another about hair, clothes, houses, and cars; but, they'll do it directly to that other man—not behind his back.

When you denigrate other women, you denigrate yourself. What do you think it sounds like to others? It makes other women wonder what you'll say about them when they're not around. It reinforces to men that women can't act interact professionally with one another. And, it makes everyone hesitant to trust you.

CASE HISTORY

During the suffrage movement, some of the northern white women were afraid of losing the support of some of the southern white women if they insisted on including black women. That split in the ranks delayed the passage of the nineteenth amendment by at least a decade. A defeat for one of us is a defeat for all of us.

But women like Alice Paul—whom southern politicians labeled, "dangerous," recruited a cross section of women to lobby in Washington, D.C., creating what was described as an uneasy truce. Working together, they succeeded in getting the amendment passed. A victory for one of us is a victory for all of us.

Show thinking as well as feeling.

The other top complaint evidenced on my audience surveys is that: **Women are too emotional.** There is nothing wrong with having emotions. And, I'm not suggesting that you become something you're not. But, if you lead with you're emotions, and only your emotions, all your customers will see is the stereotype.

If you tend to lead with your emotions, learn to balance your behavior. Practicing thinking before acting. It won't change who you are; it will just give you better equilibrium. It can also keep you from doing things you'll regret.

CASE HISTORY

Dick and Jane were financial planners working for Company A. Dick had seniority and a nice office. Jane was newer to the organization; her office was tiny and somewhat uncomfortable. After Dick left to join Company B, Jane was given the office he had vacated.

Things didn't work out the way Dick had hoped, so after a few months, he decided to return to Company A. Feeling sorry about Dick's misadventure, Jane leaped in to lend support by giving him "his" office back.

By the time she realized what she had done, it was too late to rescind the offer. To make matters worse, someone else was already using her former office, so she was relegated to a cubicle. Not only would a man not have made that offer, it would also never have occurred to him to do it.

Nor should it have. Dick is an adult who made a

career choice, saw it was a wrong move for him, and had the guts to return to his former employer. He was to be congratulated for taking a risk, not pitied for making a mistake. He didn't need to be rescued. Empathizing with colleagues you care about is natural. Just learn to keep your mouth closed until your brain kicks in. Then you won't have to feel like you starred in your own version of "Dumb and Dumber."

Be aware of your body language. Women have been trained to be nurturers, even in conversation. That means using silent gestures, like nodding, and making little remarks like oh, uh huh, tell me more, to encourage the speaker. And, exhibiting other body language like heavy eye contact and head tilting. Interestingly enough, these behaviors are more prevalent in mixed-sex groups, casting you in the role of listener, because you must not have anything important to say.

Instead, think about what you can add to the conversation and look for opportunities to enter it. That's the only way you'll be heard. If you are uncomfortable with doing that, take an assertiveness training course. It will help you build valuable skills.

The goal is to make peace, not war. Such a course can teach you how to:

- Confront others positively
- Wait until you cool off before acting
- Evaluate the relationship and choose the appropriate vocabulary
- Be direct & unemotional
- Not get sucked into the mud!

What Dick & Jane should know about diversity

According to an excellent diversity video* that I've used in supervisory classes, there are six key reasons to value diversity:

- Demographics—more women, minorities, and immigrants in the workforce. The fastest growing populations in the United States are Hispanic and Asian.
- Changing marketplace—a global economy means diverse customers.
- Challenge of Change—as organizations merge or re-engineer

*The Mosaic Workplace (1990, Films for the Humanities & Sciences, Inc., Princeton, NJ. There is now an updated version.)

themselves, they can benefit from a cross-section of outlooks and perspectives.
- Creativity and Innovation—different cultures contribute a greater variety of ideas.
- Good Business—there's money to be spent.
- Survival—in a global marketplace, understanding and respecting diversity is vital for staying in business.

The odds are that you will need to communicate effectively with a mosaic of customers, suppliers, colleagues, and even bosses. So if you want to be a success, you'll learn how to board the diversity bus and ride it with ease and comfort.

A personal note: Our goal is for *Sales Coach* to be an asset to you as you pursue your career. I wish you joy and prosperity—and fun in all your adventures.

About Anne Louise Conlon Feeny

Anne Louise loves helping clients build their communication and management skills and create career paths that feed their souls. "It seemed like an odd combination at first, even to me, " she admits.

"I began as a free-lance writer, creating PR and marketing pieces for clients— and writing a ton of resumes. After I completed my Master's in Human Resources Management, clients asked me to design and deliver training in business communication skills.

"I started teaching (college) management courses, too. A fellow adjunct linked me with his new employer, an outplacement firm. What made me attractive to them was all that resume writing and training I had done. And, that I had survived being outplaced three times myself.

"During the mid-80's, I traveled the country, working with almost every major manufacturer who was downsizing. Seminars focused on job search strategies, including networking, identifying skills and marketing one's accomplishments — all communication-based skills.

"I saw these seemingly separate paths converge in ways that made perfect sense." Her clients (government, insurance, banking, hospitality, education, community and professional associations) agree.

ALB Associates/ADHOC Human Resources Consulting

Pittsburgh Office: 6529 Brighton Rd., Suite 3300, Pittsburgh, PA 15202-2111; Telephone: 412-761-6268, Fax: 412-761-6368

New York Office: 155 East 30th Street, Suite 11A, New York, NY 10016; Telephone: 212-481-8529

Company profile
Program titles for seminars, keynotes, and consulting services

Dick and Jane Communication ®—
Avoid communication backlash by learning how to speak with and be understood by the opposite sex.

Dick and Jane Business Writing ®— Get one-on-one coaching.

Dick and Jane Business Presentation ®—Get one-on-one coaching

I thought We Spoke the Same Language — Recognize four contrasting styles and develop the skills to deal more effectively with the other three.

Exploring Career/Life Choices — Identify Personal Influencing Factors and stop sabotaging yourself.

Building Tangents, Not Ladders — Steer a course using a new career model.

The Mentor in the Mirror—Master strategies for managing your career in an ever-changing marketplace.

Inspire Yourself—the Power of One!— Re-energize your commitment to achieving your dreams!

Rightfitting*— Effect strategies that enable your business to determine the workforce it needs to meet organizational goals.

Hire the Right Match*— Implement hiring and recruiting systems that build your business's competitiveness and profitability.

The Super Supervisor: The 12% Solution— Use the tools and strategies that support your toughest job: getting things done effectively through others.

* These programs are typically consulting projects.

Chapter 10

How Customer Service Relates to Sales
A CASE STUDY

by Sandie Akerman

In order for your organization to succeed in the sales arena, your people must believe customer service is everyone's job.

—Sandie Akerman

What does customer service have to do with sales? Are the two mutually exclusive? Or...are the two one in the same? We will be exploring these questions in this chapter. By the end of this chapter, you will have a better understanding of the relationship that customer service has to sales and what role you play in that relationship.

In many organizations, customer service and sales are under different management umbrellas. The processes are unrelated. If we strip sales and customer service down to the lowest level and define what purpose they serve, we will find that there is a common denominator...the CUSTOMER.

Let's start by defining the purpose of each of these functions. What is the definition of sales? There have been many books written on this subject. They all basically agree that selling is providing the customer with what the customer wants and/or needs.

What is customer service? Again, many books have been written on the subject of customer service. One characteristic they have in common is the essence of what customer service is...it is providing the customer with what the customer wants and/or needs. Satisfying customers' wants and needs may come in the form of solving a problem, providing them with information or giving them extra value. Sound familiar?

Why is it then that so many organizations view customer service and sales differently? As you can see, when we strip these two functions down to the basic definitions, they are not mutually exclusive but are the same. It is like the front and back of your hand, you can't have one without the other.

Remember the ancient question, "which came first the chicken or the egg?" The answer to that question is usually, "it depends on the situation." The same is true for customer service and selling. Which comes first? It depends on the situation.

Most businesses exist to provide a customer with an ongoing product or service. Therefore, a need exists to insure that the customer is taken care of in a positive manner. We want to make sure that customers will come back to us the next time they have a need for that product or service. Just as importantly, we want them to recommend us to others who may have that same need. If we are doing our job properly in the sales and service areas there is a stronger likelihood that additional sales and referrals from customers will occur.

In this chapter, we are going to explore the elements of both the customer service and sales processes and see how difficult it is to see where one stops and the other one begins. In this time of increased competition, customers are expecting more from their sales/customer service representatives than ever before. They aren't looking for a representative that is just trying to provide them with a product or service.

As Linda Blackman says in her chapter on Presentational Selling™, a company representative is "always selling product, concept, service or self." What customers want is a representative who will understand their wants and needs, whether personal or business, and who will provide them with excellent service. Customers want to buy and be served by a representative that recognizes the importance of building and maintaining relationships.

COMPARISON OF SALES TO CUSTOMER SERVICE

Element	Sales Process	Customer Service Process
Setting the stage	Opening the process—getting to know customers	Greeting customers putting customers at ease and letting them know that you are there
Uncovering the need	Probing/asking customers questions to uncover the want or need.	Asking questions—finding out what kind of service customers need.
Showing how you can meet the need	Presenting/explaining to customers, based on their needs, what products and services you have to meet those needs.	Explaining how you can help–sharing with customers what you can do to satisfy their want or need, solve their problem or provide them with the extra value they desire.
Concluding the interaction	Closing/asking customers for the opportunity to do business with them.	Wrapping up the conversation–checking with customers to make sure that you have taken care of their issue and bringing the interaction to a positive conclusion.
Answering objections	Overcoming objections–asking questions to uncover the area that requires more clarification or justification.	Providing customers with additional information needed to satisfy their service need.

As you can see from the chart, on the surface strong similarities exist in each element. The similarities exist primarily in the way a sales person or customer service representative interacts with the prospect or customer. Prospects or customers enjoy feeling as though their transaction is the most important business we will conduct. They need to know that whether we are selling or servicing, we recognize that the constant theme is making people feel important through knowing their wants and/or needs have been met.

Prospects and customers want to be treated individually, want their needs to be understood, and want to receive extra value. As representatives for our organizations, we create that atmosphere by treating each person as an individual, giving them our complete attention, letting them know we believe they deserve our time and attention, and providing them extra value every chance we get. Anne Louise Conlon Feeny, in her chapter, "Dick & Jane Communications," shared that "you won't always be selling to people who look and think and speak the way you do. To sell successfully to any customer, you'll need to communicate effectively with them."

The major difference in these two processes is the timing...*when* the process occurs. In the sales process, the goal is to begin building a relationship with our prospects and selling them a product or service that meets their wants or needs. After the sale is concluded, we need to focus on maintaining and expanding the relationship. According to marketing expert, Mary Maloney Cronin, each employee promotes good public relations by creating relationships with each customer. Customer service is taking care of the customer after the sale is made, setting the stage so a future sale can be made, and/or obtaining referrals.

Instant Opportunity

Think about the places that you go to buy something or receive service . Consider the whole experience from the moment you enter the door until you leave. Every interaction you have while you are there either supports the desire to continue doing business with this organization or puts a question in your mind as to whether or not you will return. With each interaction that you have as a customer and, in turn, your customer has with you, there is an opportunity to keep a customer for life or possibly lose them forever.

Customers are no longer as loyal as they used to be, and they are smarter. If you don't take care of them the way they want to be treated, they will keep looking until they find someone who will provide that

level of service. Each customer interaction provides you with an Instant Opportunity to keep the customer for another sales opportunity or send them to your competition. Perhaps the best way to understand an Instant Opportunity is to look at a case study. While I am sharing this example with you, see how many Instant Opportunities you can identify.

CASE STUDY

Carol, an associate of mine, and I went on a business trip to Philadelphia during the coldest part of the winter. The client for whom we were providing customer service training had taken care of making reservations for us at a hotel in the downtown area near their location. We arrived late in the day. As every interaction begins at a hotel, we proceeded to the registration desk.

There we were approached by a hotel clerk who asked us for our names. She located the information about our reservations and proceeded with the check-in process. After we had provided our credit card information and signatures on the registration cards, the clerk handed us our room keys and then launched into her pre-programmed speech.

"Behind you on the right is the restaurant which is open from six o'clock in the morning until 11 at night. On your left are the elevators which will take you up to the fifth floor where your rooms are located. The exercise facility is located on the fourth floor. Check-out time is noon. Welcome to the hotel and have a nice stay."

On the surface it may sound like the clerk did a good job of informing us about the hotel but what you miss because you are reading the above commentary is the tone inflection used in delivering the message. So, let me take just a moment to share that with you. Do you remember the television show, *Lost in Space*? If you do, do you remember the robot that lived with the family? When the robot communicated information to the family it was in a flat, monotone without any voice inflection. As we are all aware, robots don't display emotion but provide just the facts. Our clerk must have attended the "Customer Service School for Robots."

What about eye contact? Well, Carol and I weren't sure what was so interesting on the ceiling so we both had to look up to find out what the clerk was seeing—and guess what—there was nothing up there that we could see.

We proceeded to the elevators to go up to the fifth floor to find our rooms. When we arrived in our respective rooms each one was a bit chilly. Having traveled frequently, we were aware that many hotels turn down the thermostats in the rooms to conserve energy. The first action we took was to turn up the thermostat that controlled the temperature of our rooms.

We had some preparation to do for the next day so we decided to work in my room and order room service since it was already 8 p.m. We assumed that by the time we finished unpacking and gathered our work, our pasta dinners would be delivered. Forty-five minutes later dinner arrived. It doesn't take either Carol or me forty-five minutes to unpack.

We spent the next two hours in my room preparing our presentations for the next day. Sitting with blankets over our laps and tucked under our feet, I asked Carol if she thought it had gotten any warmer in my room. She said she didn't think it had and went to check her room. She said hers was a little better but that mine was definitely still chilly. I called down to the front desk and asked if they could send someone up to check the heat in my room.

Carol and I finished reviewing the presentation material and Carol returned to her room. While I was waiting for the maintenance person to arrive, I decided that maybe a hot bath would help to remove the chill from my bones. I ran the bath water and was looking forward to soaking out the chill. The maintenance person still hadn't arrived. About the time I was getting ready to call the front desk, there was a knock on the door. It had been 45 minutes since I first called down to the front desk. It was now 11:30 p.m.

The maintenance man arrived, didn't introduce himself or show any identification and looked somewhat put out that anyone would request his services at this hour. He walked over to the thermostat, put his hand up in front of the vent, and said "Yep, the motor is out." Then he started to leave the room. I asked him to explain to me what he intended to do to fix it. He said that it would take two hours to fix the motor. I said, "That means you won't be finished until 1:30 in the morning." He said, "Yep, that's right, but that's only if we have a motor in stock to replace it."

Well, I decided that staying up for another two hours while the maintenance man fixed the motor for the heater fan was not an option. I asked him if he could check with the front desk and see if there was another room on the same floor, with heat, that I could move to. He said he would ask.

While I was waiting for the front desk to call, I checked my bath water to see if it was still hot. Much to my surprise it wasn't. As a matter of fact, it was ice cold. I turned on the hot water in the bathtub and then in the sink and all I got was cold water. Please understand that this had been a particularly long day. I had been up since 5:00 a.m., and presenting a new course the next day was going to be stressful. I really wanted to go to sleep.

It occurred to me that it had been a while since my encounter with the maintenance man who must have gone to the same customer service robot school as the front desk clerk. I decided to be proactive and call down to the front desk to see what was happening. The clerk said that someone was on their way up to bring me a new key. Go ahead, guess how long it was from the time the maintenance man left until the security guard with a new room key arrived. You guessed it: 45 minutes.

The guard handed me the key and started to walk away. I asked him to please tell me where the new room was located. He grunted, pointed down the hall, then turned and walked away. Well, just to keep you up-to-speed, it was now 12:15 a.m. I was anxiously looking forward to being in a warm room, taking a hot bath and jumping into bed as quickly as possible.

I began collecting my belongings and started moving them down to the new room. I turned up the heat; it kicked on and warm air began to blow out of the vent. Progress!

It wasn't until I took my toiletries down to the new room that I turned on the light in the bathroom. Guess what? This was a handicapped-equipped room. Another fact that is important for you to know is that I am 4 feet 11 inches tall and the toilet seat in the handicapped room came up almost to my waist. In order for me to sit on the commode, I would need a step ladder or a crane. I turned around and guess what else I discovered. You've got it...no bathtub.

At this point, I was beginning to think that this just wasn't my night. I still had a lot of my belongings to move since we were going to be in Philadelphia for a week. I decided against moving and thought I

would just use the covers from both beds for warmth and stay in the original room. I also thought that by morning the water would be hot and that a shower would thaw me out and wake me up. It was 1:00 a.m. by the time I finally went to bed.

When the alarm went off at 5:00 a.m., I thought that I had only been asleep for ten minutes or so. But it was time to wake up and get moving. I was really looking forward to a hot shower! I know, I know...you've already guessed what happened and you are right. Still no hot water. What a way to be jolted awake!

Carol and I met for breakfast at 6:00 a.m. in the hotel restaurant. I was still chilled to the bone so rather than getting something from the cold breakfast bar, I decided that a bowl of oatmeal would do the trick. Other than Carol and me, there were four people in the restaurant. We had to search for a server. When a waiter finally appeared, we had to ask twice for coffee. Eventually, we ordered. I ordered oatmeal and Carol decided to be adventuresome and order one poached egg with two pieces of dry, whole wheat toast.

After about 15 minutes, the waiter brought me a bowl and a stainless steel teapot of lukewarm water. When I asked where the oatmeal was, the waiter pointed to the cold breakfast buffet and said that I needed to go select my packet of instant oatmeal. Not quite what I had in mind. I ate it anyway because we were starting to run short on time. I was finished, (and I eat slowly!) and still the waiter hadn't brought Carol her breakfast. Finally, the waiter came over and said they ruined the first egg and were making another and it should be out soon.

Go ahead, guess how long it was from the time we ordered until Carol got her egg. You are good! Forty-five minutes later the egg and two pieces of burnt toast arrived. Before the waiter left, I said "You aren't going to charge us for this." He said, looking at me puzzled, "Well, of course we..." when I interrupted and said, "That wasn't a question, that was a statement. We aren't paying for this." He shrugged his shoulders and walked away.

When we got to the client's place of business, the first question from them was, "How was your hotel?" Carol and I both looked at each other and said in unison, "Don't ask." Of course, that prompted a barrage of questions and apologies. The client said that they would move us because that level of service is unacceptable. Carol and I agreed wholeheartedly.

When the client called the hotel to inform them of what happened and tell them that we would be checking out they said "Well, they have to be out by noon or we will charge them for another night." On our lunch break Carol and I rushed over to the hotel to quickly pack and check out. The check-out process was about as thrilling as the check-in process had been.

I always believe that all things happen for a reason. Since we were doing customer service and sales training for this client, the situation provided the perfect scenario for us to examine during class when we talked about the importance of an Instant Opportunity.

Did you keep track? How many Instant Opportunities did you notice? Let's go back to the beginning of the case study and discuss each one of the situations.

Instant opportunity review

Check-In

The first Instant Opportunity was when we checked in. What happened? Well, the clerk was more focused on process than on the human interaction. According to David Goldman, focus directs listening. He states in any situation the three places where you can focus are on yourself, the material or subject matter, or on the other person. Ideally, the focus in a customer service situation needs to be on the other person. In this situation, there was no attempt to make us feel welcome in the city or in the hotel. The lesson to learn here: first impressions.

First impressions set the stage for everything else to come. In "How to Market Yourself," Cronin corroborates with Marketing Tip #4: Always Make A Good First Impression. Did you know that on average we make eleven subconscious decisions about any given situation within the first seven seconds of the interaction? These subconscious decisions can be anything from the way the person is dressed to what they say to how they act and everything in between.

Eye contact is also a critical element of the first impression. We want our customers to know that they are important. Think about it. What do you think when someone doesn't make eye contact with you? At one end of the continuum you wonder if this person is interested in having your business. At the other end you probably wonder if this is someone you can trust and feel comfortable doing business with. Dave Jakielo, in his chapter, "Selling through Negotiation," shares that if someone is not making eye contact with you then it is a sure sign they disagree with something you said or have lost interest in the conversation.

Since customer service and sales is our business, Carol and I were definitely making a mental note of how the interaction affected us. But we aren't any different than most people who look for quality customer service when they go to a hotel.

Room Service

Eight o'clock is usually past the dinner rush. Our expectation, since we ordered pasta dishes, was that the food would be delivered within 20-25 minutes. It would have been helpful if the person who took the room service order gave us some indication of how long we could expect to wait before dinner would arrive. That was another Instant Opportunity.

The lesson learned here is to inform your customer of what they can realistically expect as far as performance. Then do everything you can to meet, or better yet, exceed that expectation.

Maintenance Man

The idea that in the winter you expect to have heat in your hotel room should be a standard expectation. As travelers there are certain basics we expect, like heat in the winter, air conditioning in the summer, and hot and cold running water from the sink and bathtub or shower. What was the Instant Opportunity with the maintenance man?

If he knew that it would take a minimum of two hours to repair the motor, he could have made the suggestion that I move to another room rather than my coming up with the idea. Also, I am not sure that he would have told me what was wrong with the heater if I hadn't asked.

The lesson here is to keep your customer informed of what is happening along the way so they can make decisions on what will work for them in any given instance. Also, provide the customer with alternatives of what you can do to take care of them. Be proactive—

anticipate what you would want in the situation if you were the customer.

Security Guard

When the security guard finally arrived with the new key, what could he have done to create an Instant Opportunity? He could have taken me down to the new room, turned on the heat for me, and offered to help me move all of my belongings. Also, if he had escorted me to the room, he would have seen that it was a handicapped designated room and would have known that the arrangement wouldn't work for me. Instead, he handed me the key and left me to fend for myself.

The lesson to be learned is to stay alert and know which alternatives will work for your customer and which won't. If you don't know, ask the customer to be sure that they are satisfied with the alternatives that you give them.

If the hotel staff had really been on their toes, they would have telephoned me to see how I was doing and ask if I needed anything else, or volunteered to compensate me for the inconvenience I had suffered. If your product or service doesn't meet the satisfaction of your customer, acknowledge that. Apologize for any inconvenience. Apologizing helps diffuse the customer's anger. Work with the customer to find a solution that will satisfy them.

Restaurant

When you go to a restaurant you expect prompt service, especially that early in the morning when there are few patrons. The service we received should have been prompt, and the food should have been attractively served and hot. The waiter didn't do a very good job of watching for customers, pouring coffee or keeping us informed of what was happening. Also, he disappeared for long periods of time.

In the winter, many restaurants serve freshly made hot oatmeal not the instant kind in a packet. The waiter should have informed me that the hotel restaurant offered only instant and if that wasn't acceptable, I could have changed my mind and ordered something else.

The waiter could have offered an alternate selection or recommended an item that the restaurant excelled in preparing.

Another Instant Opportunity in this situation was when he finally brought Carol's egg. The waiter could have been proactive and told us that breakfast was free to make up for the inconvenience and delay in being served. You have to admit that waiting forty-five minutes for one poached egg and two pieces of toast is very slow service.

You can learn lessons in every situation and apply them to your own situations. In this case, when you fail to meet the customer's expectation and you know that they are upset, offer the customer something that leaves them with a positive feeling. The waiter could have corrected the situation by offering to give us our meal free-of-charge. As Dave Jakielo stated in his chapter, "the only goal of any negotiation (or customer interaction) should be a win-win solution or no deal."

Check-Out

Since our client called and informed the hotel of our problems, there are several steps the hotel could have taken to ensure that we stayed with them for an additional eight nights. What could the hotel have done to make up for all of our problems?

Here are some suggestions. They might have offered each of us one free night which might have kept us at this hotel for the other seven nights that we were scheduled to be in Philadelphia. They might have offered to upgrade us to the concierge level for the rest of our stay. They might have offered each of us a free meal. They might have offered to move us to suites and assisted us in the move.

Now, let me ask you this. Would offering us any of these options have offset our negative experience? Probably. It depends on how they presented the options. Would any of these options cost the hotel a lot of money? Probably not. Would presenting any options have prevented negative publicity? Probably. At the very least, the story would have had a happy ending. Would they have made us feel valued and gotten our business in the future? Probably.

When we checked out, the clerk at the front desk didn't ask

"How was your stay?" She didn't inquire as to why we were checking out earlier than scheduled. If she had, she may have been able to take advantage of an Instant Opportunity.

In Jeff Tobe's C.O.L.O.R. Selling™ Model, he discusses how to ask questions that will uncover a customer's basic and specific needs. Knowing how closely related customer service and sales are, it is incumbent upon customer service representatives who want to generate repeat business to remember to ask questions that reveal their customer's problems, difficulties and dissatisfactions. And, as Tobe demonstrates, to eventually translate those basic needs into specific needs, desires, wants, or intentions to act.

What is the lesson to learn? It is this. The ultimate cost to an organization is usually much less if we take care of a negative customer service situation immediately. Did you know that when someone has a positive customer service experience they may tell three to five people? When someone has a negative customer service experience they will tell, on average, seven to ten people. My bet is, depending on how bad the experience, it will be shared with anyone who will listen.

A way to avoid having customers experience negative customer service is to make sure the employees understand the importance of providing exceptional customer service to each and every customer, each and every time they interact with a customer. On a personal level, a way to always make certain the level of customer service you provide exceeds the customer's expectation is to set a goal that reflects that aspiration.

There are two chapters that address goal setting. Steve Richards says in his chapter: "Changing your life, yourself, your job performance or anything else you desire is a matter of will...willingness to do what you know to be the right or most productive thing to do."

In this customer service story, some of the employees at this hotel practiced the techniques of good customer service, however, the delivery was done with their "head" (logically and objectively) because they knew they were supposed to be nice to guests rather than with their "heart," (intuitively and willingly) because they wanted to deliver excellent customer service.

If employees would examine their own motivation for doing a job well they would discover what Joe Killian, president and founder of Priority Training describes in his chapter as personal "success factors." Do the individuals at this hotel understand how important it is to create positive customer service experiences for the guests? Do their personal goals connect to the corporation's goals? Have they written professional goals for themselves that reflect providing outstanding customer service? I suspect they do not, or our experience would have been different from the moment we registered.

In order to be truly successful in our personal and professional lives it is important to know what is important to each of us, what is important to the company that pays our salary, and how those areas of importance fit together. As an employee who contributes to the overall success of a company, I need to examine the responsibilities of my job and merge my professional goals with the mission of my company. Joe Killian defines this as "your unique road map to success."

I can create this road map by using Joe Killian's Success Zone model. Killian's definition of your Success Zone is "the area in which you are most comfortable and most productive." After completing the model, if an individual decides their current position is not "who I am;" if an individual discovers that they cannot behave in a way that complements the goals of the company, then the individual may need either to look for another position within the company that will allow her/him to support their professional goals, or they may need to look for job with a different company for the same reason.

Killian further states that once you've clearly identified what you need from both your job and the people around you, you will be better able to seek out and recognize a good fit between your needs and a job that is a perfect fit. He adds that you will be better equipped to adjust when your needs are not being completely met.

A way to reinforce goals and reach a higher form of commitment to our jobs, according to Steve Richards, is to share your goals. In order to take advantage of Instant Opportunities, it is necessary first to understand how an individual fits into that picture.

In a professional environment, it may be appropriate to share your goals with a manager or supervisor. Another option is to share your goals with customers when you interact with them. For example, a clerk registering guests at a hotel could share a service goal with a customer by saying, "My goal is to ensure that your stay here leaves you feeling like a guest in my home. My name is Joan. If I can help you in any way, please dial zero and ask the operator to connect you to the front desk."

The important thing to remember is to honor the commitment that you have made. As Mary Maloney Cronin says under Marketing Tip #7: Do It Immediately! What better way to create support for your goals, create positive expectations for your customers, and reinforce the mission of your company?

In order to make outstanding customer service a reality, the desire to set and reach our goals is a must. "Desire is the key to a long and interesting life," says Steve Richards. When you can clearly envision how it will feel to satisfy your desire to provide excellent customer service, then taking the actions necessary to meet this goal will be accomplished more easily and will make the job more rewarding.

Well, that's it for the first part of the case study. First part, you ask? How could there be more? Wasn't that enough? That's what we thought, too. But yes, there is more.

CASE STUDY: PART TWO

As you already know, our client made arrangements for us to stay at a different hotel in the downtown Philadelphia area. After our training session, both Carol and I were exhausted and were not looking forward to settling into another hotel. All we knew was that it couldn't be much worse than what we had already experienced.

Even though the new hotel was only a few short blocks away, our client arranged for a taxi to take us there. They felt so guilty, since it had been such a long day and we already had our luggage, that they were trying to do anything they could to make up for the nightmare experience at the first hotel.

When we arrived at our new hotel, we were apprehensive, at best. We had no idea of what to expect after the last episode. As we entered the lobby of the hotel, we were greeted by a friendly and enthusiastic doorman, Brian. So far, so good. Brian was demonstrating Cronin's Marketing Tip #3: Enthusiasm Is The Source Of Achievement. He offered to get our luggage out of the taxi and put it on a cart. He told us that after we checked in he would help us to our warm, comfortable rooms. Warm...now that was a word that sounded very good to us.

As we walked through the double doors and into the lobby, the people behind the registration desk looked up at us, smiled and said, "Good evening, ladies." Carol and I were both so surprised by the warm and friendly welcome we both turned around to see who they were talking to, only to find there was no one behind us and that they were greeting us.

The registration process was a delight. They asked us why we were in town, what we do for a living, how the weather was when we left Pittsburgh, and other small talk to find out about us and our needs. When the formal part of the registration process was completed, Monica informed us of the restaurant hours, the free breakfast buffet, and information about our rooms. Then she said, "Now ladies, if there is anything, and I mean anything, that we can do to make your stay more enjoyable, please do not hesitate to ask us."

As Carol and I got on the elevator, we looked at each other and through our glazed, exhausted eyes came a glimmer of hope and joy.

What a totally pleasant experience. Different from the experience we had the day before and not like too many others we have had before or since.

As promised by Brian, the doorman, our rooms were warm and comfortable. While riding up on the elevator, Brian asked us if this was our first stay at their hotel. When we informed him that it was, he proceeded to tell us about the amenities of the hotel. We could tell that Brian really enjoyed his job and wanted to make us feel at home.

After getting us into our rooms and checking to make sure that we had everything that we needed, Brian reinforced what Monica had said, that if we need anything during our stay we should just ask.

Carol and I decided to unpack before going down to the restaurant for dinner. While unpacking, I noticed that my nightgown was missing. Oh great, I had left it on the back of the bathroom door at the other hotel. In my haste to pack and check out, I forgot to check behind the door. So, the experience lived on.

I called the first hotel and, after explaining what had happened, asked who I would speak to. The operator, without saying anything, transferred me to another telephone. A man answered, and since I didn't know to whom I was speaking I had to do some fact finding.

The man was one of the security guards who takes care of "Lost and Found." I explained to the man what I was looking for. He said my nightgown hadn't been turned in to "Lost and Found." I told the security guard that I was sure it was still hanging on the back of the bathroom door in the room where I stayed. I asked if he could go check. He said he would and suggested that I call back in 15 minutes.

I called back in 15 minutes and the guard said that there was someone occupying the room and, therefore, he couldn't enter the room. Through clenched teeth, I suggested that he call the room, ask them to check to see if the nightgown was there, and ask permission to come up to the room to get it for the previous guest. He said, "Hey, that's a good idea. I didn't think of that." At this point, I was beginning to wonder if anyone at that hotel could think. Again, the guard said that I should call back in 15 minutes. Well, at least it wasn't 45 minutes!

Another 15 minutes went by and I called again. The security guard had retrieved the nightgown. He said he was surprised at how nice the people were in the room. All he had to do was ask for their help. I told the guard that I would come to the hotel and pick it up after I had eaten dinner.

I went to Carol's room so that we could go to dinner. I told her about what had transpired over the last half hour. As we were riding down in the elevator, I got a great idea. I reminded Carol of what Monica and Brian said regarding "anything" they could do for us. I decided to take them up on their offer. At this point, what did I have to lose?

We arrived in the lobby and asked Monica if she meant what she said about doing "anything" to make our stay enjoyable. She said "Absolutely." I said, "Well then, I would like to take you up on your offer." I explained that I had left my nightgown at the previous hotel and I wanted someone to go pick it up for me.

She asked Mike, one of the bellmen, if he would go to the hotel and pick up my nightgown while we went to dinner. He said, "It would be my pleasure."

I called the guard at the first hotel and told him that Mike would be coming to pick up my nightgown and that it was okay to give it to him. I got money out of my wallet to give to Mike for the cab. He said, "Put that money back in your wallet, I have a cab voucher. This one is on us. Now, the two of you go and enjoy your dinner and when you come back your nightgown will be here waiting for you."

Carol and I couldn't believe what had just happened, especially after the nightmare experience at the last hotel. We had a relaxing dinner and on the way back to our room stopped at the front desk. When Mike saw us coming, he went up to the front desk and asked one of the clerks to hand him a shopping bag that was behind the desk.

With a big smile, he presented me with the shopping bag. He asked me to check it to see if it was the right nightgown. I did and it was. He shared with me that he had quite a time with the guard at the other hotel. Even though I called and said that Mike would be coming up to get it and that it was okay to give it to him, the guard gave him a difficult time.

Mike described the nightgown to the guard, "It's a long, white, flannel nightgown with pink flowers. I overheard Ms. Akerman tell you it was okay to give it to me, so just give it up, man, so that I can get back and deliver it to her." The guard finally gave the nightgown to Mike.

I took out my wallet to give Mike a tip for his time and trouble. He put his hand up and said, "Put your money away, Ms. Akerman. It was my pleasure to do this for you. I hope you enjoy the rest of your stay with us. And, by the way, I hope you have a good night's sleep. If there is anything else I can do for you, please just ask."

Wow!!! What a fabulous experience—and that was just the first evening of our stay. The rest of our stay at this hotel was just as positive. Whether we were in the elevator with the housekeeping staff or passing by the front desk or coming or going from the hotel, every employee spoke to us in a friendly and enthusiastic manner and offered their assistance.

Instant opportunity review

Let's take some time to review the Instant Opportunities that existed at the second hotel.

Arrival at the hotel
The first Instant Opportunity was when the taxi pulled up to the hotel and Brian greeted us and told us that he would take care of our luggage thus providing us with a warm welcome. From the lessons that we learned from the first hotel case study, what did Brian do that started us off on the right foot with this hotel? That's right, he knew the importance of the first impression. His verbal and non-verbal actions supported one another and let us know that we were important and valued in his and the hotel's eyes.

Deb Haggerty in her chapter, "Networking: Necessity or Nuisance?" reinforces that first impressions are critical. She encourages you to make sure you convey a professional image in dress and body language and that your enthusiasm is contagious! Just like Brian. He was a perfect role model.

Check-in
There were many elements of the check-in process that

reinforced the positive first impression that Brian established at the front door. The inviting way we were greeted by the registration desk personnel kept the positive first impression alive. The fact that Monica, the hotel clerk, took a genuine and sincere interest in us and the reason for our stay made us feel comfortable and again, valued.

The lesson to be learned is the importance of letting the customer know that you are genuinely interested in them and in accommodating their needs. Customers want to know that you value them and their business. Anne Louise Conlon Feeny shared in her chapter that the early 90's core emphasis targets partnering. She says "that means building long-term, high-quality partnerships—with each customer that resulted in repeat business and referrals."

Another Instant Opportunity of which Monica took advantage was when she made the offer to do "anything" to make our stay enjoyable. Even if we never had an opportunity to take her up on that offer, just knowing that the staff was ready to serve us in any way they could spoke volumes about the importance they place on customer satisfaction.

The lesson to be learned is to let your customers know that you are willing to go above and beyond the call of duty to satisfy them...and then do it...follow through. Monica was putting into use a principle that was covered in the "Dick & Jane Communication" chapter. Feeny said, "if you can tune into and meet a customer's need, and provide the necessary follow-up (translate: service) regardless of how different that customer may be from you, you'll increase your success in sales. Remember, the register doesn't ring until the deal is done. And, it doesn't keep ringing unless the need for service is continuously satisfied. Studies show that customers value service even more than price, because most of the time, good service saves them money."

Getting to our rooms

Brian made sure that we were informed about all the amenities of the hotel and that we knew the staff was there to serve us in any way that we required. He made sure we were comfortable and had everything we needed before he left us and then reinforced that help was only a call away.

What was the lesson learned here? It's that every part of your organization needs to support the goal of satisfying your customer and every employee needs to understand their role in providing customer satisfaction. Everyone must take ownership for performing that role.

The nightgown request

There were many Instant Opportunities during this part of our stay. Let's look at each one of them. The first Instant was when we approached Monica to find out if her offer of doing "anything" to make our stay enjoyable was real. Instead of making us feel like we were an inconvenience, she assertively said yes they were there to serve us in whatever way we required. The lesson here is that if you say you will do anything to guarantee your customer's satisfaction be sure you are ready to honor their request when they take you up on your offer.

The second Instant was when Mike was brought into the situation to go get the nightgown. His willing attitude to help and to do whatever was necessary to accommodate me and my situation was genuine and sincere. I didn't get the feeling that he was doing this because it was his "job" but because he understood his role in providing exceptional customer service.

Another Instant was when he didn't accept cab fare but said he already had a cab voucher. Since I was asking them to do something that I felt was above and beyond the call of duty, I was more than willing to pay for it, but the philosophy of this hotel was to go the extra mile because it will pay off down the road.

Lessons learned? We have already reviewed two lessons that apply in this situation. One is that customer satisfaction is a part of everyone's job and taking ownership is critical. The second lesson learned was that going the extra mile pays off in the long run. The other thing that Mike did was to assure us that he would take care of the situation and that we didn't have to be concerned. Be sure that you leave your customer feeling confident the situation is under control.

These lessons were again supported when we returned after dinner and Mike had the nightgown and would not let me tip him for his time or effort.

The fact that everyone in the hotel from the housekeeping staff to the registration desk personnel to the bellmen to the door man, understood and owned their role in satisfying the customer, speaks volumes about the integrity of the hotel and the depth of the staff commitment to provide exceptional customer service.

Talk about the difference between night and day in our hotel experiences! Which experience would you rather have? What type of experience do your customers have with your company? Do you even know?

The final word

Let's talk about what has transpired since this experience occurred. What we didn't know at the time that all of this was happening was that our client was in the middle of negotiations with the first hotel to have them on the preferred list of vendors.

The people in the client's travel department called to talk with us about our experience. They took this information back to the first hotel to use as leverage in the negotiation.

The travel department checked with other people associated with their company who had stayed at this hotel. What they learned was everyone surveyed had a poor impression.

Since the poor service by the hotel reflected back on the client's reputation, they made the decision that this hotel would not be on the approved list of places to stay. In order for the hotel to get back on the list, they would have to communicate what they planned to do and then demonstrate what they did to resolve the sources of the complaints. The poor quality of customer service cost the first hotel a very large sales contract. The exceptional quality of customer service of the second hotel got them on the preferred list for the first time.

I said in the beginning of the chapter that by the end you would have a better understanding of the relationship that customer service has to sales and what role you play in that relationship. The case study presented in this chapter shows the relationship that customer service has to sales.

I want you to ask yourself, "What type of experience do my customers have with every person in my company?" "What can I do to make the customer service experience better for my clients and eliminate negative experiences?" As Blackman says in her eleventh key component, "Building and Keeping the Relationship," the possibilities are endless for success if you partner and have passion for what you do.

The president of the first hotel sent us a letter of apology for the experience that we had and offered us a free night's stay in their hotel. We wrote back and said that we appreciated the offer but we are not willing to take the chance of staying with them again until they can show us what they have done to change the way they are doing business. This reinforces and supports the stipulation that our client made with them. We have not heard back from the hotel.

Until this was brought to the president's attention, do you think he really knew what type of service his customers were receiving? If he did, shame on him for not doing something about it. If he didn't, shame on him for assuming that his customers were being taken care of in a quality way.

Action plan

This example is just one of many that we have experienced first hand or heard about. Sales in every type of organization can be impacted by the quality of customer service. This section has been designed to show you how to take the lessons from both the positive and negative customer service experiences and apply them to your organization.

The lessons learned in the example can be valuable to the success of your organization. Let's review the lessons learned.

Lessons learned
- First impressions are important.
- Inform your customer of what they can realistically expect.
- Keep your customer informed of what is happening so they can make decisions about what will work for them .
- Provide the customer with alternatives.
- Be proactive.
- Check for customer satisfaction.
- Volunteer to compensate the customer for any inconvenience.
- Work with the customer to find a solution that will satisfy them.
- Take care of a negative customer service situation immediately.
- Let the customer know that you are genuinely interested in them and in accommodating their needs.
- Value your customers and their business.
- Let your customers know that you are willing to go above and beyond the call of duty to satisfy them...then do it...and follow through.
- Make sure that every employee understands their role in providing customer service and takes ownership for providing customer satisfaction.
- If you say you will do anything to guarantee your customer's satisfaction be sure you are ready to honor their request when they take you up on your offer.

Every time you interact with a customer there are Instant Opportunities to be captured and lessons to be learned. It is to your competitive advantage to review each customer interaction and determine where you took advantage of an Instant Opportunity and where you let one slip by. Just as important is reviewing each Instant Opportunity for the lessons that can be learned and acted upon to repeat successes or to improve for the next Instant that comes along.

Listed below are some questions to ask yourself after each customer interaction. You may want to design your own form and customize the questions to your particular situation.

Customer interaction review
- What was the situation with this customer?
- What first impression did I make with this customer? What did I do to let the customer know that I value them and their business?
- How did I go about handling this situation? If it was a negative situation, what did I do to turn it around and leave the customer with a positive experience?
- How did the customer respond to the situation?
- What did my customer expect from me? Was the expectation realistic?
- What could I have done differently?
- What other alternatives could I have offered this customer?
- Was the customer satisfied with the outcome? How do you know ? Did you ask?
- Will the customer do business with me again? How do you know? Did you ask?

If we don't review each customer interaction we won't know what we are doing well and what areas we can work on to improve. In the beginning of the chapter we reviewed the purpose of sales and customer service. We learned that both functions are important in providing the customer with what the customer wants and/or needs. If we do our customer service job well, there is a strong likelihood that we will get additional sales and referrals from customers.

"The customer is king" is an adage that we have heard many times before. This is true in both sales and customer service. Knowing that, we need to ask ourselves, "How am I doing in these areas?" and "How is my organization doing?" If our answer uncovers some room for improvement, the next step is to determine what needs to be done to make those improvements a reality.

Customer service and sales are everyone's job

Do you know what inconsistent or poor service is costing or could cost your organization? The cost may be very high. To avoid customer service pitfalls in your organization, examine each experience that you have when you are acting as the customer. Take each experience and dissect it. Was your experience positive? If it was, see if the same components that made it positive are a routine part of the service your organization offers. Did you have a negative experience? If the answer is yes, examine your organization to see if those negative pieces might exist in the service you provide. Take immediate action to eliminate any negatives that you uncover.

You need to ask yourself repeatedly, "How are my customers being treated?" One way to find out is by asking your customers what they think. They will be happy to tell you. If they say that the level of customer service is unsatisfactory, do something about it before it costs you repeat sales and/or referrals. If you feel that you consistently provide exceptional customer service, and your customers agree with your assessment, congratulations! You are among an elite class.

As I have stressed, customer service and sales go hand-in-hand. In order for your organization to be successful in the sales arena, the people in your organization must really believe that excellent customer service is everyone's job. Each person should be asking customers about the service they are receiving from your organization. If you take this simple step, your organization will always be aware of your customers' perception of your service. Remember, if you believe that quality customer service is all important, and act accordingly, the sales will come!

Special Thanks to Carol Baker Booth for her contributions and editing, Carolyn Byrne for proofreading, and Angela Love for the creative cartoon illustrations.

About Sandie Akerman

Sandie Akerman, President, Akerman Consulting & Training, Inc. began her business in August, 1995. The business is focused on assisting organizations and individuals to improve relationships with self and others.

Sandie has over twenty years of progressive management, training, and sales experience. Innovative and energetic best describe her style in working with people.

Prior to starting her own organization, Sandie was director, training and development, Architectural Finishes, PPG Industries, Inc. She won the Special Achievement Award for developing a customer training program.

Other past employers include Dictaphone Corporation, where Sandie was awarded New Sales Representative, 1983 and Top Sales Manager, 1986; United Telephone Systems, Ponderosa Training Institute, and WISH-TV.

She received Bachelor of Science degrees in Broadcast Journalism and Political Science from Butler University, Indianapolis, Indiana.

Sandie is President-Elect for Pittsburgh's Chapter of American Society for Training and Development. She is a member of the National Speaker's Association (NSA) and Pennsylvania Speakers Association (PSA).

Akerman Consulting and Training

Sandie Akerman
Akerman Consulting & Training, Inc.
602 Victory Road
Pittsburgh, PA 15237-4500
Phone: 412-635-0101
Fax: 412-635-9222
E-mail: saker602@aol.com

Company profile

Akerman Consulting & Training, Inc. specializes in assisting organizations and individuals in creating positive personal results and increasing organizational effectiveness by improving relationships with self and others. The staff of Akerman Consulting & Training, Inc. believe that people are at the heart of the bottom line and what is behind every issue is how we relate to ourselves and others.

We deploy tools and training to enhance a participant's skills by presenting customized programs in the areas of sales/sales management, customer service, relationship building and communications.

We do not believe in doing training for training's sake. We are committed to you leaving our seminars with usable information that is customized to your situation. We also believe that no matter what the seminar length, it is critical that you leave with next step actions defined in order to implement the new knowledge and behaviors immediately.

Other organizational and individual development areas: needs assessment, group facilitation, attitudes and values, change management, strategic planning, coping/stress techniques, personal listening, and team building. We are an award-winning distributor for Carlson Learning products.

Akerman Consulting & Training, Inc. works with for-profit and not-for-profit organizations. Clients include Mellon Bank, Pepsi-Cola Company, United Way of Allegheny County, Community Technical Assistance Center, Franklin Interiors, Michael Baker Corporation, Greater Pittsburgh Chamber of Commerce, S&T Bank, and RPS, Inc.

THANK YOU! We hope you enjoyed reading
THE SALES COACH...Selling Tips from the Pros and we
trust that you are now well-armed to face your sales
challenges with a new arsenal of effective, bottom-line
building, new sales approaches. If you would like **_to order
additional copies_** of this book, please fill in this form and
forward it to us.   Allow 2-3 weeks for delivery.
Note discount on volume orders.

NAME:_____

COMPANY:_____

SHIPPING ADDRESS:_____

_____

PHONE:(   )_____ FAX:(   )_____

Price per book: $19.95 usd/$27.95cdn
12+books=$16.95usd/$24.95cdn
48+books+$14.95usd/$22.95cdn

<u>Quantity</u>	<u>Cost per book</u>	**TOTAL**
_____	_____	_____
PA residents add 6% sales tax		_____
add $3.00 per book shipping		_____
TOTAL DUE		_____

PAYMENT: visa ❑   mastercard ❑
          check enclosed ❑ (payable to author's name)
* credit card billing appears under COLORING OURSIDE THE LINES
CREDIT CARD # _____
EXPIRATION DATE _____
BILLING ADDRESS ZIP CODE _____

Send order to: (AUTHOR'S NAME ON THE FRONT OF THIS BOOK)
          1144 COLGATE DR., MONROEVILLE PA 15146
OR fax to: **(412) 373-8773**
OR call toll free: **(800) 875-7106**

THANK YOU! We hope you enjoyed reading *THE SALES COACH...Selling Tips from the Pros* and we trust that you are now well-armed to face your sales challenges with a new arsenal of effective, bottom-line building, new sales approaches. If you would like *to order additional copies* of this book, please fill in this form and forward it to us.   Allow 2-3 weeks for delivery. Note discount on volume orders.

NAME:_____

COMPANY:_____

SHIPPING ADDRESS:_____

_____

PHONE:(   )_____   FAX:(   )_____

Price per book: $19.95 usd/$27.95cdn
12+books=$16.95usd/$24.95cdn
48+books+$14.95usd/$22.95cdn

Quantity   Cost per book   TOTAL

_____   _____   _____

PA residents add 6% sales tax   _____

add $3.00 per book shipping   _____

TOTAL DUE   _____

PAYMENT: visa ❏   mastercard ❏
            check enclosed ❏ (payable to author's name)

* credit card billing appears under COLORING OURSIDE THE LINES

CREDIT CARD # _____

EXPIRATION DATE _____

BILLING ADDRESS ZIP CODE _____

Send order to: (AUTHOR'S NAME ON THE FRONT OF THIS BOOK)
            1144 COLGATE DR., MONROEVILLE PA 15146
OR fax to: (412) 373-8773
OR call toll free: (800) 875-7106